GLOBAL COMMUNICATION
AND WORLD POLITICS

GLOBAL COMMUNICATION AND WORLD POLITICS

Domination, Development, and Discourse

Majid Tehranian

LYNNE RIENNER PUBLISHERS

ISEAS

To my family, friends, and students
for the journey we have taken together

Published in the United States of America in 1999 by
Lynne Rienner Publishers, Inc.
1800 30th Street, Boulder, Colorado 80301

and in the United Kingdom by
Lynne Rienner Publishers, Inc.
3 Henrietta Street, Covent Garden, London WC2E 8LU

Paperback edition also published in the Republic of Singapore by the
Institute of Southeast Asian Studies (www.iseas.edu.sg)
Heng Mui Keng Terrace, Pasir Panjang, Singapore 119614
(for distribution in India, Hong Kong, Taiwan, and the People's Republic of China,
and exclusive distribution in Southeast Asia, South Korea, Australia, and New Zealand)

Library of Congress Cataloging-in-Publication Data
Tehranian, Majid.
    Global communication and world politics : domination, development,
and discourse / by Majid Tehranian.
        p.   cm.
    Includes bibliographical references and index.
    ISBN 1-55587-373-1 (alk. paper). — ISBN 1-55587-708-7 (pbk. :
alk. paper)
    1. Communication—Political aspects. 2. Communication,
International. 3. World politics—1989–   I. Title.
P95.8.T44   1998
302.2—dc21   98-44667
                                                                         CIP

British Cataloguing in Publication Data
A Cataloguing in Publication record for this book
is available from the British Library.

Printed and bound in the United States of America

The paper used in this publication meets the requirements
⊗ of the American National Standard for Permanence of
Paper for Printed Library Materials Z39.48-1984.

5 4 3 2 1

Contents

Foreword

In 1996 in Naples, while sitting alone at an outdoor café, I was struck by the prevalence of cellular phones. At least one was visible on each table, and most tables had two or three. At the table nearest mine there were four people, and like a scene from an absurdist theater piece, each was talking on a phone while they looked idly at one another. I wondered whether they might not be talking to each other by phone, even if face-to-face. Reflecting on what all this meant, I was struck most of all by the extent to which this phenomenon of the cell phone had to do with other things in addition to perpetual accessibility. It had to do with empty lives and status and technologies that abolish distance. Once again it was evident that the medium was part of the message, and yet this message was elusive. Surely it involved the ease of contact, and quite possibly the loss of community, malaise, boredom with the familiar, and a priority of the professional over the personal. This last impression was confirmed for me on that occasion in Naples because the most avid phone users seemed to be men in the company of their wives and children, not men with one another or, for that matter, women meeting one another.

It is fair to ask how such a scene and its interpretation concern global communications and its discontents. As might be expected, I have the feeling that my experience that afternoon was emblematic. It confirmed how deeply new technologies are penetrating social spaces and entering even the sinews of intimacy and how confusing the results and their wider signification are. Far more than the impacts of these extraordinary innovations on changing patterns of power, wealth, and knowledge, there is little doubt that the newest elites around the world, including those who manage vast underground kingdoms of criminal activity, are increasingly globalized, sharing a mastery over these technologies. These developments are so amazing and rapid that it doesn't require the interpretive genius of a Goethe, Shakespeare, or Freud to inform us that what is happening on the level of technology is bound to have an instrumental and transformative effect, reconstituting the whole nature of economic, social, political, and normative (law, religion, morality) order. But how to understand the specificity of these developments and distinguish their harms from their benefits is both difficult and crucial for any successful completion of the rite of passage that awaits us as we enter a new century and a third millennium.

It is in this spirit that I welcome the publication of Majid Tehranian's *Global Communication and World Politics*. What makes Tehranian's book so special is its synoptic grasp of modernity and the traditionalist backlash against it, possibly reflecting both his professional interest in communications as an academic discipline and his experience of Iran during the past several decades, where, arguably, the collision between the shah's modernism and the Ayatollah Khomeini's traditionalism produced the loudest explosion of the century. Tehranian situates the dramatic innovations in communications within the dynamics of modernization, with its roots in the Enlightenment, the ideological foundation for the long triumphal march of reason, science, and technology, which stimulated and sustained the emergence of a Westphalian structure of world order composed of sovereign territorial states. With erudition and insight, Tehranian argues that this structure is being dissipated by the rise of a market-based globalism on the one side and by various types of communal resurgence on the other side, an increase that is generating new and frightening forms of conflict and straining to the breaking point the governance and problem-solving capacities of the state. The diagnostic portions of the book provide readers with a grand tour of this terrain.

But Tehranian does more than this. He points a normative finger at the future, and he manages to do so without either sentimentality or blueprints. It is this quality of tentativeness that makes him credible and trustworthy as a guide. Because the texture of the guidance is loose, and sensitive to the unevenness of circumstance and perception that exists around the world, each reader will derive his or her own perspective. One may hesitate to attribute an outlook to what Tehranian presents us with; with that cautionary note struck, however, it is possible to detect certain features of what is being proposed. Above all, Tehranian acknowledges a moral imperative to take suffering seriously, to look behind the abstractions of modern warfare (with its "body counts," "kill ratios," and "smart bombs") and economic globalization (with its impressive statistics of growth and rising average incomes) at the lives of people, especially those who are being left out of the capital-driven calculus of global market forces.

Tehranian also strongly advocates a dialogic approach to conflict that rests on a Gandhian foundation of principled nonviolence, an orientation for which he finds a resonance in all the great civilizational traditions of the world. So inclined, the destructive other for Tehranian is, of course,

Samuel Huntington and his notorious hypothesis of "a clash of civilizations." Fortunately, even Huntington has by now somewhat sheepishly abandoned his earlier rash call for a West united against the threat of Islam, possibly augmented by an Islamic-Confucian alliance. A consensus is forming around two interrelated ideas: First, civilizational differences and identities matter, although it is important to avoid essentialism and recognize the diversities *within* a civilization. Second, intercivilizational differences can become a source of global stability and creativity if handled dialogically rather than antagonistically.

Naturally, many of us would like to believe that Tehranian's points of departure will come to prevail, enabling a hopeful view of human destiny. Whether this can happen none of us can know. What we do know is that unless such a commitment is widely made, the results are likely to be disastrous, producing further destructive and dangerous encounters between an amoral globalism and a series of extremist ethnic, religious, and nationalist reactions to it. *Global Communication and World Politics* provides us with an invaluable interpretive mapping of this new cartography of conflict and reconciliation and identifies for us promising and treacherous pathways to the future. In the end, it helps us meet the not yet familiar challenges of this era of globalization.

Richard Falk
Albert B. Milbank Professor of International Law and Practice
Woodrow Wilson School
Princeton University

Acknowledgments

I am grateful to my students and colleagues at a number of cultural and educational institutions at which I have taught or worked during the past two decades, including Tehran University, UNESCO, Oxford University, Massachusetts Institute of Technology, Harvard University, University of Hawaii, Tufts University, Emerson College, and the Toda Institute for Global Peace and Policy Research. In particular, I wish to thank Anthony Oettinger, director of the Program on Information Policy Resources, and Lawrence Sullivan, director of the Center for the Study of World Religions, at Harvard University, where I was a senior fellow in 1994–1995. Special thanks are also due to the United States Institute of Peace, the East West Center–University of Hawaii Collaborative Research Fund, the Fujio Matsuda Scholars Fund, and the Research Relations Fund at the University of Hawaii for their support of part of the research represented in this book.

My wife, Katharine, and my children (Terrence, Yalda, John, and Maryam) have been a source of constant support and inspiration. Katharine, Terrence, and John have also provided cogent criticisms made even more palpable with their care. Andrew Arno, Ann Auman, Fred Dallmayr, Jim Dator, Richard Falk, George Gerbner, David Held, Tomosaburo Hirano, Jim Kim, Lynne Rienner, Everet Rogers, T. V. Sathyamurthy, Anthony Smith, and an anonymous reviewer provided useful suggestions for revisions aimed at clarity and brevity. My research assistants, Audray Holm, Kimberly Taylor, and Hau'oli Busby, have been very helpful in putting the final touches on the manuscript. Richard Larsen created the index with erudition and dispatch.

I have learned much about international communication and modernization by traveling across diverse decades, continents, and cultures, moving back and forth from spatial and intellectual centers to peripheries. But the greatest lesson of all has been to be humbled in the face of the complexities of this world. This has led me to reject pat ideologies, to realize

xi

how little we know, and to appreciate how much we need to learn from those who suffer the consequences of a violent and unjust international order. If this volume sheds any light on the problems we face, it has fulfilled my hopes. If it fails to do so, that can be attributed to the limits of human knowledge in general and my own in particular. In our passage to the twenty-first century, the Faustian bargain continues to haunt us. We could gain more scientific knowledge and yet lose our soul. It would be wise, therefore, to heed Lao-tzu's (H. Smith 1958: 209) ageless words in *Tao Te Ching* (Chapter 29):

> Those who would take over the earth
> And shape it to their will
> Never, I notice, succeed. The earth is like a vessel so sacred
> That at the mere approach of the profane
> It is marred
> And when they reach out their fingers it is gone.

Majid Tehranian

INTRODUCTION

You taught me language; and my profit on't
Is, I know how to curse; the red plague rid you,
For learning me your language!

—Spoken by Caliban to Prospero
William Shakespeare, *The Tempest*

The opening of a new century has always served as a symbolic turning point in human history. The twenty-first century is not an exception. The world stands at a historical juncture on the roads to self-destruction or self-renewal. On the one hand, an environmental catastrophe, a nuclear holocaust, a war among ethnic groups or powerful regional blocs (fortress North America vs. fortress Western Europe vs. fortress East Asia), a population explosion of unprecedented magnitude, a division of the world between rich and poor gated ghettoes, or a protracted terrorist war, armed by conventional and unconventional weapons, all seem to be distinct possibilities. On the other hand, human achievements in science, technology, telecommunication, education, and social organization have opened up new potentials for reaching new heights in human civilization. The conquest of ignorance, poverty, and suffering, the achievement of a new harmony among nations and between nature and humanity, and the development of a new sense of world community for the exploration of the outer and inner spaces all seem within reach.

However grand these achievements may be, structural violence continues to ripen our world for ideological crusades. The bad news is that over 15 million children die of malnutrition every year; some 20 million children have been killed by starvation or guns during world conflicts of the last decade, in which mostly civilians are the casualties; and over 50 million refugees have been displaced by civil, ethnic, and state wars. The good news is that the first global television news networks (CNN, BBC, and Star) are

1

bringing the stories of these conflicts into the homes of people in over 150 countries. Nearly 200 countries and over 100 million netizens (network citizens) are playing doctors through the Internet's interactive computer networks, in a global discourse on the diagnosis, prognosis, and therapy of world problems. It is timely to ask, therefore, what contributions can international communication make to the eradication of structural violence and to the fostering of peace and development?

Communication can act as a process of free and equal exchange of meaning, development of epistemic communities, and advancement of social solidarity, and hence of peace and harmony among individuals and nations. Conversely, however, communication can also systematically distort perceptions by creating phantom enemies, manufacturing consent for wars of aggression while stereotyping and targeting particular ethnic groups or nations into subhuman categories. Communication empowers, but it empowers more those with greater competence and access to the means of communication. The ethical choice in communication is therefore focused on whether the communicator is aiming toward power-free understanding or systematic distortions and powerful manipulations (Habermas 1983).

This book begins with a multiple effects hypothesis (M. Tehranian 1990a, chap. 2; 1990b). Modern communication media have immensely complicated any simple dualistic equation, the media's proverbial two sides of the same coin. In fact, there are many sides to every issue. The capital-intensive macromedia (print, telephony, broadcasting, satellites, computers, fiber optics, and a rushing array of their offshoots) have privileged the power centers more than ever before in human history. An information-perfect world is a panopticon world vulnerable to the abuses of power. Citizens today are under the gaze of surveillance everywhere through powerful databases (traffic, travel, banking, tax, and medical records) as well as listening devices and video cameras. By contrast, the labor-intensive traditional and interpersonal communication networks and the micromedia (mimeographing, copying machines, audio and video cassette recorders, transistor radios, fax machines, personal computers, modems, and electronic networks) have provided channels for counterhegemonic projects of cultural resistance, political revolution, and autonomous development. To what extent can the dualisms of power and communication be overcome to achieve peace with peaceful means? To overcome cognitive tyrannies through interactive and dialogical communication, through nonviolent resistance rather than violent struggles, for the transformation of the institutions of manifest and latent violence into those of social justice and cooperation, our entire communication systems need to be revamped toward pluralism of structures and discourses.

Focusing the international attention and discourse on the causes of manifest and latent violence, physical and structural violence, is essential to the processes of positive peace building. From 1945 to 1989, from Yalta to Malta, the world system was dominated by bipolar rivalries that focused on the ideological debates between capitalism and communism. The international discourse was therefore framed in terms of the politics of development, and the ethical choices were reduced to those between tyranny and freedom, each camp branding the other with the negative label. The First and Second Worlds thus competed for the allegiance of the so-called Third World by arguing for the market as opposed to planning strategies of development while the nonaligned world articulated a counterdiscourse of national liberation and indigenous development. Following the end of the Cold War and the demise of the Soviet Union, the world centers (largely in North America and Western Europe) have significantly shifted their emphasis from development to order. In the meantime, the world peripheries (largely in Asia, Africa, and Latin America) have increasingly been focusing on modernization, indigenous development, cultural identity, and political community formation. The Gulf War, the rise of religious and ethnic movements, and the struggles for regional common markets have demonstrated that these new shifts in power and discourse have far-reaching implications. They point to the emergence of new world hegemonic and counterhegemonic patterns and projects. This book reviews the patterns of the old and new international discourses in terms of the world struggles for power, peace, development, and democracy at the national and global levels.

The world is in a state of transition from an old to a new, as yet undefined, order torn between contradictory potentials. Stanley Hoffman has captured the essential feature of this uncertainty by using the metaphor of a bus to characterize the world situation:

> The world is like a bus whose driver—the global economy—is not in full control of the engine and is himself out of control, in which children— the people—are tempted to step on either the brake or the gas pedal, and the adults—the states—are worried passengers. A league of passengers may not be enough to keep the bus on the road, but there is no better solution yet. (Hoffman 1990: 122)

Although Hoffman's characterization of states as adults and people as children could be reversed with equal justice, his implicit point about the futility of wars and the need for cooperation is well taken. The futile wars of the past few decades (from Korea to Vietnam and the Middle East) brought no conclusive victories, but they inflicted untold death and misery. No side except the arms merchants won the Cold War. The presumed victor, the United States, is in a state of endemic social crisis characterized by widening gaps, and the vanquished, the ex–Soviet Union, presents the world's last imperial system in a state of disarray. As Paul Kennedy (1987) has argued, both superpowers extended their military grasp beyond their economic reach and have had to face the dire consequences.

In the midst of these contradictions, however, seven global megatrends seem to stand out, each characterized by inner tensions between two distinctly different tendencies and discourses (M. Tehranian 1993a and 1997). These trends may be defined as globalism, regionalism, nationalism, localism, environmentalism, feminism, and spiritualism. Accelerating processes of world communication have immensely contributed to what might be called an acceleration of history. Through travel, tourism, and the new media, global communication has hastened the downfall of empires and dictatorships. It took two world wars in this century to dissolve the Ottoman, Spanish, Portuguese, Austro-Hungarian, Dutch, British, French, and Belgian empires. The Soviet empire dissolved of its own accord within a few years through glasnost and the rapid exposure of the Soviet society to the world media, video cassette recorders, fax machines, and computer networks. This is not to claim for technology an exclusive or decisive role in revolutionary changes but to suggest that technology can empower the social forces already pressing for social change. How has world communication contributed to the contradictory potentials and choices in the seven global trends suggested above? In what way does the international public discourse reflect these trends and frame the policy choices?

Much of the literature of globalization has focused on the economic aspects of global markets, trade, and development. But it is fair to say that without global communication, there could not be a global marketplace. Communication has contributed both materially and symbolically to globalization in at least three distinctly different ways. First, global communication has provided the "infostructures" of transborder data, news, and image flows that have made possible the rise of a new pancapitalism. Second, it has raised the levels of demand through the "channels of desire" (Ewen and Ewen 1982) of global advertising. Finally, it has empowered the silent voices of the peripheries whose demands for self-determination and social justice have often taken the form of identity fetishism against the commodity fetishism of the centers.

This book focuses on these problems in the context of the post–Cold War era. The Cold War presented a dichotomous view of the world, simple to understand, providing a facile conceptual basis for formulating foreign policy. The end of the Cold War, however, has taken away the convenience of such simple dichotomies. It has brought us face-to-face with the stark complexities of a fragmented world that does not easily lend itself to such spatial categories as East and West, North and South, geographic centers and peripheries, or First, Second, and Third Worlds. With the two concurrent and contradictory trends of transnationalization of economies and tribalization of politics, the new world (dis)order baffles the mind.

Nostalgic for the simple dichotomies of the past, the international discourse on the so-called new world order has been characterized by resorting to new strategic concepts in order to explain the world complexities in simple terms. In the post–Cold War era, it has thus swung from euphoric optimism to dark pessimism. It has ranged from Francis Fukuyama's declarations of the "end of history" (Fukuyama 1989) and triumph of liberal capitalism to Samuel Huntington's thesis on the "clash of civilizations" between the Christian West and a Confucian-Islamic alliance (Huntington 1993a). Neither formulation can stand the test of evidence.

PROPOSITIONS

This book is about global communication and international relations that have been grounded for the past five centuries on the processes of modernization. The volume captures a wide range of discourses on the contradictory processes of globalism and its nemesis in equally powerful localist, nationalist, regionalist, feminist, environmentalist, and spiritualist trends. These forces will continue to intensify into the twenty-first century. Currently there are 185 United Nations member states, but the world contains 6,528 languages and peoples (Grimes 1992), many of whom have an actual or potential claim to sovereignty and statehood. In the twenty-first century, we may therefore expect to see a simultaneous process of increasing world economic integration and political fragmentation. With exploding global communication, we should anticipate more dissenting voices to be heard more often.

The three interlocking themes of the book (domination, development, and discourse) are treated in eight chapters. Each chapter deals with the same set of general themes under particular case studies. The charm of communications as a field of study and case study as a method lies in their holistic approaches. The world is not neatly divided into the academe's disciplinary boundaries and departments. Public discourse and practice cross these boundaries at random and with no respect for the reductionist methods of social science disciplines.

The underlying thesis of the book may be summarized in the following general propositions:

• Domination is a perennial fact of history that has evolved through at least three types of imperial world systems: agrarian, industrial, and informatic.

• The latest phase of domination, informatic imperialism, is characterized by control of knowledge industries and information channels, including science, technology, education, patents, copyright, data, ideas, and images. Resistance against it has had to focus on the same arenas in order to bridge the gap between the developed and the less developed.

• The historical transition from premodern to modern societies has entailed four fundamental (r)evolutionary processes: developmental, democratic, communication, and control.

• It also has led to four distinctly different roads to modernization—capitalist, communist, socialist, and totalitarian—each path privileging a different norm of the democratic revolution, that is, freedom, equality, community, and order. However, all three democratic paths have shown themselves vulnerable to the totalitarian temptations of the modern world.

• Whereas the pioneers (Britain, France, the United States) generally followed the capitalist democratic model, the latecomers (Germany, Italy, Japan, Spain, Russia, and China) resorted to progressively more centralized methods of capital accumulation and social mobilization to catch up and to build their own colonial empires.

• Strategies of mobilization for modernization have invariably entailed a pathology that may be termed "ideological purism," that is, a reductionist approach in which the complexity of social and cultural life worlds (the so-called lifeworlds) is abridged into a single and powerful myth and identity. This tendency has been historically manifested in the ideologies of Calvinism in Geneva, the Puritan revolutions in England and the United States (which focused on salvation through purity of faith and work), the French Revolution (which focused on liberation through the reign of reason), and varieties of nationalisms. Purism also revealed itself in the Russian and Chinese revolutions, which focused on the purist versions of class struggle. The Nazi and Fascist revolutions in Germany, Japan, Italy, and Spain focused on racial superiority and purity. The so-called religious fundamentalist revolutions and movements of recent vintage in the Jewish, Christian, Islamic, Hindu, and Buddhist varieties concentrate on a return to a presumed, bygone purity of faith. The modern ideological purism of nationalism, fascism, communism, and fundamentalism has thus generated mass movements and dictatorships focused on the hegemonic tasks of catching up and surpassing. They have often led to totalitarian formations characterized by fetishisms of freedom (McCarthyism and the Cold War), order (nazism and fascism), equality (Stalinism and Maoism), and community (fundamentalism).

• In the meantime, global capitalism has penetrated the rest of the world through competing colonial empires, followed by decolonization and the rise of postcolonial national elites. The postcolonial regimes have often resorted to internal colonialism to control their own dualistic societies that are bifurcated along traditional and modern economies, societies, and cultures. Among the marginalized populations of both advanced and latecomer countries, cultural resistance has manifested itself in a set of

reactions to modernization that may be characterized as hypermodernization, countermodernization, demodernization, and postmodernization.

• Global communication (from print to Internet) has played a multiple
role in this process, homogenizing and differentiating markets, centralizing and dispersing power, and integrating and pluralizing cultural identities. Generally, the macromedia have facilitated globalization. In the
meantime, the micromedia have empowered the periphery loci of resistance and opposition. By contrast, the mesomedia (journals of opinion, scientific and professional journals, the Internet, and the World Wide Web)
are linking up the communities of affinity in a global civil society. Global
communication has thus stimulated economic growth (through advertising)
and political democracy (through diffusion of democratic ideas and norms)
while fostering commodity and identity fetishisms.

• Following its first two phases of market and monopoly development,
capitalism has thus entered into a third phase of development that might be
called "pancapitalism." In this phase, information technologies have made
it possible for national capital to assume transnational proportions and
penetrate the farthest reaches of the world. Information technologies have
also offered the opportunity for some former peripheries, notably in East
Asia, to move into the forefront of the centers of economic growth. But the
East Asian economic collapse of 1997 recalls the cruelties of primitive accumulation and the current domestic and international barriers to sustained
development, as well as the inevitable busts and booms of capitalism. Rid-
ing on greed, pancapitalism is delivering the goods but dividing the world
into the gated ghettoes of rich and poor, within and among nations, living
in colliding times, spaces, and discourses.

• A consequence of global communication is thus the rise of cultural
and political resistance against globalist hegemonies (whether capitalist,
Communist, or Fascist) by emerging ethnonationalist, neotraditionalist,
and neoconservative movements that employ cultural politics to mobilize
the peripheries against the centers of power.

• Owing to an explosion of unheard voices and views, another unintended consequence of global communication is the rise of a postmodern,
skeptical, and relativist culture that is deconstructing all past metanarratives while constructing two competing metanarratives of its own, nihilism
and ecumenicalism. The former is evident in the rise of ego fetishism as
well as anomic and sporadic violence; the latter is manifested in an emerging dialogue of civilizations (Hindu, Buddhist, Confucian, Judaic, Christian, Islamic, humanist, and nativist). Nihilistic postmodernism sometimes
assumes a neo-Luddite aspect, as in the case of the Unibomber. Ecumenical postmodernism, by contrast, seeks unity in world diversity.

• Asia in general and the Islamic world in particular provide examples
of a series of responses to tradition, modernity, and postmodernity, ranging

from traditionalism to modernism, posttraditionalism, and postmodernism. In this context, the colonial and postcolonial discourse has been one of mutual recrimination. As in Caliban's parting words to Prospero, the discourse of modernity and dependency has been curseful. In the Cold War era, the language was ideologically charged with such inflaming categories as "the free world" and "the evil empire." In the post–Cold War era, the epitaphs of "great and small Satans," "barbaric," "uncivilized," and "terrorist and rogue states" have further embellished the international discourse.

A central paradox of our own times is a concurrent and contradictory process of economic globalization and political fragmentation, democratization and totalization. Beginning with a critical review of the dominant discourses of international relations, this volume offers an explanation of the continuing struggles between the deterritorialized information centers and the peripheries of wealth and power. It thus accounts for the new tribal politics of identity as well as an increasingly informatized and deterritorialized transnational economy and culture. This book also examines how information and communication technologies are contributing to the dual processes of democratization and totalization. The new world order is thus viewed in terms of the continuities and changes in the processes of global modernization. More specifically, the book shows how global communication has assumed a central position in the strategies of international conflict. It offers an alternative reading of the emerging world (dis)order, which is caught in the contradictions of combined and uneven development in an increasingly fragmented world system.

In the last 500 years, the processes of modernization have progressively incorporated the entire globe in seven successive and interlocking tsunamis (the Japanese term for tidal waves caused by suboceanic earthquakes), encompassing rural areas, cities, nation-states, empires, the planet, cyberspace, and hyperspace. The fifth and sixth modernizations have particularly sharpened the contradictions of the premodern, modern, and postmodern societies and sensibilities. These latest phases in the transnationalization of the world economy have been accompanied by exploding global communication, totalization of surveillance, democratization of politics at the semiperipheries, and tribalization of identities and politics at the peripheries. These conditions have led to globalization of the local and localization of the global. Although pancapitalism has triumphed over a variety of state capitalist economies (also known as communism and welfare socialism), the market has proved itself incapable of resolving the social and cultural contradictions of capitalism that emanate from its inherent tendency to accentuate inequalities. Periodic breakdowns and interventions in the market by the state and civil society are therefore to be expected in the new pancapitalist formations. The accelerating division of the world between the globalist forces tied into the networks of global corporations and those outside of it is pitting the libertarian, communitarian, and totalitarian capitalist formations against each other at the local, national, regional, and global levels.

ORGANIZATION

This volume thus focuses on three interlocking themes: communication, modernization, and democratization in the context of an evolving global system. Chapters 1–3 map out the emerging global system in terms of the continuing orchestration by hegemonic regimes of the processes of modernization, communication, and democratization. Chapter 1 provides a historical overview of the rise and fall of imperial systems, from agrarian to industrial and informatic varieties. Chapter 2 outlines the contemporary discourses of international relations, from realism to liberalism, Marxism, communitarianism, and postmodernism while critiquing the dominant neoliberal views of world order that emphasize the role of market over those of state and civil society. Chapter 3 offers an overview of the impact of global communication on seven arenas of international relations: military, diplomacy, trade, science, technology, education, and culture. Chapter 4 takes a theoretical detour and reviews the evolving discourse of development in terms of the dominant metaphors and models that have been invoked or pursued in the postwar period. Reflecting on an uneven and fragmented world, Chapter 5 employs a case study of the historical relations between the Islamic and Western worlds to argue that much of international communication is hostage to the histories of domination and resistance. Chapter 6 focuses on the increasing dissonance in international communication as reflected in high-intensity conflicts such as intra- and interstate wars, hostage taking, and ethnic cleansing. A case study of the Iranian hostage crisis in this chapter provides further insight into how international communication can turn into a dialogue of the deaf. Chapter 7 reviews the major discourses of the future, reflecting three scenarios: continuity, collapse, and transformation. The chapter provides a prognosis of each scenario and recommendations on how to turn international communication from a discourse of mutual exclusion and recrimination into a dialogue for mutual engagement, cooperation, peace, and development. The concluding Chapter 8 offers an epilogue to the twentieth century and a prologue to the twenty-first.

1

MAPPING PANCAPITALISM

If we were to think about a "new world order" that might embark on the
gradual development of some constitutional framework within which the
peoples of the globe would eventually share collective responsibility and
reciprocal obligations, somewhat analogous to what we expect in a traditional nation state, and if we were to think about the political mechanisms that might be developed, what actual nation, existing now or in the
past, might such an incipient world state resemble? If we were to con-
template gradually relinquishing some measure of sovereignty in order to
form not a more perfect union, but a more effective world legal structure,
what familiar political entity might be our basis for comparison?

I find my own answer stunning and embarrassing: South Africa.

We live in a world that is one-fifth rich and four-fifths poor; the rich
are segregated into the rich countries and the poor into poor countries;
the rich are predominantly lighter skinned and the poor darker skinned;
most of the poor live in "homelands" that are physically remote, often
separated by oceans and great distances from the rich.

Thomas Schelling, "The Global Dimension"

Schelling's apt characterization of the current world situation as
"global apartheid" deserves serious analysis. How has it come about,
where is it leading us, and what can be done to correct it? This chapter
problematizes the growing income and communication gaps among and
within nations, views that problem in the light of a long history of hegemony in world system development, and identifies the major sites of insecurity and resistance in the emerging world system.

This chapter is a revised version of my article "Pancapitalism and Migration in
Historical Perspective," *International Political Science Review* 19, no. 3 (1998), pp.
289–303.

A GLOBAL APARTHEID?

Migration stands at the center of the phenomenon of this global apartheid. Massive population movements are taking place all over the world despite increasing political barriers to immigration. At the top of the social structure, a growing population of nomads is roaming around the globe. Associated with transnational corporations (TNCs), transnational media corporations (TMCs), intergovernmental organizations (IGOs), alternative governmental organizations (AGOs), transnational military organizations (TMOs), and transnational tourist organizations (TTOs), these nomads act as managers, producers, guardians, and celebrants of the global economy. At the bottom of the social structure, economic and political strife has forced an increasing number of refugees away from their homelands into the vortex of transborder migration. If we add the great exodus of rural population to urban centers in the less developed countries (LDCs), migration is a major source of the postwar economic growth, urban decay, and political upheavals.

The impact of population movements on the world system has far-reaching consequences. It has created a global elite and a global underclass colliding in the major world metropolitan centers. The old world centers and peripheries were primarily conceived in territorial terms. The core in Western Europe and North America was assumed to be exploiting the peripheries in Africa, Asia, and Latin America in a pattern of "development of underdevelopment" (Frank 1969) that reproduced economic and political dependency. Despite the setbacks of 1997–1998, some former peripheries in East Asia (Japan, South Korea, Singapore, and Hong Kong) have almost reached the status of world centers, and others (Taiwan, Malaysia, and Indonesia) have been making strides. Moreover, the new world centers and peripheries are deterritorialized. The new nomads are no longer confined to particular sets of countries defined as developed or developing. A member of the global elite can be in any major world city in the North or the South and enjoy a lifestyle facilitated by luxury hotels and restaurants while plugged into the global telecommunication network. The world underclass is also making its presence felt in the slums of most major metropolitan centers, which are typified by violence, crime, and drug trafficking.

VIOLENCE IN THE GLOBAL VILLAGE

Thanks to Marshall McLuhan (1968), it has become commonplace to speak of a "global village." The global village, however, increasingly resembles a medieval world. The lords of the manors live in opulent castles—the wired corporate, government, and upper-class neighborhood centers—protected by their electronic moats of surveillance and surrounded by the squalor of life and clamor of the teeming, restless serfs working the fields, that is, the urban ghettos and rural peripheries. The poor live in panopticon societies controlled by the castles' watchmen stationed in the towering cameras of remote sensing satellites. Like the former South African apartheid regime, a global apartheid does not provide a stable system. Requiring a free flow of goods, services, capital, labor, ideas, and information, the transnational world economy is vulnerable to sabotage, terrorism, recession, and protectionism. In creating a global apartheid, the new postindustrial, informatic imperialism has thus sown the seeds of its own destruction. It should be no surprise that the serfs increasingly fight their battles with the most powerful means still left at their disposal—their primordial identities of race, ethnicity, religion, and nationality. The politicization of culture may thus be inaugurating a new cold war between the lords of the manor and the peasants far more ferocious than the old Cold War (Juergensmeyer 1994). For the coming decades, nativist movements will constitute the main forms of resistance against the dominant globalist hegemony.

The past appears as prologue. Jacques Attali (1991) and Lewis H. Lapham (1994), among others, have evocatively explored the parallels between the late twentieth century and the early Middle Ages. Similar to the fall of Rome, the dissolution of the European imperial systems in the second half of the twentieth century has turned into what appears to be a neofeudal order. In the new order, global pancapitalism allies the states and TNCs to control the markets of ideas, patents, and commodities while the localist forces of resistance and revolt fight to maintain their porous and vulnerable territorial and cultural spaces. As long as the Cold War persisted, a rough balance of power created a buffer zone in the Third World between the two global systems of capitalism and communism. With the end of the Cold War and the dissolution of the Soviet Union as the last of the European empires, the moral geographies of the nation-state system have shifted from bipolar rivalries toward a contestation among the competing cultural cartographies of globalism, regionalism, nationalism, localism, environmentalism, feminism, and religious revivalism. The global village contains its established centers in the European Union (EU), North America, and the emerging semiperipheries of East Asia, the Association of Southeast Asian Nations (ASEAN), South Africa, and certain oil rich countries, such as Saudi Arabia and Kuwait. The struggling peripheries of Latin America, the Middle East, and sub-Saharan Africa are largely disintegrating in envy and violence. The fate of Central and Eastern European countries hangs on whether they can establish firm alliances with the lords of the manor or become marginalized.

Metaphors are, of course, more suggestive than explanatory. But the metaphor of a wired global village with its castles, lords, shamans, peasants,

and jesters has the value of shocking us into the recognition of the contradictions of global modernization, democratization, and communication.
Since the sixteenth century, all three processes have contributed to the development of a global hierarchy of nations and ethnicities organized
around the moral geographies of city-states, nation-states, empire-states,
and, increasingly, global states and corporations. Individuals and groups
find their place in this hierarchy in accordance with their degree of access
to the economic, political, and communication resources of the states and
corporations at the centers and peripheries of power. The new centers and
peripheries are not territorial but bound by information. The unfolding of
this historical process has progressively incorporated the world into an
order of modernity and postmodernity in which the contradictions of the
global and the local have become a central problematic of our own age.
Lewis Lapham has captured well the ironies of the new system:

> The lords and barons of the smaller fiefs become vassals to larger hold-
> ing companies, owing their allegiance not to Britain or the United States
> but to Citibank or Bertlesmann or Matsushita, and all present (stewards,
> castellans, knights-at-arms, seneschals, waiting women, and the court
> fool) depend upon a corporate overlord not only for the means but also
> for the terms of their existence—gladly relinquishing the rights of free
> citizens in return for a greyhound and a room with view of the Rhine.
> (Lapham 1994: 9)

Lest we view this portrait as fanciful, let us remind ourselves of a few
facts of international life. Communism has failed. Socialism in places such
as Western Europe is showing signs of old age. Welfare is being disman-
tled in affluent societies such as the United States. The costs of maintaining health, education, and welfare for teeming millions victimized by
structural or cyclical unemployment are mounting beyond the ability and
willingness of the states to tax. The new institutions of electronic money
and transborder cash flows are stripping the states of their ability to tax the
rich, who can hide their wealth in offshore and secret bank accounts (Anonymous 1997b). The middle class, which carries the main burden of taxation,
refuses to be further burdened by what it considers the welfare cheats.

In the meantime, greed works. Pancapitalism is delivering the goods.
But in delivering them, it also tears apart societies into the privileged and
the poor. Primitive accumulation in the sweatshops of the newly industrializing countries (NICs) is taking jobs away from the sunset industries of
the previously industrialized countries (PICs). As the NICs attempt to
catch up, the PICs experience lowering wages and standards of living
among the working class. This, in turn, gives rise to mounting racism, anti-
immigrant sentiments, and cries for protectionism among the PICs. A new
international division of labor is emerging in which the PICs have to focus

on high-tech industries (computers, aerospace, biotechnology) and the NICs concentrate on low-tech (textiles, shoes, stationery, microprocessing). Despite their phenomenal success in growth rates, the NICs are also experiencing major social and economic dislocations. As one NIC president put it aptly, "Brazil is doing well, but Brazilians are not." The same can be said of most fast-growing countries without a safety net to support the vulnerable sectors of their population. The East Asian debacle of 1997 tore down the glittering facade of "the Asian miracle" to show the realities of a crony capitalism characterized by corruption and irresponsible social policies. Hard statistical evidence also shows that income differentials among different social classes, ethnic groups, and regions are rapidly widening in both NICs and PICs (Rifkin 1995; UNDP 1996).

Pancapitalism has found an ingenious solution to these problems: gated ghettos, factories, and residential communities. In Mexico City, New York, Los Angeles, Chicago, Bombay, and Calcutta, the ghettos for the poor are more or less defined and cordoned off geographically. It is unsafe for outsiders to wander off into these areas. The insiders live by their own rules dominated by territorial imperatives and gang warfare. In the United States, most of the victims are not the ghetto outsiders but the insiders inflicting violence mostly on themselves. The police often shy away from entering the scene, preferring to leave the ghettos to their own devices. The twin of the poor ghettos is the rich ghettos of gated residential communities cordoned off by private police and electronic surveillance. These two types of ghettos lock the privileged and the poor safely into separate times, spaces, and identities. A third type of ghetto is appearing in a new guise: the gated factory. As Fred Riggs has noted, this type of zonal capitalism is particularly characteristic of Southeast Asian countries:

> These are enclaves in a third world country like Indonesia which maximize opportunities for investors to accumulate profits in the production of manufactures (from shoes, fabrics and garments to cars, furniture and electronics) for which demand on a global level is escalating while costs can be reduced maximally by minimizing social and environmental accountability. During the period from 1989 to 1994, the number of these estates in Indonesia has escalated from about a half-dozen to almost 100, while at the same time their capital costs have shifted almost completely from the state to private capital. The trends apparent during this 5-year period seem destined to continue in Indonesia, and parallel in neighboring countries, as well as in widely scattered parts of the third world, appear likely to mushroom, with implications that stagger the imagination.
>
> These industrial estates are self-contained zones, surrounded by formidable walls, that can be entered only through a single controlled gateway that insulates them from their surrounding and heighten the possibility for owner/managers to provide optimal facilities for investors to establish productive facilities that maximize their profits. (Riggs 1997: 1)

The structural violence of such gated ghettos and factories somewhat parallels that of the company towns of an earlier era of industrialization in the PICs (K. Tehranian 1995). "I have sold my soul to the company store" was the cry of the working-class sentiments of that era. Under the democratic conditions of the Western countries, the labor union movement managed to counter such conditions in total surveillance and control. However, the decline of the unions in the PICs and their conspicuous absence in the NICs are alarming signs that gated capitalism can return and has, in fact, established itself in many pockets of the world. As wages rise in the NICs and decline in the PICs, pancapitalism can return to its original home, where, in the meantime, labor unions have been subdued. In fact, the appearance of some sweatshops in major U.S. cities such as New York and Los Angeles is testimony to the global mobility of labor and capital. In sweatshops staffed by legal and illegal immigrants, Chinese capitalists can produce cheaper goods in New York than in Hong Kong.

Despite its superficial resemblance to feudalism, however, pancapitalism is a new phenomenon. In feudalism, communication among the autonomous principalities was minimal and the economy largely survived on self-sufficiency. By contrast, pancapitalism is based on global communication and mobility of factors of production. Commodity production for the global marketplace is its sine qua non. Under pancapitalism, interdependency is a fundamental fact of life. On the negative side, environmental pollution, epidemic diseases, biological, chemical, and nuclear wars, drug trafficking, money laundering, arms races, financial corruption, and genocides all have a nasty habit of crossing borders. On the positive side, technological innovation, economic growth and prosperity, and expanding educational opportunities also slowly trickle down and across the globe.

The future of pancapitalism is not therefore necessarily all doom and gloom, as its opponents propose. Nor, as its proponents suggest, is it guaranteed to be all cheerful. The future hinges on whether or not pancapitalism can resolve its daunting problems of social disequilibrium and apartheid. Through its spectacular economic and technological successes, the pancapital regime can do far more than it currently does to remedy its excesses. Ultimately, however, it takes action by the states and civil societies through the political process to democratize the regime and institute greater distributive justice.

A HISTORICAL RETROSPECTIVE

To understand the nature of this challenge, it is useful to look back into the history of world system development. The concept of a "world system" refers to the patterns of global economic development since the sixteenth century. In Immanuel Wallerstein's usage, the world system is primarily an economic division of labor among world centers, peripheries, and semi-peripheries. His model explains the patterns of economic development that emerged after the sixteenth century and European colonization of the world, when Africa, Asia, and America served as producers of raw materials, cheap labor, and consumer markets to an industrial Europe. My usage of the term world system is more generalized. The imperial world systems prior to the sixteenth century were based on trade and political domination rather than a strict economic division of labor (Frank and Gills 1993; Abu-Lughod 1989; Chase-Dunn and Hall 1977). As the colonies and semicolonies (United States, Canada, Australia, New Zealand, South Africa, Japan, China, and Southeast Asia) each extricated themselves from European hegemony, the simple division of labor developed into new patterns of imperial domination. We are now engaged in far more complex patterns of international division of labor in which pancapital, in collaboration with the superstates (the United States, the European Union, Japan) and the Bretton Woods regime (World Bank, International Monetary Fund, World Trade Organization), chooses its trade and investment partners.

In this sense, "world system development" refers to a progressive incorporation of the entire world from the ancient agrarian, multinational empires into a single political economy in the late twentieth century. Large-scale population movements trigger this process. Ibn Khaldun (1332–1406), a fourteenth-century Islamic historian and perhaps the first world system theorist, viewed history as a continuing struggle for hegemony between nomadic and sedentary populations. Writing from the vantage point of an Islamic historian, he may be considered a forerunner of modern social science theorists. By anticipating much of the economic, social, and political theories that emerged from the eighteenth century onward under the banner of classical economics, sociology, and political science, his cyclical view of history focused on migration and social solidarity *(asabiyya)* as key factors in understanding the dynamics of Islamic history. He argued that history is a constant struggle between nomadic and sedentary populations for domination and thus provided an ingenious explanation for the rise and fall of successive dynasties in the Islamic world. But he also provided a key for understanding much of world history in terms of population movements and migrations. His perspective is useful in explaining some of the major trends of our own times, notably those of globalization, localization, and indigenization movements such as that of Islamism.

It may be argued that the world system has gone through three major interlocking phases of development. At the risk of oversimplifying its complexities, world history can be viewed in terms of the evolution of imperialism from an agrarian to an industrial to an informatic phase. Table

1.1 provides a schematic view of these three phases with respect to the changing structures of state and economy as well as their associated ideological and identity configurations. In its first phase, it may be characterized as *agrarian imperialism,* marked by the rise and fall of successive multinational empires that thrived on agrarian surplus economies, urban political centers, and capital accumulation through international trade in luxury goods (witness the Silk Road and the Spice Road). During this phase, the rise and fall of imperial systems can be more generally explained in terms of Ibn Khaldun's theory of history, namely, the periodic tribal conquests of sedentary populations who in turn conquered their conquerors. As the case of China demonstrates (Barfield 1989), the reverse also happened: Sinification of the hinterland population of the Chinese Empire was a dominant pattern. The Great Wall of China was, in fact, built to protect the sedentary population against tribal encroachments. Although it succeeded most times, it failed at other times, as in the case of the Mongolian invasion.

As a pioneering historical social scientist, Ibn Khaldun provides a telling explanation for the dynamics of the first phase. His core idea is the concept of *asabiyya,* without which no individual, group, or state can survive the struggles of life. Because of their need for mutual aid in constant movement and adaptation to hard economic conditions, tribal societies show a higher level of social solidarity than sedentary communities. When combined with the zeal of religious faith, tribal solidarity is a formidable

Table 1.1   Global System Development: Three Overlapping Phases

Mode	Agrarian Imperialism 550 B.C.E.–1648	Industrial Imperialism 1648–1991	Informatic Imperialism 1991–present
Mode of production			
Economy	Herding, agriculture	Mining Manufacturing, services	Knowledge industries
Mode of legitimation			
State	Religious	Political	Economistic
Mode of regulation			
Society	Multinational Agrarian empires, city-states, feudalism	Nation-states Multinational, industrial empires	Superstates, TNCs, TMCs, IGOs, NGOs, AGOs, unrepresented nations and peoples organizations (UNPOs)
Mode of communication			
Technology	Writing	Print	Electronic
Identity	Religious	Secular	Cosmopolitan
Community	Local	National	Global
Legitimacy	Metaphysical	Ideological	Ecological

force. That is how, within the short period of no more than 100 years, the Arab tribal armies of Islam could defeat the two ancient imperial forces of Persia and Byzantium by conquering all the lands lying between Spain, Central Asia, and India. In Islamic and pre-Islamic history of West Asia and North Africa, it was the perennial tribal conquests of the sedentary population that brought successive dynasties to power. Each time, the conquerors were "civilized," or sedentarized, softened by the luxuries of urban life, which led to their dynastic decline and another round of nomadic invasion and conquest.

More recent research into comparative world systems shows that commercial trade and political hegemony were supported by four major multinational agrarian empires: East Asia (Chinese), South Asia (Indian), Central and West Asia (Persian, Arab, and Turkic), and West (Greek and Roman). Chase-Dunn and Hall (1977) have provided a summary of much of this research with a rich diversity of mappings of the agrarian empires. In his periodization of world history, Jerry Bentley (1996) has identified the early part of this period as "the age of classical civilizations, unfolding from about 500 B.C.E. to 500 C.E." In addition to the rise of major universal religions (Confucianism, Buddhism, Christianity) and philosophies (Taoist and Greek), Bentley notes,

> the classical civilizations also organized states on a much larger scale than had earlier societies: the Han dynasty in China embraced far more territory than the Shang and Zhou dynasties, the Achaemenids dynasty in Persia dwarfed earlier Mesopotamian states, the Mauryan dynasty absorbed numerous regional kingdoms in India, and the Roman empire brought all the lands of the Mediterranean basin under its control. As a result of their larger scale of organization, the States generated by the classical civilizations pacified much larger territories than had their predecessors. (Bentley 1996: 756)

The classical age was followed by a postclassical period, lasting from 500 to 1000 C.E., that was dominated by three major imperial systems: the Tang empire in China, the Abbasid Empire in southwest Asia and North Africa, and the Byzantine empire in the eastern Mediterranean basin. However, this period came to an end by the rise of what Bentley calls "the age of transregional nomadic empires, extending from about 1000 to 1500 C.E." The most dramatic event of this period, as Bentley notes, "came during the thirteenth century, when the Mongols and their allies overran most of Eurasia and established the largest empire in human history, stretching from China, Manchuria, and Korea in the east to Russia and the Danube in the west. Even after the collapse of their Yuan dynasty in China (1368), the Mongols played a prominent role in Central Asia" (Bentley 1996: 756). Their illustrious rule in India collapsed only after the British conquered that country.

Whether originating from city-states (such as the Greek and Roman empires) or established by tribal conquests of cities and rural areas (such as the Assyrian, Median, Achaemenid, Seljuk, Mongolian, Timurid, Safavid, or Ottoman empires), all agrarian, multinational empires included a trichotomous social structure (rural, urban, and nomadic). In this structure, nomads and sedentary populations were in constant struggle for the control of peripheries. The institutions of the imperial state followed a consistent pattern of centralized control and decentralized administration (sometimes known as feudalism). Their economies were similarly characterized by rural, urban, and nomadic production in which the exploitation of the peasants mainly paid for the imperial rule and retinue. Whenever strong imperial systems were simultaneously in power across the Eurasian landmass, trade flourished along such commercial routes as the Silk and Spice Roads. The discovery of the ocean routes in the sixteenth century led to the decline of the Asian routes and their commercial entrepôts (Frank 1992). But Asian imperial pretensions continued until, in the eighteenth and nineteenth centuries, military defeats finally brought home a sense of weakness and eventual subjugation to the Europeans.

Identity structures also reflected the trichotomous social structure in which the center population identified itself with the imperial order and the periphery population belonged to the multinational religio-ethnic groups or tribes. The *millet* system under the Ottoman empire is typified by this kind of imperial cultural policy under which any subject could aspire to become an Ottoman while belonging to a particular autonomous *millet,* including the Peoples of the Book, that is, the Jewish, Christian, and Muslim communities. Multinational agrarian empires were thus built on the facts of ethnic difference rather than uniformity.

The agrarian imperialist phase came to an end by the post-Westphalian rise of a second phase. I label this phase *industrial imperialism.* Its industrial economies, nation-states, and large-scale immigration from rural to urban areas and from Europe into the rest of the world brought about a number of competing European industrial empires. Industrial empires began in the European nation-states with nationalist ideologies that attempted to homogenize their own population into ethnic uniformity. The rise of the European nation-state system provided a new political organization far more cohesive than the imperial orders of the past. When combined with the economic discipline and strength of an industrial state, the new nations surpassed even the tribes in their *asabiyya.* Expanding into the entire world, the modern European empires were thus nationally and industrially based. They also facilitated a new kind of nomadism through large-scale immigration into the territories of the Old and the New Worlds. Their Achilles' heel, however, was in the ideologies they exported. Nationalism, liberalism, and Marxism became the rallying points for the colonial peoples as ideologies with which to fight back and to shame their oppressors. In the face of such resistance, different national empires assumed different strategies. The British, on the whole, followed a policy of indirect rule, manipulating the traditional structures of authority to their own advantage. The French were the proud inheritors of a revolutionary tradition and consequently wished to export their political culture into the colonized territories through administrative centralization and cultural indoctrination. As inheritors of an anticolonial tradition, the United States was willing to turn the colonies into self-governing states or territories as in the cases of Hawaii, Alaska, Guam, and Puerto Rico.

The end of the industrial empires, however, left a postcolonial world torn by competing ethnic and nationalist rivalries. The European model of pannationalism was scarcely suitable to the premodern multitribal and multiethnic societies of the postcolonial states. Thus, during the Cold War, the two superpowers exploited such internal rivalries of the new states to advance their causes. The post–Cold War period has consequently unleashed well-armed ethnic conflicts in many parts of the world. Another consequence of industrial imperialism was the reverse migration from the colonies to the mother countries. Millions of expatriates and their native allies had to leave their homes voluntarily or by force. The influx of such immigrants into the major metropolitan centers of Europe, North America, Russia, and Japan has intensified ethnic and racial tensions. This has in turn led to a cultural backlash against Third World immigrants.

The third phase of world imperialism has yet to fully unfold. The passage of most advanced industrial economies into a postindustrial, informatic phase has facilitated a new type of capitalism and imperialism based not so much on control of land or capital but of the latest scientific patents and technologies. The new pancapitalism is global rather than national in scope; its loyalties are not to the national flag but to the global marketplace and its opportunities for profit. The role of information technologies is critical to pancapitalism's survival and prosperity. Nearly 70 percent of the gross national product (GDP) of Organization for Economic Cooperation and Development (OECD) countries is contributed by services; agriculture and manufacturing make up the rest. The bulk of these services are what might be called information services, including government, research and development, education, investment, banking, marketing, advertising, and the media. World centers and peripheries should be thus redefined on the basis of whether or not they can log in to these information networks.

The new imperial phase can be called *informatic imperialism,* characterized by global, post-Fordist, flexible accumulation, an information economy, and transnational regulatory regimes managed by such IGOs as the World Bank, the International Monetary Fund (IMF), the World Trade Organization (WTO), and the International Telecommunication Union

(ITU). The convergence of pancapitalism and informatic imperialism owes itself to three major transformations. First, the technological breakthroughs in information storage, processing, and retrieval, the rise of computer-assisted design and manufacturing (CAD-CAM), and the use of robotics have led to new structures of production and finance. The application of information technologies to production and financing has saved labor costs and facilitated global management of transnational conglomerates.

Second, the new structures have made flexible accumulation both possible and desirable (D. Harvey 1990). Flexible accumulation allows manufacturers to go beyond the rigidities of the Fordist assembly line production methods to achieve a higher degree of division of labor, dexterity, and efficiency by assigning the production of different parts of the same product to a diversity of production centers spread out globally.

Third, the combination of these two factors has led to an unprecedented decentralization of capital throughout the world to wherever lower wages, rents, and taxes and fewer government regulations can guarantee higher profits. This decentralization explains the phenomenon of downsizing, the presence of Japanese and Korean companies in remote parts of the United States and Europe, the flight of U.S. and European industries to East Asia, and the competition for entry into the newly opened markets of China, Eastern Europe, and the former Soviet Union.

Under the emerging circumstances, small or medium-sized nation-states are of marginal consequence because their economic, military, and cultural policies are largely circumvented by the new powerful players on the world scene, namely, the superstates in alliance with the TNCs and IGOs (M. Tehranian 1997, 1999). The new global telecommunication networks have created a world system of information gathering, storage, processing, and retrieval unparalleled in human history. Electronic cash transfers, satellite remote sensing, direct broadcast satellites, and instantaneous communication through faxes, the Internet, and the World Wide Web, as well as audio and video conferencing, have empowered those with access to such technologies. The new informatic imperialism or pancapitalism has no centers and peripheries; it thinks of itself as omnipresent, omniscient, and omnipotent.

Jonathan Friedman (1994) has argued that "ethnification, social and political disorder are expressions of declining hegemony in the global systems." But if we view pancapitalism as the political economy of transnationalization, it can be argued otherwise. It might be true that the individual superstates (the United States, Russia, China, Britain, France, Germany, and Japan) have each declined in the political control of their respective peripheries. In the meantime, however, the economic forces of globalization have penetrated both traditional centers and peripheries to a degree that political control can now be exerted much more subtly and indirectly. A small to medium-sized country can be brought to its knees by the IMF's structural adjustment program, the World Bank's refusal to lend, or the World Trade Organization's economic sanctions. In the superstates, the transnational forces act primarily through a combination of economic carrots and political sticks. In liberal democracies, the politicians and the state could also be hijacked through campaign financing and other corrupt practices. Hegemonic domination has thus continued, but its forms have become far more subtle and complex. Pancapitalism's strategy of control hinges on the control of information, namely, control of sources of capital, patents, and copyright, political surveillance and manipulation of politicians, and global advertising and its consuming identities (K. Tehranian 1998).

SITES OF INSECURITY AND RESISTANCE

Pancapitalism has not been able to homogenize the world. Despite its imperial power of "Coca-Colanization," informatic imperialism faces a world population that is as heterogeneous and resistant to homogenization as ever. This multicultural world is growing to be even more so because the same information technologies empower the voiceless to come to historical consciousness while asserting their cultural identities. Increasing ethnification is a direct consequence of this process.

As Fred Riggs (1998) argues, modernity by its very nature and temperament creates insecurities while privileging the new against the old, the nascent against the dying, and the strong against the weak. It thus marginalizes vast segments of the population and induces a conflict of cultures, values, and identities that cannot be easily resolved. By delinking the economy from polity and cultural production, liberal capitalism managed for a while to quarantine identity negotiations from the political realm. Although this delinkage frequently led to legitimation crises (Habermas 1973), periodic elections often managed to defuse its systemic impact. However, accelerating globalization of the markets and cultures has led to a relinkage of economy, polity, and culture. As witnessed by increasing costs of campaigning in the liberal democracies, the politicians and the capitalist state are often held hostage to the demands of the transnational market forces. Similarly, political resistance against transnational capital is increasingly taking the shape of struggles against regional economic or transnational organizations. Witness Ross Perot's campaign in 1992 and 1996, and the 1994–1996 struggle in Chiappas, Mexico, against the North American Free Trade Agreement (NAFTA), as well as the 1996 Filipino demonstrations against Asia-Pacific Economic Cooperation (APEC) and the 1996–1997 Tupac Amaru takeover of the Japanese embassy in Lima against the transnational encroachment of Peru by Japan.

As in the case of posttraditionalist (or fundamentalist) movements in India, Iran, Israel, Algeria, Egypt, Turkey, the United States, and Europe, the more recent resistance movements are also couched in cultural and identity terms. Culture has thus been increasingly politicized in many parts of the world, leading to violence in places such as Bosnia, Chechnya, Mexico, and Tajikistan. The great diversity of these conflicts cannot be fully understood unless we relate them to the larger picture of global pancapitalism.

Informatic imperialism is treading on volatile ground. The impact of pancapital on indigenous populations is a mixed blessing. Although capital brings with it new technologies, management techniques, and possibilities for export-driven strategies of development, it also uproots the traditional nexus of social solidarity and identity. Moreover, it creates dualistic societies torn apart between traditional masses and modernizing elites (witness Iran, Algeria, Turkey, Egypt, and Indonesia). It is often the transitional groups that take the lead in mobilizing the traditional, lower strata of population into a revolt against pancapitalism and its comprador elites. For this reason, it is more appropriate to call these groups post- or neo-traditional than fundamentalist or, worse yet, reactionary. When and if these groups take power, as the Islamic ulema did in the 1979 revolution in Iran, their strategy is not to go back to the status quo ante but to steer a new course of modernization based on indigenous institutions and dissociation from pancapitalism.

This strategy may or may not succeed, but the outcome is a society that is posttraditional. Conventional traditionalists are often marginalized in such revolutionary circumstances, as the conservative ulema have been in Iran. A similar situation exists in Israel, where the Orthodox Jews consider Zionism and the state of Israel illegitimate because they usurp the power of the Messiah.

Figure 1.1 puts the foregoing propositions into a schematic portrait of the polarities and spaces of identity negotiations in the postcapitalist era. In the rapidly vanishing premodern societies, the dominant cosmology is ecological and the sources of social solidarity and identity are primarily nativist (indigenous, tribal, and clannish). In modernizing societies, the race to riches is grounded in hypermodernity, the dominant rationality (cosmology) is instrumental, and the sources of social solidarity and identity are secular nationalism. In posttraditionalist societies and movements, reacting to the onslaught of modernization, the rationality is practical and identity formations are based on religious faith and networks. Finally, in the postmodern world of antinarrative narratives, the rationality is critical and pluralist while hybridity and cosmopolitanism characterize identity formation.

Figure 1.1 Polarities and Spaces of Identity Negotiations in the Pancapitalist Era

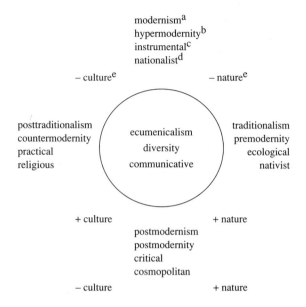

modernism[a]
hypermodernity[b]
instrumental[c]
nationalist[d]

      – culture[e]   – nature[e]

posttraditionalism   traditionalism
countermodernity   ecumenicalism   premodernity
practical   diversity   ecological
religious   communicative   nativist

      + culture   + nature
postmodernism
postmodernity
critical
cosmopolitan

      – culture   + nature

Source: Adapted from Friedman (1994: 92–93) and K. Tehranian (1998).
Notes: a. The first term in each category indicates the indentity pole.
b. The second term in each category indicates conditions.
c. The third term in each category indicates rationality.
d. The fourth term in each category indicates identity.
e. Indicates attitudes toward culture and nature.

CONCLUSION

This chapter has identified the growing gaps in wealth, income, and employment within and among nations as the symptoms of an emerging global apartheid system that causes increasing social and psychological insecurities. It has further analyzed the problem in terms of a world system that has developed from agrarian to industrial to informatic imperialism. Massive population movements have characterized all three phases. In the latest phase, however, migrations at the top and bottom of the global social structure are exacerbating ethnic and cultural conflicts to unprecedented degrees. The cultural sites of domination and resistance have become heavily politicized. Pancapitalism, or informatic imperialism, both celebrates and undermines multiculturalism. By commodifying culture, it unwittingly privileges cultural identity. However, by its inability to correct

the social and economic dislocations of growth, it gives cause for culturally grounded political resistance. The politics of identity has thus become
a nemesis of pancapitalism. Commodity and identity fetishisms are the
dual faces of the global apartheid fueling much of the current international
and intercultural insecurities.

World peripheries of power are resisting the new hegemonic globalist
trends by regionalist, pannationalist, ethnonationalist, revivalist, environmentalist, and feminist movements grounded in indigenous cultures (M.
Tehranian 1999). In the meantime, informatic imperialism has been creating two new types of nomadic populations. At the top of the social structure, there are millions of overseas TNC and IGO managers and professionals whose careers, identities, and loyalties no longer reside in one
country. At the bottom of the social structure, there are some 27 million
world refugees dislocated from their homelands because of famine, civil
wars, religious persecution, or ethnic cleansing (UNHCR 1995). These
new nomads have to reconstruct their material lives and cultural identities
in order to adjust to their new environments. Just like the old nomads in
pursuit of their worldly objectives, the new nomads also often prove more
resilient than the sedentary population. They form hybrid cultures and
identities as they are assimilated into a multicultural mainstream. Resistance against such inroads at the peripheries of centers is expressed by the
rise of anti-immigrant sentiments and policies. Informatic imperialism is
thus dividing the world between the high-tech and high-growth centers of
the global information economy and the disintegrating peripheries competing for diminishing jobs, identities, and opportunities. Overcoming an
emerging global apartheid will be the main challenge of the twenty-first
century.

2

REORDERING THE WORLD

There exists a great chasm between those, on the one side, who relate everything to a single central vision, one system less or more coherent or articulate, in terms of which they understand, think and feel—a single, universal, organizing principle in terms of which all that they are and say has significance—and, on the other side, those who pursue many ends, often unrelated and even contradictory, connected, if at all, only in some *de facto* way, for some psychological or physiological cause, related by no moral or aesthetic principle; these last lead lives, perform acts, and entertain ideas that are centrifugal rather than centripetal, their thought is scattered or diffused, moving on many levels, seizing upon the essence of a vast variety of experiences and objects, for what they are in themselves, without consciously or unconsciously seeking to fit them into or exclude them from any one unchanging . . . at time fanatical, unitary inner vision.

—Isaiah Berlin

This chapter offers a critique of the prevailing discourses of the new world order while presenting an alternative reading of the emerging dialectics of globalism, localism, and fragmentation. It argues that because of the contradictions and ambiguity of the signals of transition, the discourse has swung from euphoric optimism to dark pessimism. It has swung from declarations of a global triumph of liberal-democratic capitalism (Fukuyama 1989) to foreboding about a coming "clash of civilizations [between] the Christian West and an emerging Confucian-Islamic alliance" (Huntington 1993a). A succession of events has led us from promises to

---

This chapter is a revised version of my article "Where Is the New World Order: At the End of History or Clash of Civilizations?" *The Journal of International Communication* 1, no. 2 (1994), pp. 71–99.

27

perils. We have moved from the end of the Cold War and some vain hopes for peace dividends in 1989 to some major disasters, including the outbreak of the Gulf War in 1991, the dissolution of the Soviet Union in 1991, and the ensuing civil wars in the former Soviet Union and Yugoslavia, Somalia, Haiti, Rwanda, Burundi, Afghanistan, and Congo (formerly Zaire). The promises of peace in Palestine and Israel, South Africa, and Northern Ireland have been similarly dashed with the bitter residues of hatred. Within a very short period of time, the new world order has thus appeared as dismayingly disorderly. Some authors (Singer and Widavsky 1993) have argued that the "real world order" consists of "zones of peace" and "zones of turmoil." The zones of peace consist of a core of sixty-four advanced, industrial, liberal democratic countries, and the zones of turmoil correspond to a multitude of nations in the rest of the world caught in the agonizing pains of modernization, democratization, or transition from communist to market economies. Although this dichotomy seems to correspond more realistically to the political and economic realities of a divided world, it fails to account for the center-periphery fission within each nation and the fusion across borders. The so-called zones of peace do not appear so peaceful, and the zones of turmoil are not so uniformly in chaos.

The traditional geopolitical or spatial divisions of the world into East and West, North and South, First, Second, Third, and Fourth Worlds no longer ring true. Territories have been deterritorialized. The flows of goods, services, ideas, news, images, and data have increasingly assumed a transnational character in a global economy and culture that values whatever is novel. Cheaper goods and novel ideas emerge perhaps as much from the traditional centers as from the traditional peripheries. In the meantime, some centers have become peripherized (e.g., New York and Los Angeles slums), and some peripheries have assumed the status of industrial and financial centers (notably the four Asian tigers of South Korea, Singapore, Hong Kong, and Taiwan). This does not mean that a new reign of world prosperity and democracy has dawned. On the contrary, hard evidence shows that the world has become more differentiated and fragmented along growing gaps in social and economic equality (UNDP 1996; Maitland 1994; Tarjanne 1994). But the globalization of the world economy has brought about a new deterritorialized system of centers and peripheries based on the levels of science, technology, productivity, consumption, and creativity regardless of location. The new centers and peripheries now reside in transnational organizations and networks.

MODERNIZATION, DEMOCRATIZATION, COMMUNICATION

The dynamics of accelerating, uneven, and self-contradictory global change can be more accurately understood in light of a longer historical process that is still unfinished. For want of a better term, that process may be called "modernization and democratization." Although both terms carry a heavy baggage of ideological overtones, they still continue to have analytical value. I use "modernization" to mean a process of change that puts a primary value on scientific, technological, social, economic, political, and cultural innovations in order to achieve progressively higher levels of productivity and consumption. I employ "democratization" to mean progressively higher levels of individual freedom, social equality, and cultural community, a definition that corresponds with the French revolutionary slogan of *"liberté, egalité, fraternité."* There are thus enormous tensions between the top-down processes of modernization and the bottom-up processes of democratization. But there are tensions within each process as well. Modernization could unleash environmental disasters and cultural dislocation or, alternatively, produce a modernized harmony with nature and culture. Similarly, alternative democratization strategies could sacrifice one of the three democratic values at the altar of the others. The tensions among libertarian, egalitarian, and communitarian democracies have been historically expressed in the conflicts between the different paths to modernization, that is, modernization via the liberal democratic path versus the Communist path versus the Third World path. Through public and private discourses, communication is the arena through which the contradictions of the two processes are negotiated, resolved, or festered.

The Western Enlightenment provides the prime historical example of the dual top-down and bottom-up processes of modernization and democratization. However, its fundamental assumptions can be questioned without ignoring the urgent global needs for alleviation of economic deprivation, democratization of politics, preservation of endangered cultures, and protection of the environment. A modernization project need not be conditioned, for instance, on the infinite perfectibility of humans *or* on the absolute power of human reason, the need for the human domination of nature, the historical inevitability of progress, and the total rejection of tradition. On the contrary, successful modernization projects have often led to tradition in modernity, nurturing of nature, acceptance of the epistemological limits of human reason, and the recognition of the need for spiritual-mythological foundations in human communities.

The forces of modernization have proved to be historically cataclysmic. They have torn societies asunder in successive acts of creative destruction. Since the sixteenth century, the project of modernity has gone through many phases and faced much resistance. In the industrial centers of the world, the cultural resistance to its seemingly irresistible force has ranged from hypermodernization to countermodernization and postmodernization movements. In the agrarian and industrializing peripheries of the world, the colonial masters or the postcolonial elites have largely imposed modernization from above. It has thus been either zealously sought in hypermodernization campaigns to catch up or devoutly resisted in counter-modernization movements. In the postindustrial world, demodernization and postmodernization have begun to erode the work ethics and political hegemony of modernity.

The so-called new world order of the postwar era has thus been viewed both as progressive global integration and as chaotic global fragmentation and disintegration. As Isaiah Berlin has aptly recognized, these two contradictory perspectives reflect the subjective truths of the viewers who project their own worldviews into a presumed objective reality. By the first count, the new order is very old indeed. As commonly agreed, its seeds were sown in the rise of the modern world some five centuries ago. But as argued in this volume and by a number of other world system theorists (Frank and Gills 1993; Friedman 1994), its roots go back to the changing fortunes of all past imperial systems reflecting world systems of hegemony.

DECONSTRUCTING THE DISCOURSE

Under our own modern era of the last 500 years, the discourse of order has imposed its own order of discourse. It has divided the world between the traditional and the modern, categories roughly equivalent to the barbarian and civilized labels of the ancient world. Although modernism first appeared under the guise of commercial capitalism, it has also taken the shape of communism, nationalism, national socialism, and a variety of religious formations such as Calvinism, Puritanism, neo-Confucianism, and Islamism. By the eighteenth century, modernism had become an irresistible paradigm of most thinking in the modern world. With the force of a bulldozer, modern thought, science, and technology were paving all the obstacles that stood before them—castes, tribes, kings, bishops, myths, and dogmas. They were also founding a new myth and dogma of their own: the myth of reason and the dogma of scientism. They were establishing a new secular, globalist regime that defied the orders of universalistic religions and empires of the past. They thus stratified the world along new lines that cut across the old boundaries of religious faiths and civilizations.

In the name of reason, modernity established a new hegemony of universal science, technology, innovation, novelty, and change. By the nineteenth century, modernity was formulated into a powerful ideology of development, anchored in Darwinian evolutionary theory and the social Darwinism of classical economists, Marxian revolutionaries, and reactionary racists. In liberalism, communism, fascism, and nationalism, the four competing ideologies of modernism continue to dominate the world to this day.

Unlike the imperial and religious ideologies of the past, modernism was also armed with another powerful ideological arsenal—democracy. By challenging the divine rights of popes and kings, modernism rested on the idea of popular sovereignty. It called for the overthrow of any regime otherwise constituted, and it led to all of the capitalist, communist, and nationalist revolutions of the modern world. The democratic revolution is still unfinished and will continue well into the twenty-first century.

Above all, modernity created a new system of domination and dependency that destroyed the self-sufficient communities of the premodern world. Modernity conquered spaces with time, that is, timesaving and laborsaving mechanical, transportation, and telecommunication technologies that spread industry, people, and ideas around the world. Its globalism was thus of an entirely different order of magnitude from the globalisms of world conquerors and universalistic religions of the past. The Crusades (1095–1588) were only a dress rehearsal for what was to happen later with irresistible force. Modernist globalism first appeared after the sixteenth century in the form of colonialism, anchored in the "civilizing" mission of the "white man's burden." It led to the competing Portuguese, Spanish, British, French, German, Russian, Japanese, and U.S. empires. In the postcolonial world, the dependency patterns of colonialism gave way to neocolonial forms in which the postcolonial elites acted as surrogates for a new world system of domination and dependency.

Since modernity put the mastery of time to its own service, space became the locus of resistance against its all-conquering force. The order of modernity required accelerating technological innovation and capital accumulation as well as progressive incorporation of ever-larger spaces within its own dominion. It respected no boundaries—spatial, temporal, or intellectual. Futurism and globalism became its twin ideologies. But a total break with the past and localist loyalties proved impossible. The three competing ideologies of nationalism, regionalism, and localism provided roadblocks to the ceaseless expansions of modernist globalism. All three ideologies are based on loyalties to particular spaces to resist the leveling and homogenizing effects of modernism. Of late, however, a religious resurgence in the Hindu, Buddhist, Judaic, Christian, and Islamic worlds is reclaiming time as its chief arsenal against the modernist notions to defend spaces that have historically been theirs. Looking to the past rather than the future as the golden age of humanity, the posttraditionalist religious movements present yet another path to modernity sanctified in the name of tradition. Postmodernism also presents another challenge to the modernist hegemony: By negating all metanarratives, postmodern thought offers radical skepticism as its form of resistance. The ideological demarcations between modernist globalism and its discontents are thus drawn more sharply than ever before in the struggles for both time and space.

These battle lines are drawn everywhere, from local to global arenas, from the control of microinstitutions (e.g., the family) to macroinstitutions (e.g., nation-states). Although nonstate actors such as TNCs, TMCs, IGOs, NGOs, and UNPOs (unrepresented nations and peoples organizations) have assumed greater roles, the state actors continue to be the most visible players on the international scene. The battle for the control of states as the irreducible units of international relations will therefore continue into the future. In fact, the number of state actors may increase through the fragmentation of larger states such as Russia, the United States, Canada, India, China, and Brazil.

International discourse in the post–Cold War era has thus focused on five major themes: the problems of order and security, freedom and development, equality and social justice, community and democracy, and culture and identity. These themes are not new; they have been with us ever since the major democratic revolutions of the seventeenth and eighteenth centuries put them on the international agenda. Theories of international relations have more or less followed the logic of the five axial principles of modern democratic theory, that is, order, freedom, equality, community, and identity. However, these norms are now being discussed under the new post–Cold War conditions of accelerating globalization, multipolarity, concentrations of wealth and power, and localization and fragmentation of power in a broadening and deepening of the democratic revolution.

The world system seems to be in a state of transition that has been characterized differently by a variety of pundits. Under an assortment of rubrics, an increasing number of scholars have been speculating on the new structures of global economy, polity, and culture. Their tantalizing labels give us a glimpse of the speculative contents of each theory: "post-industrial society" (Bell 1973); "information economy and society" (Porat 1977; Masuda 1981); "post-Fordist, flexible accumulation" (D. Harvey 1990); "communitarian democracy" (Etzioni 1993; M. Tehranian 1990b); "late capitalism" (Mandel 1978); "disorganized capitalism" (Lash and Urry 1987 and 1994); "postmodernity" (Docherty 1993); "the Third Wave" (Toffler 1980); "the Fourth Discontinuity" (Mazlish 1993); and the "sixth and seventh modernizations."

The fin de siècle has also led to an alarming cottage industry of apocalyptic publications with declarations of the end of everything, from history (Fukuyama 1989) to geography (Mosco 1995), modernity (Vattimo 1991; Mowlana and Wilson 1990), journalism (Katz 1992), racism (D'Souza 1995), work (Rifkin 1995), university (Noam 1995, M. Tehranian 1996b), and diversity (Mowlana 1996). In the absence of any hard evidence, it is comforting to note that nothing seems to be coming to an end— except the twentieth century. And since time and centuries are figments of our own imagination in order to punctuate our conditions of finitude, their end also seems to be illusory. As Jean Baudillard (1994) has argued, all notions of "the end" are founded on linear concepts—of history, geography, modernity, etc. True, linearity is coming to an end in the postmodern age. But new trajectories of meaning are inventing new histories, geographies, modernities, journalisms, works, and universities.

If there is a new world order, therefore, it can be better understood in terms of the paradoxes of a situation in which we are increasingly witnessing dazzling technological and economic breakthroughs without corresponding social, political, and normative innovations (Attali 1991; Kennedy 1993; K. Tehranian and M. Tehranian 1992). These epistemological lags are leading to economic growth without employment, political democratization without political efficacy, and cultural diversity without tolerance and civility. As Adam said to Eve, we are truly in an age of transition. In order to avoid the enormous risks facing us, the challenge lies perhaps in trying to bridge the widening chasms between the exploding technological opportunities and the currently unfulfilled human needs.

The discourse of the new world order is not so new. In a computerized search at the University of Hawaii, 125 items were retrieved, including books published around the time of the two world wars, among them, Hitler's *My New Order* (1941). The conceptual framework of the discourse can be found in at least five competing theories of international relations, namely, realism, liberalism, Marxism, communitarianism (also known as institutionalism), and postmodernism. Each has, however, added some new perspectives to the old. Table 2.1 provides a synopsis of the major propositions, principles and processes, units of analysis, and methodologies of these schools. The realists have sought to find a new geopolitical category to take the place of the Cold War catechisms of the free and Communist worlds. Huntington's call to arms in his "clash of civilizations" article clearly belongs to this category. It conjures up a new enemy against whom to launch a new crusade—the fundamentalist Muslims and the godless Chinese Communists. It makes a contribution, however, to the problematization of "culture" as a critical factor in international relations. Culture was a factor largely neglected in the realist analyses of the Cold War years, but it has clearly been politicized in the post–Cold War era. Acknowledging its importance is a step forward, but turning cultural politics into a new ideological crusade serves neither the cause of scholarly understanding nor the cause of international peace.

Realists have focused primarily on the geopolitical struggles for power. They have employed the nation-state as their chief unit of analysis and considered international politics as devoid of moral consensus and therefore prone to violence. They have argued that the pursuit of national interest in the context of a balance of power strategy is the most efficient and realistic road to international peace and security (Morgenthau 1985;

Table 2.1 International Relations: A Typology of Normative Theories

Theory	Major Proposition	Axial Principle	Unit of Analysis	Methodology
Realism	IR is a struggle for power and peace through balance of power in a political environment devoid of moral consensus and prone to use of force. In such an environment, national interest and strength must be the guiding stars.	Order	Nation-state	Historical method
Liberalism	IR is a struggle for power, peace, and freedom through balance of power in a political environment in which increasing interdependencies have created a need for the rule of law and cooperation through IGOs.	Freedom	Nation-state IGOs	Historical method Game theory Simulation, etc.
Marxism	IR is a class struggle for equality between those who own the means of production and those who don't. Under the world capitalist system, the struggle has been waged between the bourgeoisie and the revolutionary working classes, peasantry, and intelligentsia. As the highest stage of capitalism, imperialism has transformed the struggle into a global class war that cuts across national boundaries.	Equality	World system TNCs TMCs revolutionary and counterrevolutionary states and movements	Historical and dialectical materialism
Communitarianism	IR is a struggle for power, peace, and community through democratic cooperation and institution building from local to global in a political environment of contesting power and moral claims that need to be negotiated through global communication, adjudication, or mediation of conflicts without recourse to violence.	Community	Civil society TNCs TMCs NGOs IGOs States	Eclectic and multidisciplinary
Postmodernism	IR is a struggle for hegemonic power through competing truth claims that need to be understood intertextually as negotiations of knowledge and power.	Identity	Culture	Interpretive

Kissinger 1994). In both theory and practice, realism has been the dominant school of thought, focusing on peace through national strength, armament, and balance of power. For realists, order is the primary normative value, and historical analysis is the soundest methodology to pursue.

Liberals, by contrast, have pointed to the integrating forces of the world market as a new reality creating considerable international interdependency in the postwar period. They have argued that increasing levels of free trade, development, deepening and broadening of interdependency, and international cooperation through intergovernmental organizations are the surest path to peace (Keohane and Nye 1989). For liberals, freedom in property ownership, politics, and trade is the primary normative value. In their studies of international relations, liberals supplement historical analysis with a variety of quantitative and qualitative methods such as time series, correlation analyses, and simulation games.

In contrast to realism, which focuses on the nation-state, the liberalist discourse focuses on the increasing economic and security interdependencies that characterize the emerging world system (Keohane and Nye 1989). It has thus incorporated the increasing role of the nonstate actors in the international regimes of energy, transportation, finance, and telecommunications. Fukuyama's contentions on the "end of history" represent the logical conclusions of over two centuries of liberal discourse on the inevitability of its hegemony. If the invisible hand of the market is what produces the most efficient and ultimately fair social and economic organization, the demise of communism in the former Soviet Union and increasing privatization in other socialist economies signal the beginning of the ultimate triumph of liberal capitalism worldwide. In this vein, Fukuyama has argued that "the essential meaning of the end of history is not that turbulence has ceased or that the world has become completely uniform, but rather that there are no serious systematic institutional alternatives to liberal democracy and market-based capitalism for the world's most advanced countries" (Fukuyama 1995: 103). Democracy in this conception is clearly viewed as libertarian rather than egalitarian or communitarian.

By contrast, Marxist and critical discourses on the new world order focus on the failure of the world capitalist system to solve its own inherent problems of boom and bust cycles, the growing gaps in wealth and income, and the breakdown of the social fabric and work ethics. Jurgen Habermas (1973) has characterized the world capitalist system as a permanent legitimation crisis born out of its delinkage of the economic and political systems, leading to contradictory results. World system analysts such as Immanuel Wallerstein (1974), Frederick Jameson (1991), and David Harvey (1990) have sought to show how capitalism has entered a new post-Fordist phase of "flexible accumulation," producing new economic and cultural crises. The more dire predictions point to the possibility of a worldwide economic breakdown and the rise of neo-Fascist movements (Attali 1991, Barber 1995).

Although in decline politically, Marxists and neo-Marxists continue to present powerful theoretical arguments that have an appeal in the peripheries of the world. They view international relations primarily in terms of class conflict within and among nations and argue that since the sixteenth century, capitalism has increasingly incorporated the peripheries into a world system of domination and exploitation through imperialism, colonialism, and neocolonialism (Wallerstein 1974; Schiller 1981 and 1985). The social revolutions in Russia, China, Cuba, Vietnam, and many LDCs have been attempts to break away from the fetters of the world capitalist system. However, these countries are being reincorporated by an international regime orchestrated by transnational corporations, the World Bank, the IMF, the General Agreement on Tariffs and Trade (GATT), and its successor, the newly formed WTO. But Marxists further argue that internal contradictions, wars, and revolutionary struggles will continue to challenge the dominant capitalist system. For Marxists, equality is the primary normative value, and historical materialism and dialectics are the dominant methodologies.

A fourth school of thought and discourse on the new world system may be labeled as institutionalist or communitarian. The transformation of the GATT into WTO, which can set the rules of world trade and adjudicate conflict, suggests a new level in international integration. As exemplified by many regional organizations, the new emphasis on regionalism provides further evidence for the communitarian perspective. The EU, NAFTA, Commonwealth of Independent States (CIS), APEC, ASEAN, South Asian Regional Cooperation (SARC), and Economic Cooperation Organization (ECO) have each made contributions toward greater regional peace and prosperity. But the communitarian perspective goes further in emphasizing the critical importance of social capital as distinct from economic capital in fostering economic development (K. Tehranian and M. Tehranian 1992).

The communitarian perspective has been articulated by a diversity of political theorists and activists (Deutsch 1966a and 1988; Gandhi 1957; Khomeini 1981; Etzioni 1993; Haas 1992; M. Tehranian 1990b; K. Tehranian and M. Tehranian 1992). Although the ideologies of its proponents differ, the centrality of civil society as expressed through community formations, in contrast to the nation-state and social classes, is what unifies this theoretical perspective. As expressed in its cultural, communal, and institutional formations, civil society thus serves as the underlying unit of analysis. In the traditional literature of international relations, this school of thought is closely linked to the institutionalist and regionalist perspectives emphasizing the integration processes of world and regional systems.

However, it also has manifested itself in a variety of anticolonial, nationalist, tribalist, localist, ethnic, and religious movements focused on mobilizing the common historical memories of the peripheries in waging a cultural and political struggle against the centers. The communitarians thus emphasize the centrality of political community as a condition for a durable peace at local, national, regional, and global levels. Community is thus the primary normative value to be pursued, and institution building for world economic, political, and cultural integration is the policy recommendation.

A fifth school, postmodernism, has called into question the truth claims of all grand theories of histories, replacing their ideological pretensions with the hermeneutics of suspicion. It has left no metanarrative of history unscathed from its scornful and skeptical criticisms. Michel Foucault and his postmodernist disciples have questioned the validity of such claims as the inevitability of progress, the march of history toward a classless society, or the pretensions of the powerful. They have argued that a deconstructive strategy of unmaking ideologies serves the interest of human liberation better than constructing yet another ideological metanarrative. By leaving no place for power to hide, Foucault and his disciples have provided a radically relativist view of international relations that examines intertextual relations for the understanding of world politics. In this view, cultural and identity formations take a central place in the analysis of international and intertextual relations (Derian and Shapiro 1989).

Postmodernism is the latest theoretical perspective to have influenced international relations theory. Emanating from the poststructuralist and deconstructionist schools of thought, postmodernism is deeply imbued with linguistic analyses of knowledge and power. It therefore highlights the central importance of identity as an axial principle in the globalization and localization of knowledge, truth claims, and power struggles. Generally committed to radical relativism, postmodernism interprets contemporary international relations as a process of negotiation of knowledge, power, and identity through military, economic, and cultural arsenals of influence. Although some tendencies in postmodernism are nihilistic, others seek out those universals in global knowledge that could unify an otherwise fragmented world (Vattimo 1991). Plurality of meanings, tolerance of differences, fluidity of identities, and recombinations of ideas and images from totally different eras and civilizations are thus the postmodern foci of analysis (Derian and Shapiro 1989).

Although each theoretical discourse has its own unique set of assumptions and conclusions reflecting competing interests in the international community, global communication has forced them into a grudging dialogue. Table 2.1 confines itself to a typology of the main conceptual strands. However, there are many theoretical hybrids that have enriched international discourse on world order. Significantly, the axial principles of the five schools of thought together constitute the five democratic goals of order, liberty, equality, community, and identity in the modern world.

POLITICIZING THE DISCOURSE

The effects of global communication on the evolution of international relations theory have been twofold. On the one hand, global communication has empowered the peripheries of power to engage progressively in the international discourse on the aims and methods of the international system. In this way, liberalism challenged the traditional state-centered, protectionist, mercantilist policies of the sixteenth to eighteenth centuries with its revolutionary doctrines of laissez-faire in international trade and protection of property and liberty in domestic life. However, it also incorporated much of the geopolitical realist view of power politics in its justification of the colonial and imperial orders while increasingly emphasizing the role of IGOs in the management of the international system. Similarly, Marxism challenged liberalism's dominance in the nineteenth and twentieth centuries by its mobilization of the peripheries against the colonialist and imperialist orders. However, in practice, Communist regimes often cynically followed realist geopolitical doctrines while paying lip service to international proletarian solidarity. Through appeals to democratic values, liberalism in turn undermined the Communist regimes by its control of the global flows of capital, trade, news, and data.

In a world system dominated by state and corporate bureaucracies, communitarianism is the latest phase in a continuing theoretical and ideological struggle by the peripheries to put the collective human rights of the oppressed on the international agenda. In its preoccupation with the collective rights of community, however, communitarianism cannot altogether ignore the realist focus on political order, the liberal preoccupation with individual freedom, and the Marxist concern with social equality. Postmodernism deconstructs the truth claims of all of the foregoing schools by casting doubt on their metanarratives. But it also posits its own metanarrative of relativism as a truth claim. Tensions among the five theoretical schools clearly reveal the conflicts among the competing aims of democracy: order, freedom, equality, community, and identity.

On the other hand, global communication has also served as a channel for theoretical integration. Political leadership in international relations has increasingly come to mean moral leadership in global debates on such issues as colonialism, development, population, environment, nuclear weapons, human rights, and the status of women and minorities. Global communication has thus historically broadened and deepened the parameters of discourse from realism to liberalism, Marxism, communitarianism, and now postmodernism. Each school of thought has had to respond to the concerns of new layers of the international community as they have emerged from conditions of oppression and silence. International relations theory has thus progressively incorporated the new democratic claims for equality, self-determination, and cultural identity.

For example, the slogan of "new world order" has gone through several mutations in this century. For the Axis powers in World War II, it meant a new world system making room for the imperial ambitions of Germany, Italy, and Japan. For the Allies, it meant a reorganization of the world around the UN principles of collective security policed by the five permanent members of the Security Council. The dichotomies of the war and the Cold War periods, however, have given way to greater multipolarity and complexity. Views of the international system and its most urgent reform needs are thus as fractious as the world itself. The complexities of the world demand international relations theories that can focus on growing gaps and interdependencies, conflicts and cooperation, violence and peace building. They also call for policies recognizing that global communication plays a central role in defining problems and negotiating solutions. But meaningful international communication calls for technical competence and equality of access to the means of communication—a requirement that is sorely lacking in today's world. For example, as long as the whole continent of Africa has fewer telephone lines than the city of Tokyo, global communication will largely continue to flow one way. Industrial countries as a whole have over eighteen times more telephone lines per 100 people than all the developing countries (UNDP 1996: 193). Since telephones are the linchpin of the emerging global communication system, this situation exacerbates the existing communication gaps in the world. Theory building in international relations clearly requires greater multicultural dialogue in order to build bridges among the competing cultural constructions of world conflicts.

For a discourse to have political efficacy, it must organize itself around collective interests. Table 2.2 presents a genealogy of the more recent discourses, their metanarratives, and their constituencies. It demonstrates how, like a chameleon, the slogan of "new world order" has historically changed its colors in order to organize competing political aggregations of interest. Depending on who has used the slogan when, it has conjured up vastly different images. To the Group of 77 at the UN calling for a new world economic order in a 1974 General Assembly resolution, the new order meant a revamped international economic system to redress the terms of trade in favor of the LDCs. When a small group of oil-exporting countries managed to quadruple the price of crude oil in 1973 through the collective action of the Organization of Petroleum

Table 2.2 The New World Order Discourses and Metanarratives: A Genealogy

The Political Discourses

1974–1984 New World Economic Order
Proponents: Group of 77
Opponents: Group of 7 led by the United States

The long-term deteriorating terms of trade between the industrial goods–producing countries of the North and the raw material–producing countries of the South have systematically deprived the LDCs of their chances for self-sustaining development. To correct these inequities, a new world economic order is needed to redress the terms of trade by collective bargaining, to provide access for the LDCs to the markets of the more developed countries (MDCs), and to facilitate transfers of science and technology. Outcomes: the Brandt Report and North-South negotiations at the UN Conference on Trade and Development (UNCTAD).

1974–1984 New World Information and Communication Order
Proponents: Group of 77
Opponents: Group of 7 led by the United States

The media concentration in the hands of a few transnational corporations from a few advanced industrial countries has created a severe imbalance in the flow of news, images, and data against the LDCs. The consequence of these imbalances is that the LDCs are often stereotyped as places where natural and man-made disasters are rampant. The genuine efforts of the LDCs for development are rarely noted. To correct these imbalances, a NWICO is needed in which the free flow of information is matched by a greater balance between LDCs and MDCs. This requires South-South cooperation and assistance from the North to build up the information and telecommunication infrastructure of the LDCs. Outcomes: the MacBride Report and the establishment of the International Program for the Development of Communication (IPDC) at UNESCO.

1989–1993 New World Order
Proponents: The United States and Gulf War allies
Opponents: Iraq and sympathizers

The end of the Cold War has unleashed a variety of new threats to international peace and security by such small or medium powers as Iraq, Libya, Iran, North Korea, and Serbia. To counter this threat and to establish a new regime of international law and order, the great powers, through the UN or independently, should police the world by active intervention in situations of conflict. Outcomes: UN intervention in the Gulf War, Somalia, Bosnia, and Haiti. The limited efficacy of such interventions has led to a decline of the discourse of the new world order.

The Academic and Policy Discourses

1945–present Modernization Theories
Proponents: Liberals
Opponents: Marxists

As exemplified by the historical experiences of the West, the transition from traditional to modern societies is an inevitable historical process. The LDCs can best succeed by emulating that experience. The best policies to pursue are breaking the traditional cultural barriers to progress, democratizing their polities, liberalizing their markets, and encouraging foreign trade and investment.

1945–present Dependency and World System Theories
Proponents: Marxists
Opponents: Liberals

Capitalist penetration of the LDCs has progressively impoverished them materially and culturally, creating a dependency status for most. Some periphery nations such as Japan and

(continues)

Table 2.2 continued

South Korea have escaped this fate by joining the ranks of capitalist nations in a world system primarily run by transnational corporations. Others may also join the ranks, but the system of capitalist exploitation will continue until socialist revolutions can abolish the class system.

> *1973–present   Postindustrial, Information Society Theories*
>   Proponents: Liberals
>   Opponents: Marxists

In the advanced industrial countries, a progressive shift from manufacturing to service and information sectors has ushered in a new postindustrial society in which the greatest percentage of the labor force is engaged in the production, processing, transmission, and application of knowledge and information. The resulting information economy and society are international phenomena facilitated by global transportation and telecommunication technologies. To catch up, the LDCs must follow a strategy of technological leapfrogging by the adoption of the latest industries and technologies.

> *1989–present   End of History and Clash of Civilizations Theories*
>   Proponents: Fukuyama and Huntington

The end of the Cold War, the collapse of the Soviet Union and Eastern European Communist regimes, and the introduction of market economies in the remaining Communist countries signal the global triumph of liberal, democratic capitalism. History as Hegel defined it (the battlefield of ideas) has thus come to an end. The rest will be devoted to the boring details of the global application of the liberal democratic capitalist principles. This process, however, is encountering some resistance from other incompatible civilizations. The next world war, therefore, may be a war of civilizations between the Christian West and an emerging Confucian-Islamic alliance.

> *1980s–present   Late Capitalism, Postmodernist Theories*
>   Proponents: *Marxists and post-Marxists*

Late capitalism is exhibiting a number of features, including global expansion, flexible accumulation, deterritorialization, disorganization, and displacement, with postmodern cultural consequences. The process may be viewed either as potentially emancipatory in the unfinished project of the Enlightenment (Habermas 1983) or as a new stage in the development of capitalism in which deconstructionist and antinarrative strategies are most effective in leaving power no place to hide (Foucault 1980). Whereas the former strategy calls for a politics of meaning focused on creating alternative normative structures, the latter implies a politics of antipolitics.

Exporting Countries (OPEC), it appeared for a fleeting moment that the nations exporting raw material might be able to redress the deteriorating terms of trade between the developed and developing countries. To the UN Educational, Scientific, and Cultural Organization (UNESCO), which picked up the discourse in the 1970s and 1980s under the banner of a new world information and communication order (NWICO), it meant balance as well as freedom in world news and information flows. The Brandt (1980 and 1985) and MacBride (1980) Commission reports set out those policy agendas (Traber 1986; Galtung and Vincent 1992; Frederick 1993). Following the largely fruitless North-South negotiations of the 1980s, the discourse of the new order was resurrected and co-opted by President

George Bush. To mobilize international support for a war effort against Saddam Hussein, Bush employed the slogan at the wake of the Gulf War in 1990–1991 with maximum effect. It now meant a new international regime of "law and order" under the aegis of the UN supported by the unanimity of the five permanent members of the Security Council and, if that were to fail, under alliances such as the North Atlantic Treaty Organization (NATO) or ultimately superpower action.

Francis Fukuyama's essay (1989) belongs to the early phase of post–Cold War optimism. "What we may be witnessing," he argued, "is not just the end of the Cold War, or the passing of a particular period of postwar history, but the End of History as such: that is, the end point of mankind's ideological evolution and the universalization of Western liberal democracy as the final form of human government." The Hegelian notion of history as the battlefield of ideas, Fukuyama was proposing, has thus come to an end. According to Fukuyama, all that is left to accomplish now is the boring details of working out the implementation of the liberal-democratic capitalist agenda throughout the world.

The proposition was reminiscent of what Daniel Bell (1960) had argued a generation earlier. Unfortunately for their prophetic merit, Bell's *The End of Ideology* and Fukuyama's *The End of History* were published just before a new surge of ideological contestations on the world scene. The Cold War between the United States and the Soviet Union and between the Soviet Union and China characterized the 1960s. So did the countercultural movements in Europe and the United States. The 1990s are similarly characterized by the reemergence of secular nationalism and religious revivalism to fill the ideological vacuum left by the end of the Cold War. It is true that in the postindustrial phase, societies become more technically driven while ideology takes a backseat to technical and incremental solutions. But scientism and technicalism are themselves ideologies. They rationalize the collective interests of the "experts" and managerial elite who are placed at the helm of major public and private organizations. The lesson seems unambiguous. Ideological contestations are a perennial part of human conflict. As long as conflict continues, ideologies will persist in order to adorn material interests with moral legitimacy while providing new myths for social solidarity and action. To be effective, however, ideologies have to cast their own particular myths into universal narratives.

The end of history thesis points to the global expansion of the market economy and its liberal-democratic metanarrative. Huntington's clash of civilizations comes as the first phase of post–Cold War euphoria is giving way to a new phase of sober realism and even Hobbesian pessimism. Huntington is appropriately skeptical of the triumph of liberal democracy. He ominously forecasts, however, that "the clash of civilizations will dominate global politics. The fault lines between civilizations will be the battle lines of the future. . . . The most prominent form of this cooperation is the Confucian-Islamic connection that has emerged to challenge Western interests, values and power" (Huntington 1993a: 22). Huntington's thesis harks back to the historical memories of the Crusades and hence is possessed of unflinching mythological power. The religious resurgence in the Judaic, Christian, Islamic, Hindu, and Buddhist traditions and the increasing economic and political cooperation between East Asian and Islamic countries also provide it with some plausibility. However, to frame the complex and continuing gaps and conflicts of interests between the deterritorialized centers and peripheries in strictly geopolitical terms is one-dimensional, simplistic, and misleading. Notwithstanding Huntington's call for peaceful coexistence, it may also serve as a justification for launching another crusade. We define our images of the world, and our images of the world define us.

If the articles by Fukuyama and Huntington were simple expressions of the optimistic and pessimistic temperaments of two solo scholars, there would have been no cause for concern. However, the U.S. foreign policy establishment has celebrated both articles as major intellectual breakthroughs in defining the post–Cold War era. The Council on Foreign Relations and its quarterly, *Foreign Affairs,* the U.S. Institute of Peace, and a number of conservative, private think tanks in Washington, D.C., have held numerous conferences to celebrate the two authors. Fukuyama became the focus of much media attention in 1989–1990 (M. Tehranian 1989), and the editors of *Foreign Affairs* compared the significance of Huntington's article to another published in that journal in 1945 by a Mr. X (George Kennan). The latter had defined and shaped U.S. policies in the Cold War for the next forty-five years. Just as Kennan's proposed "containment" policy hardened the U.S. position vis-à-vis the Soviet Union in the Cold War years, the Fukuyama and Huntington articles seem to propose a U.S. hardening toward China and the Islamic world. The two articles serve several complementary functions. They fill the ideological vacuum left by the decline of communism by identifying a new ideological enemy. Whereas Fukuyama argues that the triumph of liberal democratic capitalism is inevitable, Huntington suggests that some residual resistance is still left (Chinese tyranny, Islamic bigotry) against that progressive movement of history.

In the face of such early groping for ideological clarity in historical contradictions and confusions, a neoliberal ideology has gained ascendance in North America, Western Europe, and, until recently, in East Asia and the former Soviet Union. The fundamental premise of this ideology, advanced by Ronald Reagan and Margaret Thatcher and later partially adopted by Bill Clinton and Tony Blair, is that the state must change its orientation from demand-side to supply-side economics, from welfare support to market support, and from protectionism to unfettered international competition, trade, and investment. The neoliberal gospel is actively supported by the dominant Bretton Woods institutions of the World Bank, the IMF, GATT, and the recently established (1995) World Trade Organization. The combined power of transnational corporations, Anglo-U.S. diplomacy, and the three intergovernmental organizations persuaded some middle- to low-income countries in Eastern Europe and East Asia to tailor their policies in accordance with the neoliberal gospel. But the East Asian debacle of 1997 and the continuing East European stagnation are casting serious doubt in the minds of statesmen and citizens alike on the validity of the new doctrine of globalization.

The Clinton administration has clearly been torn between these two competing discourses. On the one hand, its pro–free trade policies follow the logic of Fukuyama's end of history thesis. On the other hand, its human rights policies reflect Huntington's prescriptions on a clash of civilizations. Nowhere are these contradictions more apparent than in the case of policies toward China. As possibly the world's largest economy and consumer market in the twenty-first century, China cannot be ignored economically. However, China's economic seductions must be weighed against its political threat to the U.S. hegemony in the Asia-Pacific region. Competing domestic interests also argue for two different sets of policies vis-à-vis China. Large TNCs greatly favor compromises, whereas smaller producers of consumer durables competing against Chinese imports opt for censuring China. China's most-favored-nation status has thus become hostage to its human rights record. In the meantime, China and Russia, the two old Communist rivals, are forging a new strategic alliance to balance U.S. hegemony in world politics.

The academic discourse on the postindustrial, postmodern, post-Fordist information society has been equally controversial. The optimists and pessimists have similarly dominated the field. While liberal analysts such as Daniel Bell, Mark Porat, and Yoneji Masuda provide generally optimistic scenarios, the Marxist world system theorists (e.g., Wallerstein 1974 and others) present a rather pessimistic view of the emerging world order. At issue is the fate of the peripheries of power, whether situated in the urban ghettos of the First World or in the rural hinterlands of the Third World. The optimists argue that a new phase of "postindustrial, information society" will eventually "trickle down" its benefits to the lower-income groups, whereas the Marxists point to the structural impediments that will keep certain regions, societies, and sectors of population perennially underdeveloping (Frank 1969; So 1990).

In the cultural arena, however, the left has become divided between the old and the new. Whereas the old left scholars tend to argue that the media conglomerates are homogenizing national cultures into the expanding global capitalist channels of consumer desires (Schiller 1976; Hamelink 1983; Mattleart 1983; Ewen and Ewen 1982), the new left points to the increasing participation of the peripheries in a global, multicultural, postmodernist pastiche of migrating meanings and identities. To capture the fluidity and irregularity of such transnational exchanges, Arjun Appadurai (1990: 6–7; 1993) has suggested a number of channels, including "ethnoscapes, mediascapes, technoscapes, finanscapes, ideoscapes." Whereas the old left points to the narrowing of the public sphere of discourse (Habermas 1983), the new left suggests that power is everywhere to be seized by the deconstructive guerrilla tactics of postmodernism (Foucault 1980). Finally, the old left recommends a new politics of meaning focused on creating "ideal speech communities" and "alternative normative structures" (Habermas 1983), and the new left calls for a deconstructive politics of antipolitics (Foucault 1980).

GLOBALIZING THE LOCAL, LOCALIZING THE GLOBAL

Under the impact of global communication, a dual process of globalization of the local and the localization of the global has made isolationism and dissociation virtually impossible for any nation, even for those that have devoutly attempted it for some time, such as China, Saudi Arabia, Burma, and Iran. Globalization is fundamentally a top-down process: localization, bottom-up. The agents of transnationalization are the global hard and soft networks facilitated primarily by the nonstate actors. The hard networks consist of transportation, telecommunication, and tourism (TTT) facilities from around the globe that connect the core in networks of communication. The soft networks provide the programs that negotiate and integrate the competing interests and values of the global players. These include global broadcasting, advertising, education, and exchanges of information. At the same time, the localization processes are working through their own hard and soft networks, at times employing the core networks and at other times developing their own independent periphery systems. The agents of localization and tribalization consist of the nationalist, religious, and ethnic movements and leaders voicing the peripheries' interests and views. In contrast to the core's macromedia, these agents often employ low-cost, accessible, and elusive micromedia, such as low-powered radios, audiocassettes, video cameras, copying and fax machines, and personal computer networking. Their soft network consists of the rich heritage of primordial myths and identities embedded in the traditional religious, nationalist, tribal, and localist ideologies.

However, the infrastructure of global civilization is quickly growing through transnational media events and transnational networks such as

CNN, BBC World Service TV, Star TV, MTV, the Internet, and NGOs. Whereas media events and television networks are largely one-way, top-down channels, the Internet and NGOs provide interactive, bottom-up, international communication channels. The media events (Dayan and Katz 1992) of the last few decades have brought about a new global consciousness of the common human destiny. Such well-televised events as the landing on the moon, Anwar Sadat's visit to Jerusalem, the Tiananmen Square demonstrations, the Gulf War, and the handshake between Yitzhak Rabin and Yassir Arafat have heightened a sense of globality in locality.

Since 1985 the steady growth of CNN into the world's first global news network has provided the elites in most parts of the world with a stream of live broadcasts in English, Spanish, Japanese, Polish, and soon French and German. In 1987, to counter the Western bias of its news, CNN started airing the CNN World Report, providing uncensored and unedited news reports from local broadcasters all over the world. By 1992, 10,000 local news items had been aired on the World Report, originating from a total of 185 news organizations representing 130 countries. CNN's internationally-distributed satellite signal is within reach of 98% of the world's population (Pai 1993; McPhail 1993; Flourney 1992). CNN has thus become more than a news medium; it is also serving as a channel for public diplomacy, often working faster than the private channels of traditional diplomacy. Many heads of states and responsible officials watch CNN during crises in order to directly assess the events abroad while gauging the impact of those events on domestic and international public opinion. Fidel Castro is reported to have been one of the first world leaders to regularly watch CNN. During the Gulf War, President Bush indicated at a press conference that he would telephone President Turgut Ozal of Turkey, who at the time was watching CNN's live coverage of the conference; a few minutes later, when the telephone call came through, President Ozal was waiting for it. Peter Arnet's reporting from Baghdad during the Gulf War filled some of the communication gaps between Saddam Hussein and the rest of the world. CNN, however, provides a global picture primarily through a U.S. prism. Britain is trying to emulate the CNN success story through the BBC World Service Television, and Japan has considered the establishment of an NHK-led (Japan's public broadcasting) Global News Network (GNN) (C. Lee 1993). Star Television, acquired by Rupert Murdoch's News Corporation in 1993, covers most of Asia through direct broadcast satellite (DBS).

Similarly, MTV is exporting youthful, whimsical, irreverent, postmodernist U.S. cultural values into Europe, Asia, Africa, and Latin America. Although possessing universal appeal, MTV is following a localization strategy wherever it goes. Stimulated by the example of a popular program that promotes the sale of the music it plays, local record companies have been quick to take up the challenge. India's Megasound spent only $5,000 to produce a video featuring India's first Hindi rap tune by artist Baba Segal.

> The album ended up selling 500,000 copies. Darren Childs, MTV Asia's head of programming, said that the Asian content of its programming has risen from 5% when the channel first aired, to as high as 50% at certain times of the day. The station has "broken" formerly unknown acts and turned them into regional stars. In addition to the regional stars, the VJ's (Video Jockeys) of MTV Asia are another important reason why viewers tune in. They are all Asian or part Asian and provide Western wackiness while toning down the grungy, street-smart image of MTV VJ's elsewhere to ensure that local audiences can still identify them." (C. Lee 1993)

MTV is thus contributing to the creation of an intended or unintended global, postmodernist subculture with far-reaching consequences.

The Internet is another fast-growing transnational network that connects millions of computer hosts in a global network of networks (Anderson 1995). Users seem to double every two years. At that rate, the network will have several hundred million users early in the next century. With the proliferation of such major commercial online services as Prodigy, America Online, Delphi, Dialogue, and Compuserve, that figure may be surpassed even sooner. In 1992, *The Whole Internet Users' Guide and Catalogue* sold 125,000 copies. A dozen other guides currently compete for the market, including *Zen and the Art of Internet* (Anonomyous 1994). It is no wonder that marketers are viewing the network as a potential electronic gold mine. However, attempts at commercializing the network initially faced serious resistance by the users. As Steve Stecklow notes:

> Residents of "cyberspace," as the online computer galaxy is known, are a world apart. They do not take kindly to sales pitches or electronic cold calling. Many view themselves as pioneers of a new and better vehicle for free speech. Unlike television viewers, radio listeners or newspaper readers, they are hooked up to the message sender and other Internet parties interactively—meaning that an offense to their sensibilities can result in quick, embarrassing reports viewed by countless of the network's . . . users. (Stecklow 1993: A1)

Commercialization of the Internet, however, has proved to be inevitable. In addition to an explosion of commercial users, the new network nation consists of computer-literate professionals from all continents and all fields. Internet users are united in the fine arts of chatting, gossiping, exchanging information, and collaborating in a variety of projects from scientific research to lifestyle preferences, dating, financial transactions, and social movements. The National Science Foundation (NSF), which subsidizes the network, has no control over a number of other data lines that are also part of the Web. The NSF phased out its $11.5 million annual subsidy in 1994; however, the U.S. government and businesses stepped in. Rupert Murdoch's News Corporation has announced that it will acquire Delphi Internet Services Inc., an online service that provides Internet access to consumers. Continental Cablevision, the third-largest cable television company in the United States, is offering Internet access to its cable subscribers. AT&T is making the Internet available to some data communication customers via a nationwide, toll-free telephone number (Stecklow 1993). Some commercial Internet service providers have taken a further step by supplying free access if commercial advertisements are allowed to piggyback the e-mail messages. "Free" Internet, like "free" TV, will be an exponential expansion of channels of desire. An oligopoly of seventy global conglomerates now dominates the world entertainment markets (Duncan 1998).

The Clinton administration has promised that by the year 2000, every school and public facility will have the capability of logging on to this vast network. On September 15, 1993, Vice President Al Gore unveiled a plan to coordinate the public and private sector efforts in building a national "electronic superhighway." This plan has raised the perennial question of the trade-off between efficiency and equity in telecommunication. Although the U.S. National Information Infrastructure (NII) plans remain ambiguous, they aim at creating a more efficient flow of communication and information. Similar to an earlier drive for the construction of transcontinental, interstate superhighways under the Eisenhower administration, the metaphor of "electronic superhighways" under the Clinton administration promises greater mobility and productivity. However, it cannot necessarily guarantee greater equity. Just as the transportation superhighways facilitated the transfer of population and resources from the U.S. Northeast to the South and the West, the new electronic superhighways will also redistribute wealth, income, and information access. The transportation superhighways facilitated the industrialization of the South and the West and the deindustrialization of the Northeast. They also were a factor in the migration of African Americans to the northern cities, the outmigration of upper- and middle-income white groups from the cities into the suburbs, the consequent erosion of the urban tax base and urban decay, and the creation of an urban underclass. Unless public policy vigorously pursues the achievement of equity and universal access, a consequence of the new electronic superhighways could be the creation of a permanent information underclass.

The new global information marketplace includes five major components: (1) the owners of the highways, the common carriers, paid for by the private or public sectors; (2) the producers of information hardware such as telephones, televisions, and computers; (3) the producers of information content such as the press, broadcasters, libraries, and "infopreneurs";

(4) the producers of software programs; and (5) information consumers who seek efficiency, equity, privacy, affordability, and choice. In response to the convergence of information and communication technologies, the U.S. Telecommunication Act of 1995 removed most of the barriers to entry into any particular sector of the market. This has already led to mergers and acquisitions aiming at the full technological and economic integration of the print, film, broadcasting, cable, telephone, cellular phone, computer, and database industries—a process that has already begun by the emergence of new giant multimedia conglomerates.

In another speech on January 11, 1994, Vice President Gore outlined the following five principles that will guide U.S. legislation and regulation concerning communication industries. The administration wants to (1) encourage private investment, (2) provide and protect competition, (3) provide open access to the network, (4) take action to avoid creating a society of information haves and have-nots, and (5) encourage flexible and responsive governmental action (CRTNET, #915, January 12, 1994). Given these policy principles, will the coming information superhighway be accessible to everyone regardless of their income? The vice president was reassuring on that question:

> The principle of universal service has been interpreted in the case of telephone service to mean that what we now have is about 93–94 percent of all American families have telephone service and it is regarded as affordable to virtually—by virtually everyone. Our definition of universal service, once the cluster of services that are encompassed is agreed upon, is that approximately the same percentage should have access to the richer information products as well, so that a school child in my hometown of Carthage, Tennessee, population 2,000, could come home after class and sit down and instead of playing a video game with a cartridge, plug into the Library of Congress and learn at his or her own pace according to the curiosity that seizes that child at the moment—not just in the form of words, but color moving graphics and pictures. (CRTNET, #900, December 22, 1993)

Despite these assurances, in the United States, most Internet users have proved to be younger, professional white males. In the United States, the most wired nation in the world, a growing, but minority, segment of the population is wired to the Internet. That percentage is even lower worldwide.

GROWING GLOBAL COMMUNICATION GAPS

The EU, Japan, and other major countries have constructed similar information superhighways. These will also probably bypass the poorer regions of the world and create a global information infrastructure (GII) and its underclass. Telephones are the linchpin of the new integrated telecommunication systems. Without telephones, the less developed countries and regions of the world would not be able to log on to the global electronic super-highways and, hence, new databases and networks. Yet the global distribution of telephony is more lopsided than any other modern medium. In 1992 some fifty countries accounting for over half the world's population had a teledensity of less than 1, that is, less than one telephone line per 100 inhabitants. Whereas the high-income countries have 71 percent of the world's 575 million main phone lines, upper-middle-income countries control 15 percent, lower-middle-income 10 percent, and low-income only 4 percent (Tarjanne 1994). Some NICs in East Asia are closing the gap, but many other LDCs are falling behind. On the whole, world telephone distribution patterns have remained relatively unchanged in the last 100 years. In light of this fact, is information hegemony replacing military domination and repression? Or will the two be mutually reinforcing as in the past? An international movement has expressed the same concerns for information access and equity for a NWICO (P. Lee 1985; Traber and Nordenstreng 1992; Galtung and Vincent 1992). As the advanced industrial world has moved ahead, the gap between the information haves and have-nots has demonstrably grown on a global scale. Except for a handful of East Asian countries (Japan, South Korea, Singapore, Hong Kong, and Taiwan) and low-population and high-income oil-exporting countries (Saudi Arabia, Kuwait, United Arab Emirates), other LDCs have so far been unable to catch up.

One relatively hopeful sign in this bleak picture is the role that NGOs are playing (Boulding 1988). The convergence of NGO computer networks and low-cost information technologies is offering opportunities for social movements to develop their own news services and information dissemination systems. In the late 1980s, the Association for Progressive Communication (APC) was established as a nonprofit network to facilitate global communication among NGOs. As Howard Frederick notes:

> Comprising more than 20,000 subscribers in 95 countries, the APC Networks constitute a veritable honor roll of organizations working in these fields, including Amnesty International, Friends of the Earth, Oxfam, Greenpeace, labor unions and peace organizations. There are APC partner networks in the United Sates, Nicaragua, Brazil, Russia, Australia, the United Kingdom, Canada, Sweden and Germany and affiliated systems in Uruguay, Costa Rica, Czechoslovakia, Bolivia, Kenya and other countries. The APC even has an affiliate network in Cuba providing the first free flow of information between the United States and Cuba in thirty years. Dozens of FidoNet systems connect with the APC through "gateways" located at the main nodes. (Frederick 1993: 97)

APC affiliates now broadcast more than twenty alternative news agencies, twenty newsletters and magazines, four radio station news scripts, and a wide variety of specialist files to which nonconventional voices contribute news and opinion. There are also over 30,000 NGOs enlisting millions of people around the world working for a vast variety of civic goals, from protection of the global environment to the defense of human rights. These social and technological networks together constitute a global civil society that provides, to some degree, a countervailing power to that of national states and transnational corporations (Commission on Global Governance 1995).

We need not be technological determinists to recognize the unmistakable links between the communication media and cultural change through history (see Table 2.3). Each medium has created or privileged a particular sector of the communication elites of society. The oral traditions privileged the shamans and soothsayers as the paramount historical memories and voices of the community. The invention of writing created a new class of scribes by the establishment of priesthoods acting as the custodians of the Holy Scriptures and the newly formed religious institutions. The introduction of print brought about a new secular priesthood in the form of modern intelligentsia challenging the authority of monarchies and religious institutions. The rise of the mass media (newspapers and radio) contributed to the emergence of mass movements in the nineteenth and twentieth centuries led by a new class of ideologues (Lenin, Hitler, Mussolini, and Roosevelt), providing them with platforms to preach their Communist, Fascist, or social democratic gospels to mass audiences. The rise of computer technologies and their impact on every aspect of economic and social life have created a new class of "technologues." The diffusion of the micromedia of communication has boosted the power and influence of the traditional communication elites (the priests, the mullahs, the monks, the community organizers), that is, the "communologues," who can speak in the vernacular of common folk. The demystifying rise of visual media (television, cable, and VCRs) seems to have led to a new and skeptical generation of communication elites who see through the pretensions of the ideologues, a new class we may call "jestologues." The rise of virtual reality is beginning to create a new generation of communicators who could be called "visualogues."

The culture of postmodernity is relativistic, episodic, antinarrative, despairing, ecstatic, playful, self-mocking, and jestful. It privileges the jestologues. The battle between communologues and jestologues, between modernity and postmodernity, was dramatized by Ayatollah Khomeini's death warrant on Salman Rushdie. Most interpretations of the confrontation have missed the point by portraying the ayatollah as the traditional, religious bigot and Rushdie as the modern, freethinking intellectual. But the two figures and what they stand for in the contemporary world can perhaps be better understood if we view each in terms of the distinctions

Table 2.3 The Layering of History: Communication Revolutions and Educational Evolution

Social System	Communication Technologies	Cultural Paradigms	Communication and Educational Elites	Communication and Educational Institutions
Bands and tribes	Speech	Magic: supernatural	Shamans, oracles, poets, soothsayers	Oral histories and historians
Agrarian feudalism	Writing	Religion: revelation	Priesthoods and philosophers	Temple, church, pagoda, mosque
Commercial industrialism	Print	Science: reason	Public intellectuals and scientists	Modern universities
Manufacturing industrialism	Audiovisual media	Ideology: action	Ideologues and persuaders	Mass media, mass movements, mass organizations
Technocratic industrialism	Computers, satellites	Technology: program	Technologues	National and global technocracies
Communitarian industrialism	Informatics	Community: human agency	Communologues, jestologues, visualogues	Global and local area networks (GLANs)

Source: M. Tehranian (1990b: 67).

made between the premodern, modern, and postmodern. The ayatollah represents a type of posttraditionalist modernism, ideologically committed to the sacred mission of realizing the kingdom of Allah on earth, whereas Rushdie voices the postmodern jester who mocks all sanctities. The ayatollah is more of a modernist than traditionalist Islamic leader in his totalizing strategy of fusing the state and the mosque into a single theocratic regime. Rushdie may be considered a postmodern critic in his deconstructionist strategy of mocking traditional as well as modern sanctities.

The postmodern strategy is to shock, to startle, and to decenter in order to dethrone the sacred and the naturalized. Its paramount medium is the musical video; its message is "I want my MTV!" Its heroes are the deconstructionist antiheroes (Beavis and Butthead), the new self-mocking shamans of electronic rock music (e.g., Sting and Bono), or the glittering stars of multiple identities and sexualities (e.g., Madonna and Michael Jackson).

The conflict among the premodern, modern, and postmodern is thus part of the cultural landscape of a developmentally uneven, historically schizoid contemporary world. Table 2.4 presents a schematic view of the contrasting tendencies of premodern, modern, and postmodern cultural orientations. It focuses on the dimensions of time, space, being, science, technology, and aesthetics to suggest a series of differences that, when politicized, can lead to irreconcilable obstacles to communication. That is a central paradox of our time. Premodern, modern, and postmodern sensibilities are juxtaposed in a complex variety of configurations in daily life. Increasing channels in international communication have provided arenas such as the Internet listservs and chat lines for the confrontation of these contradictory worldviews that lead to bizarre conversations. Without the bonds of epistemic community and face-to-face social solidarity, the international discourse in this arena as well as in the larger arena of world politics has come to resemble a dialogue of the deaf.

CONCLUSION

This chapter has (1) mapped out the current discourses on the new world order, (2) presented a historically grounded view of the current global changes and continuities in international discourse, and (3) drawn out the implications of those for modernization, communication, and democratization.

As the absence of a consensus on the shape of the new world order demonstrates, we are in an age of paradigm shifts. Our political, economic, and cultural institutions are clearly lagging behind the accelerating pace of scientific and technological change. That, in turn, has led to the dramatic breakdown of some political and economic systems such as those in Central

**Table 2.4   Premodern, Modern, and Postmodern Worldviews:
A Schematic Perspective**

	Premodern	Modern	Postmodern
Time	Circular	Linear	Multilinear
	Eternal	Material	Ephemeral
	Past-oriented	Future-oriented	Present-oriented
Space	Hierarchical	Functional	Anarchic
	Organic	Designed	Vernacular
	Closed	Enclosed	Open
	Home/office	Home vs. office	Home + office
	Fixed	Fluid	Modular
Being	Supernatural	Natural	Ecological
	Heaven	Society	Community
	Sacred	Secular	Self
	Transcendent	Material	Immanent
Power	Feudalism	Fordism	Flexible accumulation
	Land	Capital	Knowledge/information
	Gold	Paper money	Electronic money
	Authoritarian	Representative	Participatory
	Matriarchal	Patriarchal	Androgyny
	Mother church	Fatherland	Community
Science,	Practical reason	Instrumental reason	Communicative reason
technology,	Exegesis	Interpretation	Deconstruction
and aesthetics	Fate	Determinacy	Indeterminacy
	Fusionism	Universalism	Particularism
	Mystification	Rationalization	Demystification
	Metaphysics	Paradigm	Syntagm
	The wheel	The steam engine	Telematics
	Form	Multiform	Antiform
	The Holy Book	Genre/boundary	Text/intertext
	Holy relic	Art object	Performance/happening
	The Creation	Narrative	Antinarrative
	Trans-history	*Grande histoire*	*Petite histoire*
	Classicism	Design	Chance
	Sanctification	Centering	Dispersal
	Divinity	Totalization	Deconstruction
	Logos	Purpose	Play
	Traditional	Modern	Eclectic

Source: Adapted from K. Tehranian (1995).

and Eastern Europe. The zones of peace (what peace? one might ask) in the United States, Western Europe, and Japan are not immune from the current cataclysmic changes. As the current trends in industrial downsizing, welfare cutting, and immigrant bashing demonstrate, the transition from national capitalism to pancapitalism is undermining the social fabric of advanced industrial societies. The zones of turmoil are spilling over from the peripheries of the peripheries (the rural areas in the LDCs) into the centers of the peripheries (Cairo, Tehran, Bombay, Manila, Mexico City) and into the centers of the centers (New York, Los Angeles, Berlin, Frankfurt, London, Tokyo) and their newly established sweatshops. The zones of peace and turmoil are thus inextricably tied together in an increasingly complex, global web of economic, political, and cultural interdependencies. Complacency (undue optimism) or alarmism (excessive pessimism) are not warranted in the current transition to a new world order, whatever that turns out to be. In fact, the very fluidity of the situation allows us more room for greater human agency. If wars represent failures of human imagination, the price of peace with justice is human vision and action.

The future of the world depends, in large measure, on how modernity can be tamed to ensure a continuing production of wealth without disastrous consequences for the global natural, social, and cultural environments. That in turn vitally depends on how humanity can balance its competing and complementary interests in the search for common norms, laws, and sanctions. The emerging world order is caught in the contradictors of uneven and combined economic, political, and cultural modernization. Economically, modernization has achieved stunning achievements in the establishment of a world market of trade and development that is threatened only by increasing environmental pollution, international and intranational inequalities, exclusionary regional blocs, and the political upheavals that may result from those. Politically, modernization has created a multipolar power in which no single great power can rule the world with impunity. It has also unleashed democratic forces that in societies with sizable middle classes have led to the institutionalization of freedoms of speech, assembly, and organization. Culturally, however, modernization has produced contradictory effects. The history of modernization so far has been a history of the dominance of instrumental reason against practical, critical, communicative, or ecological reasons. To some extent, though, modernization has been tamed by the diverse spiritual and cultural traditions of civility. These traditions have provided countervailing perspectives on how to universalize and localize knowledge at the same time. The antagonisms between the global and the local have led too frequently to the tyranny of one against the other. What is urgently needed is creative tension and dialogue between the modernists and traditionalists.

As for the processes of international relations, the most significant change of the last few decades appears to be in the stunning expansion of channels of global communication. This has proved to be a mixed blessing. On the one hand, it has led to the hearing of new voices—the Kurds, the Shiites, the Palestinians, the Tatars, the Tibetans, the Abkhasians, the Uighurs, and hundreds more. On the other hand, it may be stereotyping "the other" to a point that international communication is becoming a dialogue of the deaf (M. Tehranian 1982b). Marshall McLuhan's "global village" is looking more and more like a neofeudal manor with highly fortified and opulent castles (centers of industrial, financial, and media power) surrounded by vast hinterlands of working peasants clamoring for survival and recognition.

The debate on NWICO has been largely polarized between those who wish to give new means of self-expression to the peasants and those who consider the media monopoly of the lords to be a greater guarantee of freedom and traditions of civil discourse. As in any debate, the two sides may have oversimplified a more complex reality. The new media, like the old, tend to have multiple effects, dispersing and centralizing, democratizing and controlling, pluralizing and homogenizing. Whereas the state and corporate institutions are using the new media largely for surveillance, legitimation, and persuasion, the NGOs and unrepresented peoples are employing them to resist, organize, and mobilize. As storytellers, the media mediate in the top-down and bottom-up processes of global governance and communication. They construct the global realities that frame the global events feeding the media constructions of global realities. The emergence of Somalia, Bosnia, and Chechnya to the top of the international agenda of the 1990s may have been in part considered the work of Cable News Network International (CNNI). By focusing on the tragedies of famine and ethnic cleansing, the world media embarrassed these governments into taking action; however, the media could not lead them to appropriate action. In fact, aid and communication fatigue are leading the media away from those trouble spots. Setting agendas is a powerful media function, but it does not necessarily lead to resolving problems.

A NWICO can be best constructed by developing communication competence for the voices that are not heard through increasing media access, ownership, management, and control by the NGOs and unrepresented peoples. Pluralism in voices requires pluralism in structures of media access. No single system of media control (governmental, commercial, public, or community) can guarantee that plurality of voices. A balance among them might use the expanding channels of communication for broadening a plurality of voices that are more reflective of the international community. The project of a new world order calls for a free and balanced flow of communication among the 5.5 billion inhabitants of this planet, who are caught between the imperatives of the premodern, modern, and postmodern worlds to which they belong (see Table 2.4). It calls for the beginning rather than the end of history for the two-thirds of humanity who were hitherto primarily objects instead of subjects of history. The redefinition of modernity in consonance with the traditions of civility embedded in most world religions and civilizations calls for a dialogue rather than a clash of civilizations. The challenge is to tame the forces of modernity for the fulfillment of human needs in rather than against nature, for the celebration of democratic freedom rather than its defeat, for cultural pluralism rather than cognitive tyranny.

A NWICO may be conceived of as a network of networks among the NGOs to mobilize the global civil society. It can mean the empowering of the deterritorialized peripheries in the urban centers and rural hinterlands and the enhancement of their communication competence and media capabilities. Such empowering can lead to fruitful negotiations among the state and nonstate actors, the IGOs and the TNCs, in order to redress the conditions of dehumanizing poverty and violence, manifest and latent, so characteristic of our world.

3

RISING GLOBALISM

"Privatization" and "deregulation" are inadequate to describe the enormous upheaval that is unfolding before our eyes. Along with the creation of vast new wealth, the map of global economy is being redrawn. Indeed, the very structure of society is changing. New markets and new opportunities have brought great new risks as well.

—David Yergin and Joseph Stanislaw, *The Commanding Heights*

As argued in the previous chapter, global communication has significantly contributed to the rise of globalism in the economic, political, and cultural arenas. This chapter further substantiates that argument by providing an overview of the impact of global communication on international relations in the military, diplomatic, economic, scientific, educational, and cultural arenas. The chapter also draws out the global implications for national cultural, information, and media policies.

Global communication at the turn of the twenty-first century has had multiple effects. On the one hand, it has blurred technological, economic, political, and cultural boundaries. Print, photography, film, telephone and telegraphy, broadcasting, satellites, and computer technologies, which developed fairly independently, are rapidly merging into a digital stream of zeros and ones in the global telecommunication networks (Carr 1990; Campbell-Smith 1991; Anonymous 1995). Economically, separate industries that had developed around each of these technologies are combining to service the new multimedia environment through a series of corporate

---

This is a revised version of my article "Global Communication and International Relations: Changing Paradigms and Policies," *International Journal of Peace Studies* 2, no. 1 (January 1997), pp. 39–64.

mergers and alliances. Politically, global communication is undermining the traditional boundaries and sovereignties of nations. DBS is violating national borders by broadcasting foreign news, entertainment, educational, and advertising programs with impunity. Similarly, the micromedia of global communication are narrowcasting their messages through audio- and videocassette recorders, fax machines, and computer disks and networks, including the Internet and the World Wide Web. Culturally, the new patterns of global communication are creating a new global "Coca-Colanized" pop culture of commodity fetishism supported by global advertising and entertainment industries (Duncan 1998).

On the other hand, global communication is empowering hitherto forgotten groups and voices in the international community. Its channels have thus become the arenas for contestation of new economic, political, and cultural boundaries. Global communication, particularly in its interactive forms, has created immense new moral spaces for exploring new communities of affinity rather than vicinity. It is thus challenging the traditional top-down economic, political, and cultural systems. In Iran it facilitated the downfall of a monarchical dictatorship in 1978–1979 through the use of cheap transistor audiocassette recorders in conjunction with international telephony to spread the messages of Ayatollah Khomeini to his followers within a few hours of their delivery from his exile in Paris (M. Tehranian 1979c, 1980b, and 1993c). In the Philippines, the downfall of the Ferdinand Marcos regime in 1986 was televised internationally for all to witness while alternative media were undermining him domestically. In Saudi Arabia a BBC-WGBH program, "The Death of a Princess," banned by the Saudi government as subversive, was smuggled into the country by means of videotapes the day after its premiere in London. In China, despite severe media censorship, the 1989 democracy movement in Tiananmen Square spread its messages around the world through fax machines. In the Soviet Union computer networkers who opposed the Moscow coup of 1991 and were sympathetic to Boris Yeltsin transmitted his messages everywhere despite severe censorship of the press and broadcasting (Ganley and Ganley 1987; Ganley 1992 and 1996). In Mexico the Zapatista movement managed to diffuse its messages of protest against the government worldwide in 1994 through the Internet. In this fashion, it solicited international support while embarrassing the Mexican government at a critical moment when it was trying to project a democratic image for admission into NAFTA. In Burma, or Myanmar as it is officially known, both government and opposition have employed the Internet in their political struggles. E-mail has been used to achieve rapid global mobilization for the withdrawal of Western companies from Myanmar in protest against the government's repressive policies (Anonymous 1996: 28).

These are only a few examples; however, they demonstrate that accelerating technological advances in telecommunications and their worldwide dissemination are profoundly changing the rules of international relations. On the one hand, they are facilitating transfers of science, technology, information, and ideas from the centers of power to the peripheries. On the other, they are imposing a new cultural hegemony through the "soft power" of global news, entertainment, and advertising (Nye 1990). Globalizing the local and localizing the global are the twin forces blurring traditional national boundaries. The conduct of foreign relations through traditional diplomatic channels has been both undermined and enhanced by information and communication resources available to nonstate actors. The emergence of a global civil society in the form of over some 30,000 NGOs, some 37,000 TNCs, and numerous TMCs is a significant aspect of this phenomenon. The addition of the nonstate actors alongside nearly 200 state actors as well as over sixty IGOs and autonomous bodies has added to the complexity of international relations (Commission on Global Governance 1995). Telecommunication is contributing to changes in economic infrastructures, competitiveness, and trade relations, as well as internal and external politics of states. It also affects national security, including the conduct of and deterrence against wars, terrorism, civil war, the emergence of new weapons systems, command and control, and intelligence collection, analysis, and dissemination. The Gulf War provided a glimpse of what future wars might look like. The emergence of an international politics of cultural identity organized around religious, ethnic, or racial fetishisms suggests what the future issues in international relations might be.

Global communication is thus redefining power in world politics in ways that traditional theories of international relations have not yet seriously considered. More specifically, it is bringing about significant changes in major arenas of hard and soft power (Nye and Owens 1996; Cohen 1996). "Hard power" refers to material forces such as military and economic leverage, and "soft power" suggests symbolic forces such as ideological, cultural, or moral appeals. But major changes seem to be taking place in both hard and soft power conceptions and calculations. First, information technologies have profoundly transformed the nature of military power because of emerging weapons systems dependent on lasers and information processing. Second, satellite remote sensing and information processing have established an information power and deterrence analogous to the nuclear power and deterrence of an earlier era. Third, global television communication networks such as CNN, BBC, and Star TV have added image politics and public diplomacy to the traditional arsenals of power politics and secret diplomacy. Fourth, global communication networks working through NGOs and interactive technologies such as the Internet are creating a global civil society and pressure groups (such as Amnesty International and Greenpeace) that have served as new factors in international relations. Although no theoretical generalizations on the dynamics of hard and soft power are yet possible, trends indicate that the latter is assuming increasing importance.

THE MILITARY ARENA

The multiple effects of global communication are perhaps most visible in the military arena. Military technologies have become increasingly information and communication intensive. Historically, most communication technologies have immensely benefited in their research and development phase from military investments, but their declassification has often led to rapidly diffused civilian applications. All adversaries have also quickly adopted them. Table 3.1 provides a schematic view of the most important communication technologies and world orders. As Harold Innis (1950) has persuasively argued, world political systems closely correlate with world communication systems. Without reliable command, communication, and control, power centers cannot effectively manage their peripheries. However, every communication system also empowers the peripheries. Print, for example, facilitated the political and cultural hegemony of the West from the fifteenth century onward, but its spread also gave rise to increasingly potent resistance via nationalist movements throughout the world.

In the military arena, the double-edged sword feature of communication technologies has led to the paradox of more is less: More security has meant less security. A few examples illustrate the point. Nuclear weapons have been assumed to be a powerful deterrent force; however, their proliferation has meant a greater probability of accidental or intentional nuclear war. Remote sensing by satellites has created a global surveillance system at the disposal of the superpowers, but commercialization of such information is now leading to its availability to those adversaries who can afford the price. Moreover, direct broadcast satellite communication through such global television networks as CNN and BBC is bringing the news of adversaries' strengths and weaknesses to each party far more quickly than was ever possible before.

In warfare, the technological system is having two contradictory consequences. The conduct of war and resistance against domination are both becoming increasingly robotized and globalized. This is so because the technological system is at once global and local as well as both powerful and vulnerable. Terrorism, both state- and opposition-sponsored varieties, has thus been on the ascendancy locally and globally. It has manifested

Table 3.1 Communication Technologies and World Orders

Date	Command, Communication, and Control Systems	World Orders
550 B.C.E.	Postal system equipped by relay stations with fresh horsemen	Persian Empire
500 B.C.E.	Postal system manned by postal runners	Chinese Empire
350 B.C.E.	Voice and fire signaling	Greek Empire
44 B.C.E.–476 A.D.	Road system from center to peripheries, some 90,000 miles	Roman Empire
632–1259	Surface mail by horses and airmail by pigeon carriers	Islamic empires
1500–1970	Print	European empires
1844–1914	Telegraph	European empires
1900–1945	Radio broadcasting	Competing empires
1945–1989	TV, satellites, computers, and the Internet	Bipolar system
1989–present	Strategic Defense Initiative (Star Wars), cyborgs	Globalist system

itself on the West Bank as well as at the New York World Trade Center, in the Armenia-Azerbaijan region as well as at Turkish and Armenian embassies around the world, and at the Oklahoma City federal building as well as in Washington, D.C., and Lima, Peru.

The idea that stockpiling weapons of mass destruction can gain commensurately higher levels of security for those who possess them is thus proving to be an illusion. As military technologies have augmented their hit:kill ratios and communication technologies have improved their powers of surveillance, conditions of permanent insecurity seem to have become more prevalent at the centers and at the peripheries of power. The policy implications of this phenomenon for the pursuit of power and peace are far-reaching and yet not fully explored. Old-fashioned security thinking still goes on at the top levels of policymaking and media punditry (Anonymous 1997b: 15–16)

THE DIPLOMATIC ARENA

In addition to traditional intergovernmental diplomacy, global communication seems to have generated three new types of diplomacy: public, people, and virtual. The global reach of broadcasting seems to have led to a shift of emphasis from power politics to image politics (M. Tehranian 1982b; Livingston and Eachus 1995). Public diplomacy has thus assumed an increasing importance in the conduct of foreign policy. Realists such as former U.S. ambassador George Kennan (1993) and former U.S. secretary of state James Schlesinger (1993) have, in fact, decried this tendency as tantamount to emotionalism in the policy process. James Schlesinger (1993: 17) has argued that the U.S. policies in Kurdistan and Somalia were in particular driven by the impact of television images of those human tragedies. John F. Kennedy once summed it up: A videotape is more potent than ten thousand words.

Public diplomacy, however, complements rather than supplants traditional diplomacy. Steven Livingston and Todd Eachus have challenged the facile presumption of a "CNN effect" on such U.S. humanitarian interventions as those in Somalia or Kurdistan (Livingston and Eachus 1995: 413). However, the debate over the role of the media in international relations cannot be settled by a few case studies. Judging by the media's role in such post–Cold War crises as the Gulf War, Somalia, Bosnia, and Chechnya, there seems to be a symbiosis between governments and the media in the coverage of international affairs. Governments can enhance, restrict, or manipulate the media's access to information and coverage, and the media can play multiple roles in the formation of foreign policies. In their coverage of international affairs, the media—particularly commercial television—tend to dichotomize, dramatize, and distort. In this process, they follow a pattern of storytelling that has been well established in U.S. Western movies with enormous success at the box office, that is, pitting the cowboys against the Indians in a dramatic struggle between the forces of good and evil. Given government license to cover a certain story, the media may legitimate prevailing policies, or accelerate, impede, or prioritize them. This is often known as the agenda-setting function of the media; the media focus more on what to think *about* than *what* to think. But agenda setting prioritizes, that is, it accentuates, impedes, or legitimates. In the case of the Vietnam War, the first television war in history, the media initially legitimated and accelerated U.S. government policies. However, as the body bags came home and the atrocities of the war were televised into U.S. homes, the media gradually turned against government policies, to a certain degree impeded them, and finally contributed to a change of priorities from war to peacemaking. In the case of the Gulf War, the first government-managed television war in history, about 80 percent of the U.S. public receiving its news from television supported the war effort. Television coverage of the plight of the Iraqi Kurds and Shiites in the aftermath of the war may have accelerated the U.S. government's decision to provide relief and air cover, but it was not decisive in the adoption or execution of that policy. The media may thus be viewed as neither powerful nor powerless but power linked.

Public diplomacy is an auxiliary instrument to traditional diplomacy. The use of television as a channel for sending messages to the opposite side has significantly increased. Such usage occurred during the Gulf War and subsequently in the conflicts between the United States and Iran and Israel. The employment of CNN as a source of information and intelligence gathering by foreign and defense policy leaders and the testing of trial balloon proposals via the mass media are examples of such uses of public diplomacy in other times of crisis. None of these examples can conclusively suggest that in their foreign policy making, states have become hostages to the media. However, they do suggest that governments are increasingly aware of the potential and risks of the media.

In contrast to public diplomacy, which is essentially top-down, people diplomacy is a bottom-up process. Improving global transportation and telecommunications have increasingly made it possible for ordinary citizens to engage in a game that has been historically reserved for foreign policy experts. In their efforts to mediate and resolve international conflicts, such prominent citizens as Jimmy Carter, Jesse Jackson, and Ramsey Clark reflect the possibilities and constraints of people diplomacy. Many other individuals and groups are also engaged in such efforts; among the best known is Amnesty International, an organization devoted to the freedom and humane treatment of political prisoners around the world. Foreign policy establishments often resent such interventions in the policy process and regard them as intrusive. However, people diplomacy can serve as a corrective to the governments' narrow or nationalist objectives (Mandelbaum 1996; Hoffmann 1996).

Virtual diplomacy is of more recent vintage. Although many organizations and people active in people diplomacy are employing the new information technologies, virtual diplomacy has broadened and deepened the opportunities for diplomatic interventions through a more diverse variety of channels. Global audio, video, and computer teleconferencing has allowed numerous official and unofficial contacts on a routine basis. The institution of a hot line between the White House and the Kremlin in the aftermath of the missile crisis of 1962, closed-circuit video teleconferencing by the U.S. Information Agency through its Worldnet, and other similar facilities demonstrate that diplomacy has new tools at its disposal. But the explosion of the Internet into a worldwide, interactive communication network has also provided numerous opportunities for expert groups to act as intermediaries, advocates, or advisers in international conflicts. At Harvard University's Conference on Information, National Policies, and International Infrastructure (January 1996), Henry Perritt reported on the project Virtual Magistrate jointly sponsored by the Cyberspace Law Institute and the American Arbitration Association. The project provides expert mediation services to parties at conflict through the Internet and the World Wide Web. Another example of virtual diplomacy is the Internet listserv Gulf2000, directed by Gary Sick, a retired member of the U.S. National Security Council. The list includes over 400 leading experts on the Persian Gulf. It provides both a forum for the discussion of current issues and a channel through which opinions are formed. Many other expert groups, such as the Toda Institute for Global Peace and Policy Research, also employ the

Internet for international conflict resolution projects that aim at identifying the parties in a conflict, engaging them in a dialogue, and searching for common ground. The possibilities for virtual diplomacy through the Internet as well as audio or video teleconferencing are thus immense and will no doubt be exploited further in years to come.

THE ECONOMIC ARENA

The impact of global communication on the world economy is perhaps the most studied and best known (Schiller 1981 and 1985; Nordenstreng and Schiller 1993; Wriston 1992). This impact has reshaped the processes of world production, distribution, trade, development, and financing. Expanding global transportation and telecommunication networks in recent decades have clearly enabled TNCs to decentralize their production and distribution networks while seeking higher profits in regions of the world with lower wages, rents, and taxes and less government regulation. World trade and financing have also been profoundly affected by the transborder data flows that facilitate airline and hotel reservations, cash and capital transfers, and international trade in capital markets. In developing economies, the new information technologies have made technological leapfrogging possible in such world trade centers as Singapore and Hong Kong, which now boast some of the world's highest per capita incomes and penetration of telecommunication facilities. Other Asian tigers such as South Korea, China, Taiwan, Thailand, Malaysia, and Indonesia have similarly found in telecommunications an engine of rapid technological leapfrogging and economic growth.

The economic consequences of the current worldwide information revolution are, however, less well known and more controversial. Is the information revolution leading to global leveling of wealth and income or to a new class system of information haves and have-nots within and among nations? In creating and destroying jobs, is the information revolution leading to the "end of work" (Rifkin 1995) or to a system of structural employment prompted by the disappearance of middle management and downsizing? Is the nature of employment and career changing fundamentally from a pattern of one-life-one-career to one of one-life-many-careers-and-jobs?

The most visible impact of information technologies on the world economy is the rise of a new type of capitalism: pancapitalism. This new world political economy is driven by some 37,000 transnational corporations of diverse national origins but increasingly multinational ownership, management, and control. It has led to new forms of capital accumulation labeled by David Harvey (1990) and others as "flexible accumulation."

The TNCs go wherever political security, low wages, taxes, and rents, less government regulation, and fewer environmental controls promise them higher profits. Their loyalties to their national governments are therefore minimal. Information technologies and robotics also allow them to engage in distributing the production process among a number of sites by flexible accumulation and production. Thus, computer chips may be produced in Malaysia, monitors manufactured in Taiwan, logic boards made in Hong Kong, and the entire system assembled somewhere in the Silicon Valley.

Pancapitalism thus comes into frequent conflict with national capitalisms. Clearly, the transfer of industries and jobs from higher- to lower-cost areas within and among nations has led to new policy dilemmas that have been hotly debated among experts and politicians. As witnessed in U.S. presidential politics, the debate has particularly focused on internationalism versus protectionism in trade. However, issues of efficiency versus equity, national security versus economic freedom, and development versus social and environmental health are also at stake in the debate. World trade has become increasingly dependent on information flows and patent and copyright protection. The new economic policy dilemmas therefore involve issues such as transborder news and data flows versus national information sovereignty; industrial espionage and piracy versus the rights of industrial patent and copyright holders (Branscomb 1994); and global advertising and consumerism versus national saving and investment needs.

THE SCIENCE AND EDUCATIONAL ARENAS

The experiences of latecomers to the industrial revolution, such as Japan and China, have abundantly illustrated that the acquisition of modern science and technology is the key to catching up. In this process, the role of information technologies, from print to the Internet, cannot be overemphasized. Since the rate of obsolescence in scientific and technological knowledge is also increasing, information technologies are assuming a function in addition to that of transferring knowledge: They have made lifelong and open learning systems more likely and readily available (Noam 1995; M. Tehranian 1996b). What are the relationships between traditional educational institutions and new systems? Can scientific internationalism and technological protectionism coexist? Does leapfrogging from low-tech (e.g., typewriters) to high-tech (e.g., global computer networking and DBS) undermine cultural sovereignty and identity? Which is more important in the processes of economic development, financial or human capital? If the latter is more important, as the evidence tends to show (UNDP 1992 and 1996), what is the place of science and technology policy in an overall development strategy? What are the implications of all these issues for a global science and technology policy? These questions clearly have no easy answers. But they present the beginnings of any serious international discussions on information, science, technology, and educational policies.

THE CULTURAL ARENA

The impact of global communication on international cultural life is perhaps the most visible of its effects. Traveling along the Silk Road in 1992, I found CNN, BBC, and Star TV to be ubiquitous. Coca-Cola, Michael Jackson, and Madonna were also there wherever I went—from the Great Wall of China to Urümqi (capital of Xianjiang, China's western province) to Almaty (capital of Kazakhstan), Dushanbe (capital of Tajikistan), Tashkent (capital of Uzbekistan), Ashkhabad (capital of Turkmenistan), Baku (capital of Azerbaijan), and Tehran. In Almaty, in August 1992, I encountered Jimmy Swaggert preaching the Gospel in fluent Kazakh on national television. In Tehran, in June 1994, courtesy of CNN and DBS, I witnessed O. J. Simpson on the run on the Los Angeles freeways. And despite Islamic edicts, MTV videos with their postmodern messages of sensuality, pluralism, and skepticism were reaching into the sanctity of Islamic living rooms. This was viewed by Iranian government authorities as a cultural invasion no less menacing than the U.S. armed fleet off the coasts of the Persian Gulf.

It would be misleading, however, to think of media effects as unilinear and uniform. Technological effects are always socially mediated and constructed. Each new technology has to find its own cultural space in the life of a society before it can have any meaningful impact on social relations. In the case of the media, where technologies range from the simplest to the most complex and from the readily accessible to those accessible by only a small elite, the effects are even more complex and ambiguous. A distinction between macromedia, mesomedia, and micromedia might illustrate the point. The macromedia of communication (satellites, mainframe computers, the Internet, and its offshoot, the World Wide Web) seem to be acting as agents of globalization. Through global satellite and computer networks, transborder data flows, scientific and professional electronic mailing, and commercial advertising, the macromedia are supporting the globalization of national markets, societies, and cultures. The mesomedia of communication (print, cinema, and broadcasting) are primarily under the control of national governments or commercial and pressure groups and therefore function mostly as agents of national integration and social mobilization. The micromedia of communication (telephony, copying machines, audio- and videocassette recorders, musical tapes, personal computers, and the World Wide Web) have primarily empowered the centrifugal forces of dissent at the peripheries of power. All three types of media, however, are closely interlinked via social networks of governments, markets, and civil societies (see Figure 3.1). Without contextualizing their social and political functions in historically and culturally specific situations, media effects would remain largely mystifying and incomprehensible.

COMPETING PARADIGMS AND POLICIES

We live in a complex world, and global communication is not making it any less so. But if we view modernization as the overall theme of international relations in the last 500 years of world history and possibly the next 500, we may consider the paths to modernity to have fluctuated within four political paradigms: capitalism, communism, totalitarianism, and communitarianism. Figure 3.2 remaps the conventional half-circle political spectrum into a full circle around these four polarities. World politics has been characterized by a struggle among the proponents of these four paths. The Blues, or the pioneers of the industrial revolution (England, France, and the United States), took the liberal democratic, capitalist road. The industrial bourgeoisie, preoccupied with the rights of private property and individual freedom, led the transition by following a high accumulation

Figure 3.1 Global Policy Stakeholders

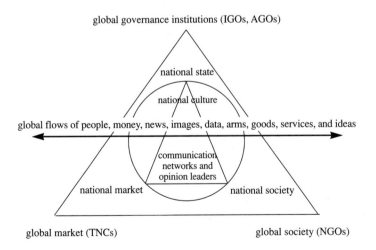

Figure 3.2   Remapping the Global Political Spectrum

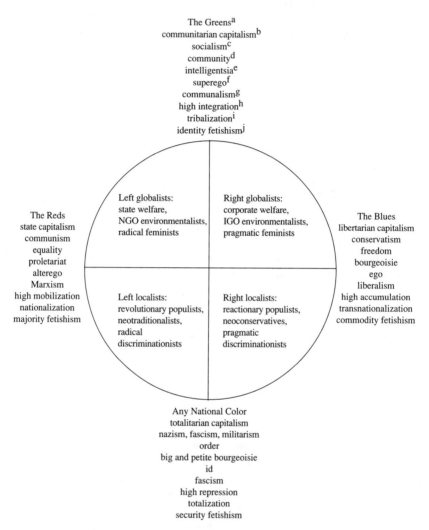

Source: Adapted from M. Tehranian (1990b).

Notes: a. The first term in each category indicates symbolic color.

b. The second term in each category indicates social system.

c. The third term in each category indicates political party alignment.

d. The fourth term in each category indicates axial principle.

e. The fifth term in each category indicates leadership.

f. The sixth term in each category indicates psychic energy.

g. The seventh term in each category indicates ideology.

h. The eighth term in each category indicates development strategy.

i. The ninth term in each category indicates process.

j. The tenth term in each category indicates pathology.

strategy of development and free trade policies designed to open up the markets of the rest of the world. The Reds, the Communists, were led by the revolutionary working class and intelligentsia aiming at the same goal of industrial revolution through national planning with a focus on social equality, national self-sufficiency, and high mobilization strategies of development and self-sufficiency. The Greens, led by the intelligentsia, have argued for socially, culturally, and environmentally responsible strategies of development prizing community and high-integration strategies of development. The communitarians range in perspective from Gandhian revolutionaries in the LDCs (India, South Africa, and Sri Lanka) to the social democratic and Green parties in the West. As Figure 3.2 shows, this conceptual map situates a complex range of right and left globalists as well as right and left localists in the international political spectrum. However, all three democratic paths have shown themselves prone to totalitarian temptations. The fourth path to development has thus assumed the national colors of totalitarian movements. Capitalism in the United States (during the McCarthy era), Germany, Italy, and Japan; communism in the Soviet Union and China; and communitarianism in Israel (since the occupation of the West Bank), India (under Hindu militancy), and Iran (under the Islamic regime) have all succumbed to that temptation. In particular, the totalitarian regimes of the latecomers to the industrial revolution (Germany, Japan, Italy, Spain, Argentina) employed their national or party colors (brown for nazism, black for fascism, yellow for Japanese militarism) to mobilize their societies around a new, highly repressive order that glorified national myths of superiority.

As Figure 3.2 illustrates, global communication has already placed the democratic norms of order, freedom, equality, and community on national agendas. The central task of the media in democratic societies may be considered to be twofold: (1) to allow for the diversity of voices in society to be heard and (2) to channel that diversity into a process of democratic integration of public opinion and will formation. Without free and vigorous debate among competing views, no nation can achieve the level of integrated unity and determination necessary for democratic societies to act on public issues. Generally speaking, media pluralism would serve these purposes better than a media system exclusively dominated by state, commercial, public, or community media. Pluralism in structures of ownership and control is therefore needed in order to obtain pluralism in perspectives and messages. Separation of editorial from ownership structures may guarantee some measure of editorial autonomy, but evidence shows that such separations more often lead to editorial self-censorship than autonomy. In any case, structural pluralism is hostage to the presence of independent market institutions and voluntary associations (political parties, trade unions, religious and civic organizations). The existence of a strong civil society to counter the powers of the state and the market is therefore a precondition for media pluralism.

In formulating national communication policies, three sets of interlocking policies are at stake, namely, cultural, information, and media policies (see Figure 3.3). The overarching policy questions concern freedoms of conscience, speech, association, and assembly. Cultural policies include the questions of not only national values, heritage, and identity but also freedoms of religion, language, and schooling. Information policies concern the production and dissemination of public information by such institutions as government agencies, public libraries, and value added networks (VANs). Media policies cover the whole gamut of mediated modes of communication, from print to cyberspace.

Cultural Policies

The central dilemma of how to balance cultural diversity with national unity is a perennial problem for any national cultural policy. Perhaps the most important issue in cultural policy is how a country defines itself with respect to its cultural identity, heritage, goals, and values. Although most democratic governments pay lip service to cultural diversity, national unity is often a higher priority. Even in North America and Western Europe, where cultural diversity has been accepted as a democratic value (witness the motto on the Great Seal of the United States: *e pluribus unum*), multiculturalism has come under attack in recent years (Schlesinger 1993). Under communism, the Soviet Union defined itself as a bastion of the international proletariat. Composed of over 100 nationalities, however, it had to deal with the problem of nationality. Under Stalin, the Soviet empire was divided into fifteen autonomous republics based on nationality. Soviet cultural policy, however, constantly vacillated between the primacy of proletarian solidarity under the banner of a Soviet culture as defined by the Soviet Communist Party and homage to the religious and ethnic diversity of its vast population. But to divide and rule, the Soviets drew the boundaries of most republics in such a way as to include significant ethnic and religious minorities. Voluntary and forced migration also significantly contributed to the multiethnic character of the population in most republics. Although Soviet policies succeeded in maintaining the hegemony of the Soviet Communist Party for over seventy years, they could not destroy ethnic and religious loyalties. It is no surprise, then, to witness the resurgence of such loyalties to fill the vacuum that is left by the delegitimation of the Communist ideology. As a result, in the newly independent republics, national histories, identities, goals, and place and family names have been revamped to fit the new circumstances. Such cultural restorations included a reversion from Leningrad to St. Petersburg, Leninabad to Khojand, Khodanazarov to Khodanazar.

Figure 3.3 Taxonomy of Cultural, Information, and Media Policies

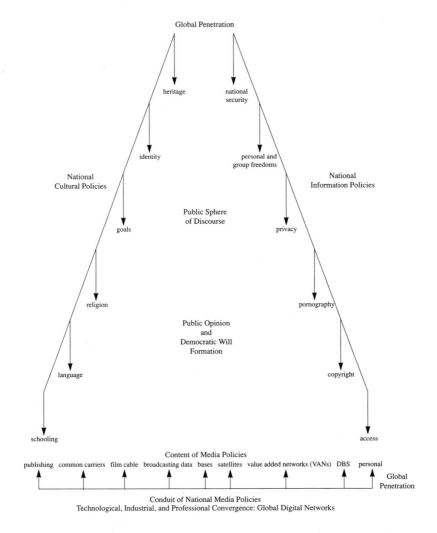

Competing myths and historical memories powerfully shape the cultural configurations of society. They are preserved in national monuments, libraries, national and religious rituals, textbooks, and the literature of a country. Cultural policy determines what myths and historical memories to preserve, which to discard, and what to repress. In monarchical Iran, for instance, the myths and memories of the pre-Islamic Iranian monarchy were glorified, whereas in Islamic Iran, they are being repressed at the same time that the Shia Islamic myths and memories are revived and embellished (M. Tehranian 1979c and 1993c). The religious policy of a state has profound consequences for its cultural policy. Whether a state adopts a national religion, as in England, or pursues a policy of separation of church and state, as in the United States, has important implications for the type of schooling allowed or subsidized. Similarly, language policies affect educational practice. Since its independence in 1917, Finland has required Swedish language instruction in its schools. However, Finland's entry into the European Union has raised questions about the value of Swedish in contrast to English or French as a bridge to the European community. By adopting bilingualism, Canada has attempted to keep Quebec within its federation. But Quebec's refusal to require bilingualism within its borders has undermined Canadian unity. To protect and enhance European identity vis-à-vis U.S. TV programs, the EU is imposing limits on the proportion of foreign programs on television.

Information Policies

The dilemma of how to reconcile freedom of information with the dictates of national security and rights of privacy seems to be at the heart of any democratic national information policy. A telling example of this dilemma is the controversy in the United States on the clipper chip and the V(violence)-chip. In 1993 the National Security Agency (NSA) introduced a new encryption technique to be used for security and privacy on the National Information Infrastructure. This new eneryption technique, commonly known as the clipper chip, was designed in secret by the NSA and remains classified, so its inner workings are unknown. It has a feature that allows the government to wiretap any Internet user it wants. This proposal met with nearly universal opposition from the public and industry. In January 1994 many of the world's top cryptographers and computer security experts wrote to President Clinton asking him to withdraw it. Public concern with pornography and violence has clashed with First Amendment rights in other arenas as well. The U.S. Communication Decency Act of 1995 made the dissemination of pornography on the Internet a criminal act. It also required the installation of V-chips in TV sets, allowing parents to control the programs their children watch. However, in 1996, U.S. courts declared as unconstitutional any infringement of freedom of speech proscribed in the act.

Cyberia, otherwise known as cyberspace, is thus becoming a technologically visible panopticon society as well as a public arena for contestation among policies. In a society such as the United States, which is committed to freedoms of conscience, speech, association, and assembly, the new technologies are raising fundamental questions on how to protect the First Amendment. Questions of national security also touch on the protection of sensitive scientific and technological information. Since a great deal of science and technology development takes place at research universities, which are generally committed to academic freedom and publication, tensions between the government and institutions of higher education are clearly inevitable. In the 1960s, the *New York Times* published the Pentagon Papers, documents relating to the Vietnam War that were released by Daniel Ellsburg, a former official of the U.S. Department of Defense. The government sued the newspaper for its breach of national security. The courts decided in favor of the *Times*, but the question of who defines national security and its breach of information remains.

The management of news is one such issue. During the Vietnam War, reporters had direct access to the battlefront. From a power point of view, the consequences were disastrous. Vietnam was the first major U.S. war to be covered by television. As the images of the bloody battlefields reached U.S. homes, the Pentagon's claims of victory were increasingly questioned and antiwar sentiments among the public forced the government to finally withdraw from that country. Government information policies on war subsequently changed. Ever since Vietnam, U.S. reporters have been denied direct access to battlefronts. In the invasions of Granada, Panama, and Iraq, reporters received most of their information through Pentagon briefings. Under these circumstances, the news media have had only limited opportunity to independently examine the veracity of Pentagon claims.

To turn to another policy arena, the question of patent and copyright protection is primarily a commercial issue. However, it has important consequences for a country's international obligations. In recent decades, the United States has been in direct conflict with a number of countries, including Hong Kong, Thailand, Taiwan, China, and Singapore, for their breach of copyright laws of the United States. Textbooks, computer hardware and software, and musical recordings have been systematically pirated for profit without payment of copyright royalties. However, as long as a country has not signed the Geneva Convention on Copyright, it can continue reproducing intellectual properties without compensation to authors and publishers. The United States has brought considerable pressure on some of the Asian countries to sign and abide by the Geneva Convention. Some have; others continue to refuse to sign on the grounds that their Asian heritage has been pillaged for centuries without compensation and it is now their turn to borrow or steal. In this instance, the interface between national information and foreign policies could not be any closer. Foreign policy can no longer confine itself only to issues of military security; it must also develop positions with respect to cultural identity and security, media freedom and security, and information trade and security (M. Tehranian and Reed 1996).

A democratic information policy would support public libraries and the rights of citizen access to public information, both of which are turning mostly into electronic databases. Some sunshine laws in the United States provide for this. However, a thornier issue is the question of the rights of access of an individual to the information held about her or him. A variety of government and business files such as tax, credit, employment, and court records contain errors or facts that may be detrimental to an individual. The central policy dilemma here revolves around the question of how far the law should extend the individual rights of access and reply before government or employer rights are compromised.

Media Policies

Many of the dilemmas of cultural and information policies also confront those who shape national media policies. However, in multicultural societies, the dilemma of how to allow freedom of speech without encouraging hate speech is the central question. Different media philosophies would, of course, respond differently to this question. Authoritarian media policies often follow the dictates of the ruler(s) or a single political party or clique. In multinational imperial systems, such as the premodern Islamic and European empires, the level of tolerance for religious and ethnic differences was relatively high. As long as allegiance was paid to the central authorities, each cultural community was largely left to its own devices. In the Islamic empires, in fact, the *millet* system ensured a high level of internal autonomy. As Islam expanded into Iran, the Indian subcontinent, and southeast Asia, Zoroastrians, Hindus, and Buddhists also were accepted into the fold.

Libertarian media policies tend to value free speech above politically correct speech. Proponents of a ban on hate speech, however, argue that it is equivalent to crying "Fire!" in a crowded theater and thus constitutes a "clear and present danger." Hate speech should not be tolerated because it seriously threatens ethnic and racial peace. As the Report of the Project on Ethnic Relations in Eastern Europe and the Former Soviet Union suggests, the problem can be tackled in several ways: (1) through constitutional checks and balances; (2) through intermedia checks and balances; (3) through journalists' own codes of ethics; (4) through better historical and cultural education for journalists; (5) through better coverage of news contexts in relation to news events; (6) through shaming the aggressors by publicizing information about the political persecution of minorities provided by such organizations as Amnesty International; and (7) through bringing international pressure to bear on violators of human rights.

Communitarian media policies face a different set of problems in ethnic and religious conflicts. By definition, such policies value one religion or language or ethnicity over others because they consider it of vital importance to national unity. Other religions or cultures are either repressed or not equally valued. Iran's persecution of the Baha'is, Turkey's persecution of the Kurds, Iraq's persecution of the Shiites and the Kurds, and Israel's persecution of the Palestinians all fall within this category. Global communication can make a contribution to human rights through international censure for such systematic violations of its provisions (Manasian 1998).

Totalitarian media policies, by contrast, leave little room for international or domestic remedies until the regime reaches a point of self-destruction. The introduction of market forces in China, Iran, the Philippines, the former Soviet Union, and Eastern Europe suggests, however, that a civil society may emerge sooner or later even under the tightest of controls. A civil society can, in due course, bring about the freedom of public discourse necessary for a democratic regime.

National policies are often formulated in the context of global forces and policies. But who decides global policies? There is no global sovereign government comparable to national governments. Instead, we have a complex variety of players or stakeholders on the global scene, each taking part in formulating policies that inevitably enhance or constrain national governments in the pursuit of their goals. Figure 3.4 provides a schematic view of the major stakeholders on the global scene, including states, markets, pressure groups, financial groups, civil societies, and media. States regulate, markets allocate, lobbies try to persuade, civil societies resist and mobilize, financial institutions accumulate, and the media (de)legitimate policies. It is in the context of such forces and policies, as well as their respective media outlets (state, public, commercial, community, advertising, pressure group, and trade and investment media), that global, national, and local discourses take place.

Table 3.2 (p. 79) provides a schematic view of global policy formation suggesting the roles of aforementioned stakeholders in the processes of problem definition, policy formulation, policy legislation, policy legitimation, and policy implementation, regulation, adjudication, and evaluation. The table views the policy process from the top-down, bottom-up, and mediating perspectives. From a top-down perspective, the interests and policies of the great powers and the TNCs primarily drive global policies. From a bottom-up perspective, small and medium-size powers as well as revolutionary and opposition parties and NGOs influence policies. From a mediation perspective, the global communication networks and media act as negotiating arenas among conflicting authorities, legitimacies, and identities of governments and opposition groups. The table spells out the possible roles of the stakeholders in these three processes. National and global policies can therefore mitigate or exacerbate, regulate or unleash, prolong or resolve conflicts. In this light, modernization and democratization may be viewed as contradictory top-down and bottom-up processes mediated

Figure 3.4   Global Networks and Networlds: A Schematic View

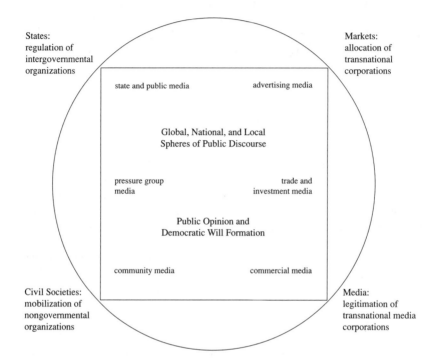

States:
regulation of
intergovernmental
organizations

Markets:
allocation of
transnational
corporations

state and public media   advertising media

Global, National, and Local
Spheres of Public Discourse

pressure group   trade and
media   investment media

Public Opinion and
Democratic Will Formation

community media   commercial media

Civil Societies:
mobilization of
nongovernmental
organizations

Media:
legitimation of
transnational media
corporations

through communication channels. Because all three processes have been significantly transnationalized, Table 3.2 provides a schematic view of the global policy formations with respect to each. The table is based on the following premises: Power is ubiquitous; even the most powerless have the power to resist; hegemonic power is never absolute; and hegemonic power always has to negotiate with, adjust to, and incorporate the interests of the effective oppositions. The table presents the public communication channels as the arena for such mediation and policy negotiations. Broadening the base of global governance and democratization of communication thus go hand in hand.

The structures and processes of international relations should be examined in reforming global governance. The structures of the international system consist of the states, IGOs, and at least four increasingly powerful nonstate actors: TNCs, NGOs, unrepresented nations and peoples organizations (UNPOs), and the global communication networks (GCNs). The processes of international relations may be viewed in terms of the problems of conflict regulation, conflict management, and conflict resolution. These involve such processes as exchange (trade agreements), negotiation

Table 3.2   The Global Policy Formation Process: A Schematic View

Top-Down Process: Generated by the interests and policies of the great powers and TNCs

Resources	Problem Definition	Policy Formulation	Policy Legislation	Policy Legitimation	Policy Implementation, Regulation, Adjudication, and Evaluation
Natural, technological, and human resources	Think tanks, foundations and commissions (e.g., Rand, Rockefeller, and Trilateral Commission)	Great powers and TNCs (e.g., G7 plus Russia and China, Exxon, AT&T, British Telecom, Mitsubishi)	National legislatures and IGOs	Politicians, publicists, press, and broadcasting	TNCs, IGOs, national government agencies, regulatory commissions, and the courts

Mediation Process: Generated by the media constructions of reality and discourses in response to governments and opposition

Resources	Problem Definition	Policy Formation	Policy Legislation	Policy Legitimation	Policy Implementation, Regulation, Adjudication, and Evaluation
Global telecom networks	Global elite press (e.g., *International Herald Tribune, Wall Street Journal, The Economist*)	Media owners and editors	National media laws, international covenants on copyright, spectrum and orbit allocation, and technical standards	Global media networks (e.g., elite press, CNN, news agencies)	Media associations (e.g., International Press Institute, International Publishers Association)

(continues)

Table 3.2 continued

Bottom-Up Process: Generated by the small and medium powers and revolutionary and opposition parties and associations

Resources	Problem Definition	Policy Formulation	Policy Legislation	Policy Legitimation	Policy Implementation, Regulation, Adjudication, and Evaluation
Human, natural, and technological resources	Revolutionary movements, NGOs, and related foundations, think tanks, and civil-religious networks (e.g., Amnesty International)	Small–medium powers and global lobby groups (e.g., G-77, Physicians for Social Responsibility, American Friends Service Committee, Greenpeace)	States in exile, revolutionary movements (e.g., PLO, Tibetan government in exile, unrepresented nations and peoples organizations, World Council of Churches)	The alternative and underground media, the informal networks of gossip and rumor, and civic and religious associations	Voluntary associations, labor unions, religious institutions, and out-of-power political parties

(diplomacy), adjudication, arbitration, mediation, public (mis)communication, and violent and nonviolent struggles.

CONCLUSION

This chapter has catalogued the problems, puzzles, and policies associated with the impact of global communication on international relations, an impact that has been significant and wide ranging. It has been so particularly in the rise of a new pancapitalist world system that considers the globe its playing field, engaging in capital accumulation, production, and marketing activities in a flexible mode and seeking higher profits wherever there are lower wages, rents, and taxes, fewer environmental controls, and less government regulation. However, in the absence of persuasive evidence, such claims as the end of history, journalism, work, university, or modernity and the emergence of an information society, global village, or electronic democracy should be considered with skepticism. I have emphasized the multiple effects of information technologies while cautioning an emphasis on any single effect. The only exception to this rule may be considered to be the following argument: Although each technology brings forth its own bias to the social scene by extending this or that human power (e.g. cars extend speed, computers extend information processing), it is the social mediations, constructions, and applications of technologies that ultimately determine their social effects. Radio communication has a bias for two-way communication, but when introduced into a commercial or government-controlled social environment, it assumed the character of one-way broadcasting. It was not until the introduction of the cellular phone that the two-way potential of radio communication was fully exploited.

In international relations, global communication seems to have encouraged both globalism and its discontents, that is, nationalism, regionalism, localism, and revivalism (M. Tehranian 1993a; see Chapters 5–6). Because of the uneven levels and rates of economic development of nations, resistance against globalism may be considered a chronic problem. As a force in modern history perhaps as powerful as globalism, nationalism was initially fostered by print technology (B. Anderson 1983). However, the other spatial forms of resistance against globalism are also facilitated by communication technologies. Historically, the ideological thrust of nationalism was toward uniformity in religion, language, and ethnicity. It is no wonder, then, that the major wars of the twentieth century revolved around clashing national identities. The Cold War temporarily shifted the emphasis to ideological issues. The post–Cold War era is clearly marked by a return to national, ethnic, and religious rivalries and conflicts. In the meantime, expanding global communication networks with English as the lingua franca facilitates globalism.

At the threshold of the twenty-first century, the world is faced with many contradictions, our awareness of which owes much to global communication. On the one hand, as Francis Fukuyama (1989) has argued, liberal capitalism appears to have triumphed to put an end to the history of ideological contestations. On the other, history has just begun for those marginalized nations whose growing access to the means of global communication is bringing them to the attention of the rest of the world. Some 6,000 languages and potential nationalities around the world are increasingly clamoring to be subjects rather than objects of history. We may thus expect the twenty-first century to be an arena for competing territorial and moral claims. The hegemonic pancapitalist system will continue to be challenged by sporadic but persistent acts of resistance unless the world learns to respect and celebrate diversity by devolution of power to smaller aggregates of human community.

As Samuel Huntington (1993a and 1993b) has argued, a "clash of civilizations" is characterizing our own era because new economic and communication power is enabling the ancient civilizations of Asia to challenge the truth claims of the relatively new nations of Europe and America. However, thanks to global communication, a new dialogue of civilizations is also being conducted via the international communication networks. Communication technologies are enabling the silent voices of the past to be heard in a global Tower of Babel characterized by old and new ethnic and racial hatreds. But global communication networks are also fostering a new ecumenicalism leading to the negotiation of new global identities and communities.

In the absence of a more egalitarian world, Marshall McLuhan's global village has proved to be a place not of harmony but of colliding moral spaces and sporadic violence. The lords of the electronic castles and the rebellious serfs, shamans, and jesters surrounding them have confronted one another in physical, political, economic, cultural, and environmental clashes. In this context, global communication channels can serve the cause of world peace and reconciliation only if they can be turned into channels of international and intercivilizational dialogue. In place of exclusive national sovereignties, the global commons of outer space, ocean resources, geostationary orbit, and electromagnetic spectrum must come under inclusive global sovereignties. In place of zones of protracted violence, such as Palestine, Kurdistan, Kashmir, and Israel, zones of peace and shared sovereignties must be built. To turn global communication into global dialogue, however, we need to rethink the problems of sovereignty, governance, economy, human rights, civic responsibilities, and media systems in order to accommodate human unity in diversity. That diversity can be ignored only at our own peril.

4

RETHINKING DEVELOPMENT

I have struggled for a long time with the concept and practice of development. Emerging from the western citadels of learning (Cambridge, Yale, Harvard) in the 1950's, I was armed with the firm neo-classical conviction that the real purpose of development was to increase national income—and all it required was an increase in saving and investment. . . . [But] what really happened was that while national income had increased human lives had shriveled, as the benefits of growth had been hijacked by powerful pressure groups. . . . After producing seven global Human Development Reports, I had to face the sad reality that the real challenge of human development lay back home.

—Mahbub ul Haq,
the late founder of the UNDP *Human Development Reports*

Communication and development became the focus of theoretical attention only in the post–World War II period. As a result of rapid diffusion of the mass media into the less developed countries, social scientists began to consider the media as possible engines of cultural diffusion and economic development. The pioneers in this first phase were Daniel Lerner and Lucille Pevsner (1958), Wilbur Schramm (1964), Lucien Pye (1963), David McClelland (1961), Everett Rogers (1962), and Frederick Frey (1973). In a second phase, inspired in part by the dependency theories of development and underdevelopment, a more critical approach on the role of the media was adopted. The main theorists included Everett Rogers (1976), Herbert Schiller (1976), and an increasing number of Third World

This chapter is a revised version of my article "Communication and Development," in *Communication Theory Today,* David Crowley and David Mitchell, eds. (Cambridge, UK: Polity Press, 1994), pp. 274–306.

scholars such as Paolo Freire (1972). In the third phase, in response to the rapid technological breakthroughs in telecommunication and information processing, the theoretical debates have taken three new distinct turns. First, theories of information society (Bell 1973) and information economy (Porat 1977) have posited a new evolutionary stage theory introducing the concepts of "postindustrial," "information," or "mode of information" society (Poster 1990). Second, in response to the growing international gaps in income and information, the LDCs have rallied around UNESCO's MacBride Report (UNESCO 1980) calling for a new world information and communication order with a dual emphasis on freedom as well as equality-cum-balance in information flows. Third, the critical and neo-Marxist theorists have increasingly turned to theories of poststructuralism and postmodernism (D. Harvey 1990; Waught 1992) for explicating the conditions of a media-saturated and information-intensive postindustrial world.

This three-way theoretical split roughly corresponds to the pre–Cold War division of the globe into the First, Second, and Third Worlds of development. However, in the post–Cold War era, the three worlds can no longer be defined spatially in terms of Western Europe and North America, the Sino-Soviet bloc, and Africa, Asia, and Latin America. The ethnic, regional, and class divisions within the countries also are rupturing into the open. For instance, India (a nation of over 900 million) may be viewed as three distinctly different but interlocking nations at three different stages of development: (1) an underdeveloping agrarian and semiurban population of about 400 million; (2) a developing industrial population of about 100 million, placing India among the top ten industrial countries; and (3) a struggling middle class of about 400 million torn between the seductions of an industrial society and the fetters of caste, class, ethnic, and religious warfare. The United States, a country of over 250 million, also is increasingly divided among the superrich (about 5 percent of the population), a struggling middle and lower class (approximately 75 percent), and an underclass (about 20 percent) characterized by functional illiteracy, drug addition, high crime rate, malnutrition, poor health, unemployment, and unemployability (Bartlett and Steele 1992). Although the United States ranks highest in per capita income and communication development and sixth in overall human development among the industrial countries, it also places as one of the highest in human distress and weakening social fabric (see UNDP 1992: 127, 188, 194). This suggests that U.S. society is deeply torn along five major social fault lines, those of class, racial, gender, generational, and regional divisions. Aggregate national communication and development indicators thus reveal in international comparisons as much as they conceal in intranational disparities.

The production of theoretical knowledge on communication and development is similarly following a more complex pattern, reflecting the increasing levels of differentiation of the world into interwoven patterns of centers and peripheries that defy simple spatial boundaries. Following three decades of theoretical and research productivity at the centers (mainly in the United States) generated by Cold War rivalries and the U.S. Agency for International Development (USAID) funding, the field went into decline in the 1980s (Samarajiwa 1987). Reflecting this decline, an African scholar declared it dead in the mid-1980s (Okigbo 1985). In a subsequent autopsy, an international group of scholars brought together by the Asian Mass Communication Research and Information Center (AMIC) found the subject still alive but in need of resuscitation (Jayaweera and Amunungama 1987). The worldwide appearance of several journals mostly or exclusively devoted to the problems of development communication also indicates that the field was alive and expanding. It now has proliferated into a diversity of fields such as political economy (Hamelink 1983; Jayaweera and Amunungama 1987; M. Tehranian 1990b); popular culture (Wang and Dissanayake 1985; Robinson, Buck, and Cuthbert 1991); rural development (McAnany 1980; Hornick 1988); news flows (Arno and Dissanayake 1984; Galtung and Vincent 1992); and peace and security (K. Tehranian and M. Tehranian 1992).

Without attempting to review the foregoing history in detail, this chapter focuses on three sets of critical issues, including the definitional, theoretical, and policy problems of development communication. In conclusion, I pose what appear to be the major theoretical and policy challenges and opportunities facing the field.

SOME CONCEPTUAL QUAGMIRES

Communication and development are both concepts without precise boundaries and therefore in need of some operational definition. "Communication" is viewed here as the process of exchange of meaning by verbal and nonverbal signs operating through cosmologies, cultures, contents, and conduits. This definition avoids media centrism by including the ideological formations, the cultural expressions (both verbal and visual), the content of messages, and the conduits of communication from primary (interpersonal) to secondary (organizational) and tertiary (mediated) channels. It therefore places the role of the modern media of communication in the larger context of human communication. Earlier literature of development communication, however, emphasized the media to the neglect of interpersonal and organizational networks of communication, including such vital links as the traditional and religious networks.

"Development" is defined here as the process of increasing the capacity of a social system to fulfill its own perceived needs at progressively higher levels of material and cultural well-being. This view somewhat differs from the evolutionary concepts of development that consider the process as universal, inevitable, and wholly positive. Employing an organic metaphor, evolutionary development suggests progressively higher levels of differentiation and complexity as well as integration and order. Such concepts primarily focus on the progressive rise in a set of universally applied economic, social, or cultural indicators, such as per capita income, industrial output, urbanization, literacy, life expectancy, or TV sets per 1,000 of population. Without rejecting the quantitative measurements, the proposed definition problematizes them by asking whether they can be universally applied without attention to the uniqueness of particular circumstances. It thus shifts the burden of proof for development from the exogenous categories of achievement to the endogenous perceptions of development. In many LDCs, a rapid rise in some development indicators such as gross national product and per capita income has often entailed environmental pollution, income maldistribution, and serious social and psychological dislocations. Recent studies of development indicators are attempting to correct the excessive emphasis on physical output in favor of a greater emphasis on the human dimensions of development (Caracas Report 1990; UNDP, annual since 1990). If we consider such factors as literacy, life expectancy, Gini coefficient (indicator of income distribution), and access to health and educational facilities, nations significantly rank differently from the traditional hierarchies of per capita income (see UNDP 1992: 127–129).

Concepts are often better understood in terms of their opposites. The opposites of communication are silence or noise; decay may be considered the opposite of development. Silences are essentially of two kinds, communicative and noncommunicative. When there is virtually no contact between two persons, peoples, or cultures, the silence can be deemed as signifying nothing. However, silences become meaningful when they are administered as a conscious effort to convey approval, disapproval, or neglect. Noises may be regarded as analogous to electrical static in the environment often disrupting the flow of meaningful messages—"sounds and furies signifying nothing!" Decay suggests the declining capacity of a system to fulfill its own perceived needs. Economic decay suggests declining productive capacity. Social and political decay suggests the declining capacity of a national system to respond to its citizens' perceived needs. When rising expectations considerably outpace rising income (the situation that prevails in many LDCs), frustration, aggression, and political repression may follow. Repression is often exercised when political mobilization has outstretched the institutions of political participation. Under such conditions, political decay may be defined as the failure of the political system to channel expectations into channels of political communication and consensus building. Since democracy has become a broadly shared aspiration in the modern world, it may be argued that its fulfillment vitally depends on public communication on the goals of development and is severely retarded by noise and distortion. In contrast to other forms of rule, democracy is government by discussion and consensus building. In this fashion, communication, development, and democracy present profoundly intertwined theories and practices.

Abraham Lincoln's classic definition of democracy as government *of* the people, *by* the people, and *for* the people can be usefully applied to these concepts of communication and development. Development *of* communication may be defined as expanding the channel capacity of the communication system. Development *by* communication might mean employing that capacity to provide social services such as tele-education, telemedicine, telelibraries, telebanking, etc., alongside the traditional services. Development *for* communication might be interpreted to mean power-free and dialogic communication among government, business, and civil society so that public policy decisions are based on communicative rather than instrumental rationality. Thus defined, development communication means increasing levels of economic democracy (productive employment), political democracy (access and participation), social democracy (expanding equal opportunities), and cultural democracy (pluralism of meanings).

MODERNITY AND ITS DISCONTENTS

Ever since the eighteenth-century European Enlightenment, the concept of development has constituted an overarching metanarrative of modern discourse appearing throughout the world in a variety of ideological guises, such as nationalism, liberalism, Marxism, and religious messianism. The idea of progress, anchored on human rationality and perfectibility, has had a spellbinding effect on the history of the last two centuries. However, we may be coming to the end of that optimistic road. It has taken two devastating world wars, a long Cold War, and the disillusionments of a post–Cold War state of world disorder to put the concept of the inevitability of progress on trial. The critiques of the idea have taken many forms. Some have rejected it altogether, others have attempted to modify it, and still others have proposed alternative concepts. The discourse on development thus has been rich in content and variety. This chapter will review three sets of theoretical debates that reflect the historical, ideological, and paradigmatic levels of discourse on modernization, corresponding to the surface, subsurface, and deeper levels of the global discourse on development.

Theory building on communication and development has faced some insurmountable problems. The root of the problem appears to be historical in nature. Can there be a general theory of communication, development, and democracy to explicate the diverse historical experiences of so many different nations? The stark reality is that nations of the world stand at many different stages of development. Their rates of progress toward universally defined indicators of development are also varied. In fact, the last three UN Decades of Development have witnessed a growing gap among nations. As a UNDP study (1992: 1) reports, "In 1960, the richest 20% of the world's population had incomes 30 times greater than the poorest 20%. By 1990, the richest 20% were getting 60 times more. And this comparison is based on the distribution between rich and poor *countries*. Adding the maldistribution within countries, the richest 20% of the world's people get at least 150 times more than the poorest 20%."

The same report suggests that restricted or unequal access to global markets costs developing countries some $500 billion annually—about ten times what they receive in foreign assistance. The same pattern of lopsided distribution is also reflected in media ownership: some 10 percent of the world's population owns some 90 percent of the world media (UNESCO 1980). Despite this relative deprivation, the less costly media, such as transistor radios, television, and audio and video cassette recorders, along with Western programs, have rapidly penetrated the LDCs in absolute numbers.

Faced with the demonstration effects of mass consumption standards in advanced industrial societies, which are effectively transmitted through global media, the LDCs have resorted to three strategies of defense vis-à-vis the world capitalist system: (1) hypermodernization and assimilation; (2) countermodernization and dissociation; and (3) selective modernization and participation. In addition, the more-developed countries, entrapped by the rising problems of hyperindustrialism, have shown two distinctly different critical reactions against modernization: (4) demodernization and deindustrialization and (5) postmodernization and accommodation. The entire Enlightenment project of modernization has thus come into theoretical and practical question through these five reactive discourses and practices.

Hypermodernization strategies are typical of the latecomers to the industrial revolution. Two different types of discourse, separatist and assimilationist, often characterize it. In the cases of Germany under Adolf Hitler, Italy under Benito Mussolini, Japan in the interwar period, the USSR under Josef Stalin, and China under Mao Tse-tung, the dominant theme of their crash industrialization programs was how to build, defend, or expand separatist fortresses under siege by the more advanced industrial West. In the case of periphery countries such as Japan in the postwar period, Iran under Shah Mohammad Reza Pahlavi, and the Philippines under Ferdinand Marcos, the dominant theme was an effort to catch up with the West within a compressed period of time by imitating its ways. Assimilation into the world capitalist system is often the result of such strategies. Both strategies are, however, characterized by a zealous commitment to the idea of progress. In their critiques of liberalism, totalitarian ideologies thus became more Catholic than the Pope, more committed to industrialism than the industrial West.

In contrast, countermodernization is a strategy of dissociation from what is perceived to be the sinful ways of modernity—too much greed, too many disparities, too few benefits, and losing the soul while not necessarily gaining the world. It is a reaction typical of the earlier stages of industrialization, the period of primitive accumulation. It can take either naturalist or messianic forms. In its naturalist forms, it may be regarded as a Rousseau effect; in its messianic forms, it may be viewed as a Khomeini effect. It was Jean-Jacques Rousseau, the romantic French philosopher, who first formulated a naturalist response to the Enlightenment project. "Man was born free, but he is everywhere in chains," he declared in *The Social Contract* (Rousseau 1968). Rousseau's proposals were to return to nature, to the original innocence, to the unity of the general will of the political community rather than the fragmented will of all in representative governments. Although individualism rather than communitarianism was at the core of their philosophy, U.S. transcendentalists also showed some of the same reactions. Love of nature, rejection of industrialism, distrust of government, and resistance against authority were their philosophical hallmarks. The Russian Narodniks also demonstrated similar romantic tendencies toward a return to the land and soul of Russia. In the Third World, however, countermodernization is deeply tied to anticolonialism, antiurbanism, and antisecularism. Mahatma Gandhi and Ayatollah Khomeini provide the two most well known and radically different faces of the same set of reactions. Recapturing a historic past while attempting to reconstruct authentic religious or national traditions is the motivating force. Proposals for self-reliant and indigenous forms of development are the strategies for the future.

Selective modernization and participation (in the world capitalist system) constitute the third major reaction to the challenges of modernization in the Third World. As exemplified by the development strategies of Korea under its postwar military regime, China under Deng Xiaoping (since 1976), and Iran under Ali Akbar Hashemi Rafsanjani (since 1997), this strategy combines relative economic freedom with political dictatorship (B. Smith 1997). The state thus hopes to launch an economic revolution with a combination of market incentives and government regulation. There are strong indications that Russia and some of the Eastern European countries might be taking a similar road toward constructing market economies. Selective participation in the world capitalist system, if carefully planned, can provide opportunities for capital and technology transfers without unduly appending the national economy to foreign sources of control.

By contrast, the reactions to modernity in the postindustrial West have ranged from demodernization to postmodernization. Demodernization seems to be characteristic of the stage of late industrialism that often leads to de-industrialization. Postmodernization represents a range of strategies from cultural accommodation to cultural guerrilla warfare against the dehumanizing effects of hyperindustrial information societies. Demodernization was best crystallized in the counterculture revolutionary movement of the 1960s—a "soft revolution" (Berger 1977) led by middle-class intellectual revolutionaries who were at once the beneficiaries and critics of the industrial system. Its slogan of "I am a human being—do not bend, staple, or mutilate me" captured much of the sentiment of the youthful revolt against the stupendous and anonymous technostructures of modern industrial society that were reducing the individual to an IBM card in a huge and impersonal information-processing machine. Its cultural weapons of rock music, free speech, antiwar demonstrations, communes, and drug experimentation scandalized respectable bourgeois society. However, much of the movement's cultural innovations have been gradually incorporated into the more pluralist cultural patterns of postmodern societies. In fact, the process of incorporation has given a new lease on life to the cultural industries exploiting the artistic talents of rock musicians, film directors, and multimedia producers.

The failure of the demodernization movement to produce any structural changes in the capitalist system has led to postmodernization as a new cultural revolt. Following the student revolts of 1968 in the United States and Europe and their failure to bring about significant political change, the strategy of the new cultural revolt is antipolitics. Although the intellectual origins of postmodernism are rooted in the demodernization protests of the 1960s, its cultural relativism and political nihilism are uniquely its own. In the words of its high priest Michel Foucault, a postmodernist critique of society and politics "leaves no room for power to hide" (Foucault 1980). It unmasks all ideological claims as self-serving conceits. Epistemologically, postmodernism is founded on a tradition of sociology of knowledge that considers all reality to be socially constructed and therefore subject to social negotiation. This tradition, however, can take two distinctly different theoretical and practical turns. In the works of Jurgen Habermas (1983) and Anthony Giddens (1984), it has led to theories of communicative action and structuration in which democratic discourse and human agency can combine to change the social structure in more desirable directions. Giddons, in fact, has provided the idealogical direction for the Labor Party's Third Way that is presumably paved between capitalism and socialism in Britain. In the works of Foucault and Jacques Derrida, however, such optimism does not seem warranted. The structures of postmodern society appear to be so mindless and pervasive that only two recourses remain: (1) a deconstructionist strategy that voices the despair of the individual in self-mocking expressions of cultural and political criticism but does not necessarily offer positive alternatives and (2) an escapist strategy such as that of the Heaven's Gate group in San Diego, whose members committed collective suicide in early 1997 in order to escape the bondage of this world, to liberate their souls, and to reach out to a heavenly spaceship hiding behind a comet.

Development as the metadiscourse of the modern world has thus come under severe doubts and criticisms from numerous quarters. The concept continues to be the operative principle for most of the ruling global institutions (including the TNCs, the World Bank, the International Monetary Fund, and the UN). But its legitimacy has been seriously challenged at two political and cultural extremes: (1) the religious revolts calling for a return to the purity and simplicity of premodern life and (2) the demodernist and postmodernist revolts against the tyrannizing and dehumanizing effects of modernity. Neither revolt, however, has yet succeeded in dethroning modernity. On the contrary, evidence suggests that modernity and its material rewards continue to be desperately sought after in the deprived parts of the world still struggling to achieve the conditions of basic nutrition, housing, health, and education. The central question still appears to be one of *how to* and not *why* develop. Communication about development is therefore as important today as development of communications. As Patricia Waught has put it aptly,

> To argue at a theoretical level that all assertions are the fictions of incommensurable language games is to deny the fact that most people do, indeed, continue to invest in "truth effects." If we continue to invest in "grand narratives," such narratives can be said to exist. Grand narratives can be seen to be ways of formulating fundamental human needs and their "grandness" is a measure of the urgency and intensity of the need. They are unlikely, therefore, simply to die, though they may need to be profoundly transformed. I suspect that Postmodernism will increasingly come to be seen as a strategy for exposing oppressive contradictions in modernity, but I would wish to resist the idea that we have all embraced it as an inevitable condition. We can work with it, I would suggest, in some contexts shaping our behavior through universal emancipatory ideals, in others recognizing the lurking cultural imperialism potentially involved in any such position and thus drawing on the postmodern as a strategy of disruption. Freud argued that maturity is the ability to live with hesitation, ambiguity and contradiction. Perhaps to grow up is to live suspended between the modern and the postmodern, resisting the temptation for resolution in one direction or the other. (Waught 1992: 2)

FIVE NORMATIVE THEORIES

Development, democracy, and communication are normative concepts; they suggest certain desirable processes of social change. It is no surprise, therefore, that theories of development, democracy, and discourse (communication) also are normative and often ideological in orientation. Table 4.1 provides a schematic view of the dominant postwar schools of thought on the linkages between the three concepts. In its first four decades, development communication as a field of study was clearly polarized by the Cold War ideological battles into the liberal and Marxist schools of thought (Blomstrom and Hettne 1984; So 1990). The liberal theories have argued for a modernization paradigm that tends to be idealist in perspective, emphasizes individual freedom as its normative preference, assumes a consensus model of social change, and focuses on the nation-state as its chief unit of analysis and on the internal dynamics of the developmental process. These theories also tend to be empirical in method of research, drawing conclusions partial to market solutions and transnational corporate penetration of Third World economies. The liberal theories also provided a typology of the theories of the press (F. Siebert and E. Siebert 1974) that, in its simplicity, reflected the Cold War divisions of the world. The authoritarian, libertarian, social responsibility, and Communist ideologies framed four different media systems. Table 4.1 provides an alternative view linking the development, democratic, and discourse theories with the different commercial, single party, state, community, and pluralist media systems and strategies of communication.

The Marxist theorists, by contrast, have largely operated on the basis of a dependency paradigm that critiques the modernization theories for their failure to account for the structural factors at the national and international levels and for their procapitalist bias. The dependency paradigm tends to be materialist in orientation, emphasizes social equality as a normative preference, assumes a conflict model of society, and focuses on the world capitalist system as its chief unit of analysis and on the center-periphery dynamics of development. Dependency theories also tend to be critical in their research methods, arguing for structural change and social revolution. Modernization theories see the role of communication in development primarily in terms of promoting modern as opposed to traditional consciousness through media participation, psychic mobility, and diffusion of innovations. By contrast, dependency theorists critique the capitalist strategies of development as inducing lopsided development characterized by unfair divisions of labor, unequal distributions of income, media imperialism, titillating global advertising, and social and cultural dislocations that inevitably lead to social revolutions. However, as a result of the apparent success of some East Asian nations (Korea, Taiwan, Singapore, Malaysia, Indonesia) in breaking through the cycles of dependency and underdevelopment in order to join the ranks of industrial countries, the dependency paradigm has declined in importance. Immanuel Wallerstein, Andre Gundar Frank, and Janet Abu-Loghod have led the way in developing

Table 4.1 Normative Theories of Discourse, Development, and Democracy

School	Philosophy	Norm:Media	Model	Unit of Analysis	Focus	Methodology
Modernization	Idealism	Freedom: commercial media	Consensus	Nation-state	Internal	Empirical
Dependency	Materialism	Equality: party media	Conflict	Class	External	Critical
World system	Materialism	Equality: mixed media	Hegemony	World system	Internal/external	Political economy
Totalitarian	Voluntarism	Order: state media	Hierarchy	Race, dogma	Will	Engineering
Communitarian	Interdependency	Community: community media	Construction	Culture	Emancipation	Eclectic
Postmodernist	Skepticism	Plurality: multiple media	Discourse/practice	Knowledge/power	Resistance	Interpretive

a world system model of development that emphasizes interdependencies and cyclical shifts in domination and dependence.

In the post–Cold War era, the axis of debate seems to be shifting in a new direction, focusing on a conflict between totalitarian and communitarian perspectives. Historically, the totalitarian paradigm has been as important as the liberal and Marxist paradigms, giving shape and legitimacy to the development policies of the Nazi, Fascist, Stalinist, Maoist, and other totalitarian states. However, following the defeat of the Axis powers in World War II and the disgrace of Stalinism in the postwar period, totalitarian theories have not enjoyed intellectual respectability and have consequently appeared only in disguised ideological forms.

Nevertheless, totalitarian political theory is vast in its reach and rich in its variety and can be studied in both its classical statements and its modern renditions. This literature tends to be voluntarist in that it views history as an arena for the exercise of human will. Friedrich Nietzsche's philosophy of the Superman is considered one of the sources of inspiration for Nazism but also the beginning of postmodern thought. The politicians of the right often invoke "law and order" as key justifications for repressive state policies. Totalitarian theories similarly focus on the primacy of order as their normative preference. For this reason, Plato's *Republic* is regarded by some as the prime example of a totalitarian model of society. Whereas Plato's republic is premised on rule by a philosopher-king and an aristocracy of virtue, totalitarian models of ideal society are based on strict notions of social hierarchy that often include theories of racial superiority (e.g., the Aryan race). Human traits other than race have also served as the basis for totalitarian legitimacy: Any particular religious faith, political party, ethnic origin, gender, or even academic degree (with Platonic overtones) can be privileged to serve as the basis for totalitarian domination. Witness the theocratic or patriarchal regimes, ethnic cleansing, or policies of academic credentials or presumed expertise as criteria for social privilege (e.g., Singapore under Kuan Lee). Totalitarian policies therefore focus on how the collective will of any particular social group (even a minority, as in South Africa during apartheid) can impose its own vision and blueprint of an ideal and disciplined society on the rest of the population. Correspondingly, the assumption is made (as in the Grand Inquisitor chapter in Fyodor Dostoyevsky's *The Brothers Karamazov*) that the masses of population are gravely in need of social guidance and social engineering from society's select elite. Cultural and communication policies under authoritarian and totalitarian regimes thus typically follow strict rules of censorship with respect to messages of the media.

Communitarianism represents a variety of social movements for alternative modes of communication and development with a diversity of emphases. The Third World liberation movements have been primarily concerned with the need for emancipation from the economic, political, cultural, and psychological dependencies of colonialism and neocolonialism. The civil rights movement in the United States concerned itself with the same set of problems in the context of internal colonialism. The indigenous rights movements throughout the world focus on their rights of self-determination. The feminist movement is primarily focused on problems of gender colonialism but has expanded into broader issues of how patriarchal societies inflict violence on nature, other societies, and themselves. The environmentalist Green movement in the advanced industrial societies has called for a restoration of the community between humans and nature, but it is also deeply concerned with the related problems of world peace, social justice, and participatory democracy. The Christian theology of liberation in developing countries emphasizes social solidarity among the poor and the need for structural changes to restore the ruptured national community. Other religious traditions also have profound commitments to the primacy of community vis-à-vis the rights of individual or property. They have inspired movements such as the Gandhian movement in India, the Sarvodaya movement in Sri Lanka, the Islamic movements calling for the revival of the *umma* (the community of the faithful), and a recent intellectual communitarian movement in the United States led by Amitai Etzioni (1993) and others.

Although the communitarian perspective emerges from a long theoretical tradition critical of the processes of modernization and industrialization, it has proved its political potency only in recent decades. Rousseau, Émile Durkheim, the U.S. transcendentalists (Emerson, Thoreau, and Whitman), John Ruskin, Gandhi, Leo Tolstoy, and the intellectual leaders of the current worldwide peace, feminist, environmentalist, and Green movements may be considered among the leading theorists of this school. Although their remedies are different, their critiques of industrialism express similar sentiments: return to nature, distrust of government, and appeals to direct democracy. Because some recent theorists focus on the preservation of community as the highest value, the school can be characterized as communitarian. This characterization contrasts with liberalism's focus on liberty, Marxism's preoccupation with equality, and the totalitarian emphasis on order. Although concerned with the preservation of individual freedom, social equality, and national security and order, communitarianism is most deeply concerned with the loss of community in the modern world. The democratic slogans of the French Revolution, *"liberté, egalité, fraternité,"* are thus revived by the goals of peace with freedom, justice, community, and security.

With respect to the idealist versus materialist debate, communitarian perspectives tend to assume an interdependency position. They thus attach a higher value to human agency than do culturally or economically determinist

views of social change. Culture and cultural constructions of reality, however, assume a central position in the communitarian perspectives. Restorations of one kind or another—of nature, of cultural identity, of the lost
community—play a critical role in the emancipatory projects of communitarian movements. In contrast to the emancipatory projects of liberalism,
communism, or totalitariansim, such emancipation is not to be achieved
through the physical or structural violence of economic accumulation,
class struggle, or exercise of national will. Rather, it is considered primarily as a spiritual and internal process that leads to its external manifesta-
tions in social peace and social cooperation for common objectives. In
some communitarian movements, however, violence has been employed to
restore what is perceived to be an oppressed cultural and political community.
The Islamic revolution in Iran is the prime example of such a movement.

Liberalism, communism, and communitarianism may be viewed as the
three faces of the general democratic movement that has characterized
world history during the past two centuries. Ranging from fascism to
nazism, Stalinism, Maoism, Japanese emperorism, and their contemporary
Third World varieties, totalitarian formations provide complex responses
to the dislocating processes of democratization by imposing centralized
and bureaucratic domination in the name of racial superiority, proletarian
solidarity, national security, or religious piety. Capitalist, Communist, and
communitarian ideologies thus have the potential to slip into a totalitarian
mold when circumstances call for them to do so. Nazism in Germany was
a reaction against the liberal democratic regime of the Weimar Republic.
Stalinism put an end to the party democracy of early bolshevism. Japanese
emperorism inflicted untold misery on its own and other Asian nations.
Maoism imposed great famine and violence on the Chinese people in the
name of the Great Leap Forward and the Great Proletarian Cultural Revolution. Khomeinism provided powerful religious justification for a prolonged war while repressing political opposition and minorities in a multiethnic and multireligious society.

In contrast to the other schools of thought, postmodernism negates all
metanarratives except for that of skepticism. As such, it may be considered
as the cultural logic of late-capitalist modernity with its market-driven
commodification of all consuming desires (Jameson 1991) or, alternatively, as the source of cultural resistance to domination through deconstructive strategies against all hegemonic powers (Foucault 1980).
Whichever is the case, postmodernism opts for pluralism in discourse and
media systems; it focuses on an analysis of discursive practices in order
to fathom the grids of power and knowledge that constitute society. Its
methodology in research is primarily textual interpretation of all social institutional arrangements, from prison systems and asylums to art, architec-
ture, and urban design (K. Tehranian 1995).

FIVE OPERATIONAL MODELS

In addition to normative and ideological rivalries, the global discourse on communication and development has also been profoundly influenced by five competing metaphors of social change. To explicate social system transformations, these metaphors have characterized the social system in terms of *supernatural, mechanical, organic, cybernetic,* and *linguistic* metaphors and models. Whereas the normative perspectives tend to be concurrent, reflecting the simultaneity of conflicting social interests, the transition from one set of metaphors and models to another has signaled major paradigm shifts in the social science discourse. Social sciences have a tendency to follow in the footsteps of the paradigm shifts in the natural sciences, and the change in metaphors and models reflects these "scientific revolutions" (Kuhn 1962). In Kuhnian terms, social sciences are always situated in a preparadigmatic state of development in which different competing paradigms coexist but one or the other predominates because of newly emerging power configurations.

The supernatural metaphors represent a prescientific cosmology, and the next three metaphors point to views of society as, respectively, a mechanistic, organismic, or cybernetic information-processing system. With the rise of linguistic metaphors, social theory is attempting to emancipate itself from naturalistic assumptions and embrace humanistic assumptions. In contrast to natural sciences, the discourse of social science is characterized by strong normative assumptions and debates directly bearing on social policy. Although debate on competing theoretical and policy paradigms follows the natural scientific paradigm shifts, it appears to be never ending, focused on such normative issues as freedom versus equality, equity versus efficiency, order versus spontaneity, individualism versus community, and conservative versus reformist versus revolutionary. This feature of the debate corresponds to what Anthony Giddens (1984) calls "double hermeneutics" or "duality of social structure." Human agents are part of the social system they observe. Through their interpretations of the system and their actions based on those interpretations, they intervene in the processes of structuration.

Table 4.2 provides a synopsis of the paradigm shifts in the pre- and postscientific discourse, with particular reference to theories of communication and social change. The table is clearly suggestive rather than exhaustive. Briefly stated, the shift from prescientific and supernatural to mechanical, organic, cybernetic, and linguistic metaphors and models corresponds to the transition from traditional and prescientific worldviews to a number of paradigm shifts in the natural sciences. These shifts occurred from Newtonian physics to Darwinian evolutionary theory, from the rise of computer technologies to cybernetics and general systems·theory, and from

Table 4.2 Changing Metaphors and Models

Development Models

Supernatural	Mechanical	Organic	Cybernetic	Linguistic
Revelation: The visible world follows the designs of the invisible and the commandments of Revelation (the Bible, the Koran) to attain moral and material progress or salvation.	Instrumentation: Perfecting the machinery of society by social engineering to achieve maximum efficiency, order, output, learning (Watson, Skinner).	Differentiation: Diffusion of higher, modern values and techniques to achieve higher levels of differentiation, order, and complexity accompanied by higher levels of income, literacy, media exposure, psychic mobility, and political participation. Stage theories posit evolutionary change or mutations (Comte, Durkheim, Marx, Rostow).	Rationalization: Information monitoring, processing, and feedback to obtain greater speed, efficiency, and accuracy in the mapping of the environment to match its complexity for social, economic, and political decisionmaking (Bertalanfy, Wiener, Boulding).	Emancipation: Deconstructive and communicative action to achieve power-free communication and emancipation of the human life worlds from the grammar of society, which is embedded in the abstract and anonymous hierarchies and technologies of power (Habermas, Foucault).

(continues)

Table 4.2 continued

Communication Models

Supernatural	Mechanical	Organic	Cybernetic	Linguistic
Metaphysical systems of world religions communicated through divine revelation or spiritual texts; active source and wayward receivers of messages.	Behavioral and stimulus-response models of communication and mass media effects (Klapper, Comstock); active senders and passive receivers of messages.	Diffusion models of communication of modern values, ideas, and techniques from higher to lower cultures, more developed to less developed societies (Lerner, Schramm, Rogers); active senders and semiactive receivers of messages.	Transmission-belt models of communication, e.g., Shannon–Weaver information theory: Sender, Message, Noise, Receiver, Channel, Feedback; or the Lasswellian model of Who Says What to Whom Through What Channels with What Effects (Shannon and Weaver, Miller, Lasswell); active senders and passive receivers of messages.	Semiotic models of society as a web of signifiers, signs, and signified supplying texts and discourses subject to a diversity of interpretations and meanings by their authors and readers (Saussure, Eco, Derrida, Foucault); active senders and receivers of messages.

Common Assumptions

Supernatural	Mechanical	Organic	Cybernetic	Linguistic
Metaphysical rationality Invisible causality Moral universality Divine determinism Human responsibility Divine guidance and human striving to reach perfection (salvation, nirvana)	Mechanical rationality Linear causality Machine universality Machine determinism Algorithmic process Change within mechanical structures	Organic rationality Evolutionary causality Species universality Evolutionary determinism Processes of genetic mutation from lower to higher species	Cybernetic rationality Multilinear causality Cybernetic rationality Probabilistic Multifinality Change within information-bound cybernetic structures	Symbolic (ir)rationality Hermeneutic causality Cultural specificity Multiple meanings Change through human agency and structuration

information theory to communication theory, reflected in the rise of semiotics, poststructuralism, and postmodernism. Significantly, some major contemporary social theorists such as Habermas, Foucault, Derrida, and Giddens have employed linguistic and communication metaphors as integrating principles in their theoretical constructions.

Although the table draws sharp distinctions, it is important to note that new paradigms in natural as well as social sciences never completely abandon the contributions of their predecessors. By employing a new set of metaphors and models, they shift the focus of attention to new conceptual maps capturing some hitherto neglected aspects of reality. In the process of incorporating the older ideas into their new theoretical vision, they also, hopefully, achieve a higher level of explanatory power. Behavioral models of communication and social change can explain certain types of rudimentary phenomena, for example, memory learning based on trial and error and corrective behavioral change. For higher levels of learning, such as explanatory understanding and innovative problem solving, there is need for greater theoretical mapping to arrive at higher levels of explanatory power (Biggs 1971: 340–341). Such theoretical formulations need not abandon the behavioral, stimulus-response insights that have, in fact, led to the invention of effective teaching machines and computer programs focused on the rudimentary principles of most disciplines and languages.

Table 4.2 also provides a key to the common assumptions and strategies of social change implied in each paradigm. The supernatural paradigms, of which the traditional religious worldviews are prime examples, are often based on the primacy of the invisible over the visible world. Visible society thus has to conform to the commands of God's revelation, providing spiritual and moral guidance for human action. Starting in the seventeenth century, the scientific paradigms dispensed with such metaphysical views of society and human action; they provided a succession of alternative metaphors and models that explained reality in material rather than metaphysical terms. The mechanical paradigm viewed society primarily in terms of the regularity and predictability of a machine. The Newtonian "clock of the universe" and "the mechanics of law" represent some of its better known metaphors. The organic paradigm sees society in terms of the rationality of an organic system. The typical metaphors are "the body politic" and "the head of the state." Whereas conservative organic theorists (e.g., Parsons) focus on the homeostatic attributions of the social organism, revolutionary organic theorists (e.g., Marx) draw attention to the genetic mutations on the historical stage, for example, the qualitative jumps from feudalism to capitalism and then to socialism. The cybernetic theorists, in contrast, employ the metaphor of an intelligent, information-processing terminal in order to portray society as a complex, adaptive, information-bound, feedback-generating, self-correcting apparatus. Their typical metaphors are "institutional memory" and "social networks." Cybernetic theorists therefore employ input-processing-output-feedback models of the economy, society, and polity.

Linguistic metaphors and models of the social system, however, take serious issue with the rationality assumptions of the mechanical, organic, and cybernetic paradigms. If there is any rationality in society, it is the linguistic rationality of a loose grammar that allows almost infinite variations within the same fundamental rules yet is open to a variety of creative configurations and subjective interpretations. As language allows poets to innovate, so do societies grudgingly allow social innovators to go beyond the rules to achieve their purposes. Societies evolve in the same patterns as languages, so the metaphor suggests. Society is viewed as a text, history as a context. Readers bring to the social text and context their own meaning systems. There is therefore no objective social reality apart from the interplay of subjectivities. Linguistic metaphors and models thus negate the metanarratives of a Logos or telos in society while celebrating epistemological pluralism.

These five ways of seeing society also imply different theories and strategies of development. At the risk of oversimplification, the central process of social change in each worldview may be said to consist of *revelation* in the supernatural models, *instrumentation* in the mechanical models, *differentiation* in the organic models, *rationalization* in the cybernetic models, and *emancipation* in the linguistic models.

Although individual theorists are typically preoccupied with multiple themes, the main foci of each paradigm suggest a different strategy of social change. In the supernaturalist weltanchauung, society must conform to an invisible world and its God-given rules of individual and social conduct. The strategy of social change is therefore primarily one of moral exhortation and purification. In the mechanical worldview, social engineering and technological manipulation are the basic approach taken in order to optimize the functioning of an efficient social machine. In the organic worldview, the evolutionary process reigns supreme. Processes of differentiation and integration of social systems are thus the main foci of analysis. Whereas the conservatives emphasize gradualist and incremental change through social diffusion of knowledge and techniques, the revolutionaries call for structural change through historical mutations by midwifing social revolutions. In the cybernetic worldview, rationalization of the system as a whole rather than in parts is the central issue. This can best be achieved through increasing the capacity of the system for self-monitoring and mapping the environment for self-correction and self-transformation. The linguistic paradigm, by contrast, is mostly characterized by a normative bias for emancipation of the human spirit from the rationalized, routinized, and bureaucratized webs into which modern industrial society entraps its members. Although some theorists are more optimistic about this prospect than others, the general thrust is toward the deconstruction of ideological mystifications of power, the strengthening of critical consciousness in society, and the enlargement of the public sphere through communicative action for mutual understanding of the life worlds.

CONVERGING THEORIES AND MODELS

Ideational formations (including theories) thus consist of two interlocking elements, cosmological and ideological. The cosmological element tends to be culture bound, while the ideological element is interest bound. This view of ideational formations sharply contrasts with the orthodox liberal and Marxist views of ideology. Although the orthodox positions have been considerably modified in the neoliberal and neo-Marxist views of ideology, the lingering view of ideology as a camouflage that needs to be unmasked remains. Whereas modernization theory provides a stress theory of ideology, the dependency school offers an interest theory (Geertz 1973). In the modernization literature, ideology is essentially considered a pathology—a disease that transitional societies catch. In orthodox Marxism, ideology tends to be dismissed as fraud—a false consciousness perpetrated by the ruling classes to mystify the realities of class struggle. In both schools, ideology is considered a passing historical phenomenon that will wither away once the rational discourse of modern science and technology overtakes "the irrationalities and distortions" of ideological discourse. In the modernization paradigm, this happens as transitional societies achieve the full status of modernity (Lerner and Pevsner 1958; Bell 1960). In orthodox Marxism, the false consciousness of the ideological discourse becomes unnecessary once social classes have been altogether abolished in a classless Communist society.

Despite such predictions, however, ideological formations have continued to persist because they are part of the human condition. Human experiences are perceived and framed through conceptual categories that are socially constructed. These social constructions of reality are bound by time, space, culture, and language. In other words, they are epistemically determined. The dichotomy between material and ideational can thus be brought into question. Human understanding of the material world should be properly viewed as mediated through ideational constructions that mutually interact with changing material conditions. Ideological constructions are thus viewed as deeply embedded in cultural traditions (Geertz 1973). In this perspective, culture is viewed as a verb, not as a noun. An epistemic community is constantly engaged in the processes of actively negotiating those visible and invisible bonds of meaning that tie it together. The society's verbal and nonverbal modes of communication are the tools through which these negotiations take place, and ideologies constitute those competing worldviews and hegemonic projects that attempt to unify a society toward a set of common myths, values, norms, and behavioral pursuits.

This perspective calls for a culture-specific understanding of ideational formations. In this sense, tradition and modernity are considered as part of the inner tensions of a single cultural system in the process of transformation. By contrast, theories of discontinuity in historical change have been handicapped by a number of flaws. By drawing sharp distinctions between tradition and modernity or feudalism and capitalism, the orthodox liberal and Marxist theories have neglected the needs for cultural continuity. By dichotomizing tradition and modernity as mutually exclusive categories, these theories render the processes of modernization a zero-sum game. The more modern a society becomes, so the orthodox theories maintain, the less traditional it is. However, historians have long considered it "a commonplace that tradition is constantly modernized and modernity is constantly traditionalized" (Von Sivers 1984: 96). No wonder that Britain and Japan, the pioneers of modernization in Europe and Asia, also continue to present the most traditional societies on those two continents. By overemphasizing the universal aspects of the transition to modern society, the theories have thus underestimated the uniqueness and resilience of cultural traditions in the processes of social change.

The processes of human communication may thus be viewed as a series of multiple, interlocking layers of consciousness, rationality, narratives, and communicative agency that can be correlated with the discursive practices. Table 4.3 correlates the layers of human communication with their corresponding layers of discursive practices, narratives, and communicative genres and agencies. "Practical consciousness" means those traditional, routinized layers of awareness that a given language, culture, and perceptual style pass on from generation to generation. The discursive practice most closely associated with this type of consciousness is the reflective monitoring of action. When asked to report on our activities, we tend to produce a simple and surface narrative of our motivations, for example, "I refused to take the exam because I was ill." This is the type of explanation that often appears in routine conversation or news stories.

"Instrumental consciousness" means those more purposive layers of consciousness aiming at the achievement of certain objectives or the fulfillment of certain plans or projects. The discursive practice most closely associated with this type of consciousness is rationalization of action, which takes three forms. In a Weberian sense, this rationalization means devising the most rational methods of reaching an objective. In a Freudian sense, it means covering up our real motives. In a Marxian sense, it might mean creating an ideological apparatus that generalizes particular interests

Table 4.3 Layers of Rationality, Consciousness, Discourse, Narrative, and Communicative Agency

Consciousness and Rationality	Discursive Practices	Narratives	Communicative Agency
Practical	Monitoring of action	Surface narrative	Conversation, news, rumor, gossip, information
Instrumental	Rationalizing of action	Subsurface narrative	Ideology, advertising, propaganda, public relations
Critical	(De)constructing of action	Deep narrative	Religion, philosophy, science
Communicative	Human-human interaction	Metanarrative	Discursive regimes
Technological	Human-machine interaction	Hardware and software programs	Cosmology, mythology, science, scientific disciplines
Ecological	Human-nature interaction	Genetic blueprints	Cosmology, mythology, science, religion
Spiritual	Human-supernatural interaction	Revelation	Holy books, visual and performing arts, literature

in terms of the more generalized and socially legitimate interests. This type of explanation presents a narrow set of interests in terms of broader interests, for example, "I refused to take the exam because I wanted to protest against unfair school conditions." The explanation refers to a subsurface narrative that needs to be articulated or deciphered. This kind of social explanation is often the stuff of ideologies and ideological struggles, but it is also typical of the more narrowly focused types of instrumental and persuasive communication, namely, advertising and propaganda.

Critical consciousness monitors routine social actions and their rationalization in order to unmask their hidden meanings and to hypothesize alternative normative structures. This type of consciousness is perhaps best associated with the kind of constructions and deconstructions of reality that are embedded in ideology, religion, and politics. It begins with the radical questioning of the origins and end of life, including the nature of truth, beauty, and goodness. The narratives behind these types of explanations are of the deepest kind that only a critical approach can attempt to deconstruct.

Communicative consciousness is closely associated with the social and interactive nature of human beings. Social interactions are therefore the central feature of the discursive practice in this mode of consciousness. As Habermas (1983) has argued, this mode of interaction requires a high degree of equality and communicative competence among the participants. Habermas's "power-free communication" may be impossible in the real world, but to the degree that its conditions are met, negotiations of meaning can take place democratically to realize a truly communicative action. The prevalent discursive regimes determined by existing power and communication configurations, however, enhance or constrain the possibilities of communicative rationality and action. Communicative action presumes common epistemic communities and discursive regimes founded on a common metanarrative, for example, the idea of progress in the modern world or the American dream in the United States.

Scientific and technological consciousness is an entirely different order of magnitude. It is closely tied to the scientific-technological system of the modern world privileging the logic of hardware and software programs embedded in technology. Its communicative agency is to be found mainly in the scientific discourse and disciplines, the predominance of expert knowledge, and the grid of technological power that increasingly dominates the world.

Although dominant in the premodern world, during the past two centuries ecological consciousness has gradually lost its position of privilege to instrumental and technological rationalities. However, since the 1960s, the disastrous consequences of mindless exploitation of nature in industrial societies have become more known and appreciated. This has resulted in a return of ecological rationality to a position of prominence in postmodern discourse and an emphasis on the creation of new scientific myths such as the Gaia hypothesis to support environmental protection. Ecological consciousness has thus found its communicative agency not only in traditional religion and indigenous cultures but also in scientific literature.

Closely allied to ecological rationality is spiritual consciousness focusing on those spheres of natural life, that is, human finitude, fragility, and failure, that have proved to be beyond scientific and ideological explanations and remedy. In recent decades, the failure of the secular ideologies of progress and the limits of scientific knowledge have led to a rise of religious consciousness throughout the world in a variety of complex movements, from fundamentalist to ecumenical.

Communicative agency in all of the foregoing modes of discourse focuses on the interactions between communication, action, and social, natural, and technological environments. Human agency therefore operates through "multiple hermeneutics" rather than "double hermeneutics." This view is drawn from Anthony Giddens's stratification model of human agency (see Figure 4.1) and should therefore be understood in conjunction with his arguments:

> The reflexive monitoring of activity is a chronic feature of everyday action and involves the conduct not just of the individual but also of others.

Figure 4.1　Giddens's Model of Reflexive Action

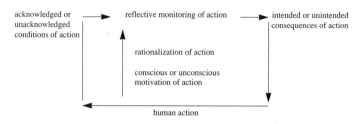

Source: Adapted from Giddens (1984: 5).

That is to say, actors not only monitor continuously the flow of their activities and expect others to do the same for their own; they also routinely monitor aspects, social and physical, of the contexts in which they move. By the rationalization of action, I mean that actors—also routinely and for the most part without fuss—maintain a continuing "theoretical understanding" of the grounds of their activity. . . . While competent actors can nearly always report discursively about their intentions in, and reasons for, acting as they do, they cannot necessarily do so of their motives. Unconscious motivation is a significant feature of human conduct. (Giddens 1984: 5–6)

THE POLICY PROBLEMS

As a result of changing material conditions in the world and their accompanying paradigmatic shifts, the five normative theories of development discussed earlier (namely, modernization, dependency, communitarian, totalitarian, and postmodernist) have each gone through enormous changes. Nevertheless, the perennial tensions among the complementary and contradictory norms of order, freedom, equality, and community continue in the processes of modernization and democratization. Whereas modernization by its very nature requires order and homogenization, democratization demands freedom, equality, community, differentiation, and pluralism. The transition from metaphysical to mechanical, organic, cybernetic, and linguistic metaphors has challenged the normative theories and has led to major reconfigurations of the axial principles of order, freedom, equality, and community. Religious movements, for instance, have borrowed heavily from secular ideologies of progress to mobilize social support on behalf of their own culturally and politically specific programs. To understand these configurations more specifically, it is useful to focus now on the development and communication policy problems.

To consider the role of communication in development policies, we may begin with the proposition that society can be usefully viewed as a process of communication and control for hegemonic domination. Figure 4.2 portrays the economy, polity, society, and culture as social institutions of communication and control of power, exchange, norms, and meaning. In this model, the developmental functions of communication and control are economic accumulation, political legitimation, social mobilization, and cultural integration. In the processes of modernization, these processes become the arenas for the conflict of competing development worldviews, ideologies, and discourses.

The current global information revolution seems to have significantly contributed to four concurrent and contradictory revolutionary processes in the world: the developmental, information, control, and democratic revolutions. Beginning with the rise of capitalism in the modern world, the developmental revolution is the oldest of the four. Through transnational corporations, this revolution has now reached the farthest corners of the globe. It has led to a transnationalization of the world economy at the centers, including Western Europe and North America, as well as the metropolitan centers of Africa, Asia, and Latin America. Global advertising and information processing have served as electronic highways in the integration of the world market economy.

The information revolution, which started with the invention of print technology, is the second oldest global revolutionary process. The more recent technological innovations in electronic media have further accelerated this revolutionary process. The widespread diffusion of the print and electronic media throughout the world has had contradictory consequences. On the one hand, it has created a global pop culture dominated by Western cultural exports. On the other hand, it has led to the deepening of national

Figure 4.2 Four Global Revolutions: Institutional Loci and Processes

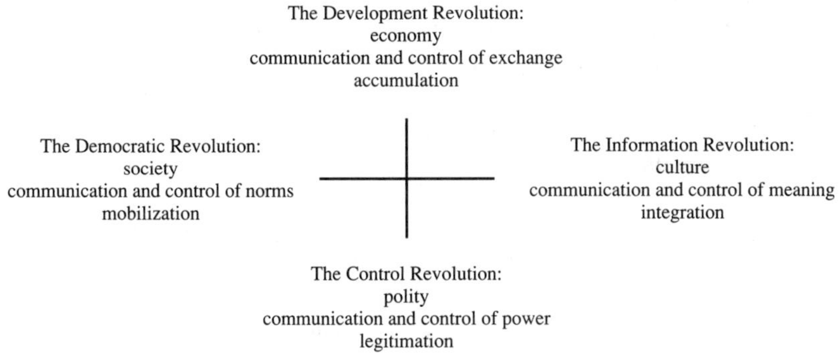

The Development Revolution:
economy
communication and control of exchange
accumulation

The Democratic Revolution:
society
communication and control of norms
mobilization

The Information Revolution:
culture
communication and control of meaning
integration

The Control Revolution:
polity
communication and control of power
legitimation

and ethnic consciousness in the remotest and most oppressed populations of the world.

The control revolution also has modern origins (Beniger 1986). This revolution consists of the rise of the modern bureaucratic state and corporation, the use of census statistics and computerized information processing, the modern systems of taxation, intelligence, and credit information gathering, and the abuses of such information for monitoring and manipulating citizens' behavior. Note the derivation of the word "statistics" from "state," suggesting the new science of statecraft. In the totalitarian regimes of the twentieth century, however, this revolution has achieved its most sinister forms when combined with the instruments of state terror. In an Orwellian world, it signals its most compelling warning. In the current technological revolution in information storage, processing, and retrieval, it presents its greatest potential for mischief in an information-perfect world (M. Tehranian, 1990a). The control revolution has thus led to a panopticon society (Foucault 1979) in which the individual's minutest behavior can be observed, analyzed, and possibly controlled by authorities.

Information technologies seem to be Janus-faced. Historically, they have contributed to both democratic and counterdemocratic trends in society. Hence there is the promise of a democratic revolution alongside the perils of a control revolution. As argued in Chapter 2, the democratic revolution in the modern world has taken at least three distinctly different roads, including capitalism, communism, and communitarianism. All three roads to democracy, however, have proved to be vulnerable to the totalitarian temptations inherent in the technostructures of modern industrial societies.

Each ideology represents an alternative path to modernization and proposes a different set of development priorities and strategies. The capitalist road tends to opt for high accumulation strategies of development, while the communist road has emphasized high mobilization strategies. As critics of both capitalism and communism, the Greens have stressed the need for the protection of the environment and social solidarity and hence have adopted a high integration strategy. Totalitarian dictatorships, by contrast, see the need for law and order on behalf of some hierarchical society as the paramount virtue. They are prepared, therefore, to pursue a high repression strategy of modernization to achieve these goals.

Table 4.4 pairs these four internal development strategies with three external communication policies—association, dissociation, and selective participation. Association policies are typical of the states following an open-door policy vis-à-vis international capitalist penetration, for example, the Philippines, Iran under the shah, Indonesia under Suharto, and Egypt under Sadat and Hosni Mubarak. Dissociation policies typify countries that have gone through a social revolution and see a need for a period of

Table 4.4 Alternative Communication and Development Strategies: A Matrix of Policies

External Communication Policies	Internal Development Policies			
	High Accumulation	High Mobilization	High Integration	High Repression
Association	Iran (shah) India (Gandhi II and III) Philippines (Marcos) Egypt (Sadat, Mubarak) Turkey (Kemalist)	Philippines (Aquino)	India (Gandhi I) Iraq (Saddam Hussaein)	South Africa (apartheid)
Dissociation	USSR (Stalin) PRC (1956–1966)	USSR (1917–1927) PRC (1949–1956, 1966–1976) Vietnam (1945–1974) Iran (Khomeini)	Japan (Tokugawa)	Burma Albania USSR (1927–1953)
Selective participation	Saudi Arabia PRC (1976–present) NICs (South Korea, Taiwan) Japan (Meiji, postwar) Indonesia (Suharto) Malaysia (Mahathir) Iran (Rafsanjani and Khatami)	Algeria (Boumeddin) Indonesia (Sukarno) Egypt (Nasser) Pakistan (Bhutto I, II)	Tanzania (Nyerere)	Spain (Franco)

Notes: India: Gandhi I refers to Mahatma Gandhi; Gandhi II refers to Indira Gandhi; Gandhi III refers to Rajiv Gandhi. PRC (People's Republic of China): 1949–1956 refers to the early revolutionary period; 1956–1966 refers to the Great Leap Forward; 1966–1976 refers to the Great Proletarian Cultural Revolution; 1976–present refers to the modernization period. NICs (newly industrializing countries) refers to South Korea, Singapore, Taiwan, and Hong Kong. Pakistan: Bhutto I and II refer to Zulfaghar Ali Bhutto and his daughter, Benazir Bhutto. USSR: 1917–1927 refers to the periods of War Communism and New Economic Policy before the rise of Stalin and Stalinism.

consolidation of power, for example, the Soviet Union under Lenin and Stalin, China under Mao, and Iran under Khomeini. Selective participation often characterizes those regimes that have passed the earlier stages of a national liberation or a social revolution and are able and willing to negotiate mutually beneficial terms for international cooperation on relatively equal terms, for example, the Soviet Union during Nikita Khrushchev's rule and afterward and China under Deng.

This theoretical perspective views development as a dialectical process of social change, involving the struggles for capital accumulation, social mobilization, cultural integration, and political legitimization (see Figure 4.1). To recapitulate, the processes of capital accumulation generate social mobilization, that is, physical mobility from rural to urban areas, horizontal and vertical social mobility, and psychic mobility in terms of multiple social roles. In turn, the processes of social mobilization generate the need for reintegration of society along certain new common values, norms, and identities. This calls for political legitimization along newly developed hegemonic projects that coalesce around competing ideologies and discourses. Development processes have historically shown a cyclical pattern of movement from high accumulation to high mobilization to high integration strategies. The intensity and duration of these cyclical swings clearly vary from country to country. Generally, the more democratic systems allow for political feedback and participation. This in turn softens the blows of the cyclical upheavals. If we define discourse as the symbolic processes of exchange of meaning to negotiate reality, the coding and decoding systems thereof assume a central position in development processes. Public discourse, whether mediated or unmediated, may thus be viewed as the social struggle for the definitions of reality and hegemonic or counterhegemonic interventions to replicate, reform, or transform it.

CONCLUSION

During the past three UN Decades of Development, the world has witnessed some stunning successes and failures in the less developed countries. The newly industrializing countries of South Korea, Hong Kong, Taiwan, and Singapore have joined the ranks of the industrial world within a generation. They have out-Japanized Japan in some respects, but in others they have lacked Japan's longer institutional experience in modernization. Other NICs, such as Indonesia, Malaysia, Thailand, the Philippines, Vietnam, and Cambodia, are more or less following the same market strategy of export-led development policies. Some of these countries seemed to be on the brink of takeoff into self-sustained growth, but the economic debacle of 1997 has put them back for years if not decades. Since 1978, when its modernization policies were set into motion, China, with annual growth rates of about 10 percent, has presented yet another stunning success story of the same strategy. Much of Africa and parts of Asia and Latin America, however, continue to languish in desperate poverty and often negative growth.

The role of communication in these successes and failures has been a matter of intense theoretical controversy. The modernization school has steadfastly held that the introduction of modern media has (1) assisted national integration, (2) provided linkages to national and international markets, (3) stimulated domestic demand for modern goods and services, (4) mobilized resources for development, and (5) diffused modern values and techniques in such areas as education, family planning, nutrition, hygiene, agricultural and industrial production, and rural and urban life. By contrast, the dependency school has argued that the penetration of the less developed countries by the Western media has (1) exacerbated their conditions of social, economic, political, and cultural dependency, (2) undermined their national identity in favor of consumerism and internalized colonialism, (3) privileged the economic and cultural interests of an urban and Westernized elite against the vast majority of semirural and rural populations, (4) encouraged conspicuous consumption through global advertising at the expense of social investments in education, health, and infrastructure, and (5) failed to create genuine development projects and perpetuated repressive and rapacious elites. The communitarian school of "another development" has called instead for the media to be employed as instruments for endogenous rather than exogenous development by focusing on (1) participatory modes of communication and development relying on both traditional and modern media, (2) horizontal rather than vertical communication channels, (3) appropriate technology rather than costly and complex high technology, (4) rural- rather than urban-based development, and (5) preservation of indigenous cultural and national identity and pride.

Historical evidence suggests that there are no panaceas, no blueprints for development applicable to all times and all places. However, successful countries seem to have gone through the historical cycles of high accumulation, high mobilization, and high integration. A subsistence agricultural economy, for instance, cannot usefully follow for its development a neoclassical market strategy that relies exclusively on market incentives for saving and investment. Low levels of income generate low savings and investment; fragmented or concentrated land tenure systems provide little incentive for investment in agriculture; lack of infrastructure discourages investment in industry. A high accumulation strategy would release labor and capital through land reform, force savings through government confiscation, and stimulate the economy through taxation and investment. Authoritarian governments with totalitarian ideologies and persuasion techniques have often employed such strategies. If successful, however, high accumulation strategies lead to high mobilization and the need for redistribution of income and investment in social services. The communication strategy in this phase often employs the horizontal rather than vertical channels, voluntary associations and networks rather than the one-way mass media messages.

Furthermore, the dislocating effects of both accumulation and mobilization create the need for national integration and unity. The role of communication in this phase of development is critical. Without the use of a lingua franca and a body of common historical memories, myths, and literature, it would be extremely difficult for a nation to absorb the disintegrating effects of the developmental process. It is no historical accident that countries with relatively homogenous populations, such as England, Japan, and Korea, have found it easier to mobilize their resources for development. But homogeneity by itself does not necessarily lead to development unless it is stimulated by external political pressures (foreign invasions in all three cases) and economic incentives (the lures of international trade). Nor is heterogeneity by itself a barrier to development, as the case of the United States, with its abundant resources, empty spaces, and immigrant population, amply demonstrates. In all cases, the developmental process creates the need for inventions of new modes of discourse based on new languages, myths, and literature. Communication has thus served as both the cause and the effect of development.

The historical lessons of the past four Decades of Development seem to have influenced theories of communication and development to move (1) from determinism to indeterminacy and human agency, (2) from idealist or materialist conceptions of development to interdependency, (3) from mechanical, organic, and cybernetic metaphors and models to linguistic metaphors and models, (4) from an emphasis on physical development to an emphasis on human development, (5) from internal or external foci to the interactions between internal and external factors in the development process, (6) from the need for technology transfer to the need for technological leapfrogging, and (7) from the centrality of the mass media to the importance of interpersonal and alternative communication networks.

5

HOSTAGES TO HISTORY

Algeria is the open port of entry to a barbaric continent with two hundred million inhabitants. . . . In His providence God now allows France the opportunity to make of Algeria the cradle of a great and Christian nation.

—Archbishop Lavigerie,
Archbishop of Algeria and Primate of Africa (1887)

Today backward and deprived, we face an economic and military giant with the moral and spiritual scruples of a flea. It is not a pleasant encounter.

—Sadeq al-Mahdi,
Prime Minister of Sudan (1966–1967)

Relations between Islam and the West have never been a model of harmony. The two quotations above are not isolated expressions of idiosyncratic opinion. They represent only one of the chapters in a long and arduous history of mutual suspicion and recrimination. This history began when the Christian West became aware of Islam's potent presence on its doorstep in Europe at the time of Charlemagne, king of the Franks (768–814) and emperor of Europe (800–814). Although Charlemagne put a stop to the advance of Islam at the heart of Europe, the borders between Christianity and Islam have remained remarkably similar ever since. The expulsion of the Muslims from Spain after seven centuries of domination (711–1492) determined the borders between Europe and Islam in the western Mediterranean. But in the eastern Mediterranean, neither the Christian

This chapter is extracted from my article "Islam and the West: Hostage to History," in Kai Hafez, ed., *Islam and the West in Mass Media: Fragmented Images in a Globalizing World* (Cresskill, NJ: Hampton Press, 1999).

Crusades from the eleventh to the thirteenth century nor the Ottoman siege of Vienna in 1683 could settle the existing borders between the two great Semitic religions that have rival universal claims and proven universal appeal.

I became disturbingly aware of this long history of mutual recrimination when a sweet, old British lady in Chipping Norton, England, asked me if Islam considers women to have souls. At the time, I was giving a series of lectures on Islam as a visiting fellow at St. Antony's College, Oxford. I was puzzled by the question, but I answered it the best way I could: "Islam considers men and women to be equal in the sight of God, both endowed with souls and moral responsibility." When I subsequently inquired about the origin of the question from my good friend and colleague at St. Antony's, the late Albert Hourani, he laughed and informed me that this idea was part of the medieval Christian propaganda against Muslims that has survived to this day.

Familiarity breeds contempt, and proximity brings about love and hate. The history of relations between Judaism, Christianity, and Islam (unlike those between Hinduism or Buddhism and Christianity) is thus replete with prejudices bordering on a will to misunderstand. The latest chapter in this history begins with the modern European encroachment on Muslim territories and thus gives rise to an unprecedented complexity of feelings ranging in variety and intensity from unadulterated fear to grudging admiration and consuming hatred. Although in many respects the Islamic responses to Western imperialism are fundamentally no different from Hindu, Buddhist, or, for that matter, Latin American Catholic responses, there are some uniquely Islamic reactions that flow from an Islamic weltanschauung. In no other "world religion" (to use a Weberian category) is the unity of temporal and spiritual realms as central a tenet as it is in Islam. For this if no other reason, militant Islam has proved to be a far more formidable force than militant Hinduism, Buddhism, or Christianity.

In its encounter with the West, militant Islam faces a twofold challenge: external domination and internal decay. Muslims have had to admit that Western domination of the Islamic world became a reality only when Islamic societies had degenerated into corrupt and fragmented entities that were ruled by the shahs or the sultans and were far removed from the Islamic ideals of piety and justice. The response of modern Islam to this dual challenge has been correspondingly twofold: external defense and internal reform. Beyond this consensus on the nature of the problem and the challenges it presents, there is considerable disagreement among Muslims today as to the strategy and tactics of the struggle. Although the Islamic revolution in Iran initially captured the imagination of many Muslims throughout the world, its mixed success with the dual aspects of the challenge has had a sobering effect on the Muslim world. There are no easy solutions in this world, no panaceas. Theocracies are as vulnerable to arrogance and corruption of power as any other regimes.

In the West, by contrast, an understanding of the Islamic responses to the challenges of independence, democracy, and development has been marred not only by past historical distortions and prejudices but also by the contemporary political and ideological mystifications of the realities at hand. The media, with their natural penchant for hyperbole and bad news, are not, however, the only culprits. The academic pundits and specialists have also faltered. This should not be too surprising. The two modern ideologies of progress, liberalism and Marxism, are strongly secular in bias and therefore predisposed to view any religious manifestation with disdain. If the religion at issue also happens to be as mystifying and threatening as Islam is perceived to be in the West, common stereotypes can easily take the place of serious analysis while policies pursue the course of shortsighted interests. We become hostages to historical prejudices without gaining a historical perspective. For instance, it is often forgotten in the West that modernity began with theocratic regimes: in Britain with Henry VIII, who declared himself the head of the Church of England, and in Geneva with Calvin. British and Japanese monarchies are to this day theocracies of sorts, with the head of the state also serving as head of the dominant religion, Anglican Protestantism and Shintoism, respectively.

THE TORCH OF CIVILIZATION

Relations between Islam and the West have to be understood therefore in the light of historical perspectives broader than the current shortsighted interests or their ideological rationalizations. These relations may be viewed as the passing of the torch of human civilization from hand to hand. The torch was transferred from ancient Mesopotamian, Egyptian, and Persian civilizations to the Greeks, Romans, and the Semites, from whom the Muslims learned their science, technology, and theology. Islamic civilization, in turn, served as a bridge to the European Renaissance, which recaptured the classical philosophy and sciences from Muslim translations and commentaries.

From another perspective, Islamic-Western history may be viewed in terms of changing power relations. These relations have gone through four distinctly different historical periods. The first period was a time of Islamic ascendancy, lasting from 622 A.D. (the year of the prophet Muhammad's exodus from Mecca to Medina and the beginning of the Islamic Era) to 1492, the year that marked the fall of Grenada and the expulsion of Muslims from Spain. This period witnessed the remarkably rapid expansion of Islam from the Arabian peninsula into the entire expanse of North

Africa and Asia. The second period represents a Western countermovement against the Muslim occupation of the Holy Land by means of a series of Christian Crusades that began in the eleventh century and continued until 1683, into the Ottoman period, when the expansion of that last Muslim empire into Europe was stopped at Vienna. The end of the Crusades could also be conceived as the beginning of a third period that finally led to Western ascendancy and the subsequent domination of the Islamic world in the nineteenth and twentieth centuries. The Industrial Revolution and the technological and economic lead it gave to the West have ensured Western political domination to this day.

The latest chapter in relations between Islam and the West is, however, characterized by an increasing Muslim resistance to Western domination that began in the nineteenth century. I will focus on the complexity of factors at work during this particular period of history to show the patterns of Western domination and Islamic resistance as they have unfolded in their dialogue. In recent years, revolutionary Islam has been one particular manifestation of this dialogue that has haunted the West. The implications of this phenomenon for the West as well as the Islamic world are a focal point of the following analysis. A realistic understanding of its import is vital for authentic communication and peace between the two worlds.

MILITANT ISLAM: CAUSES AND CONSEQUENCES

By "militant Islam" I mean a complex variety of movements that are often referred to by the Western media as "fundamentalist." The term "Islamic fundamentalist," however, represents a profound cultural misunderstanding. In the Christian tradition, "fundamentalist" applies to those groups that consider the Bible as the literal Word of God. In Islam, the Koran is considered the Word of God (*kalam al-Allah*) by all Muslims, but its interpretation is left to the ulema (the learned), who have developed the science of *kalam* (equivalent to theology) and divine law (the Shari'a). The Shari'a is based on the Koran, the tradition of the Prophet and rightly guided caliphs (Sunna), the principles of analogy (*qiyas*) and reason (*r'ay*), and the consensus of the community (*ijma'*). By this definition, all Muslims are "fundamentalist" but not in the Christian sense. Islam, like Orthodox Judaism, is a religion of law covering all aspects of life. And since law is subject to constant interpretation, the Muslim ulema undergo a rigorous education to reach the status of a *mujtahid,* who can exercise *ijtihad* (struggle) to interpret the Shari'a. Issuing a *fatwa* (religious decree) is thus the prerogative of only a handful of leading Islamic jurists.

Militant Islam is unified in its consensus that Islam is the key to the salvation of Islamic societies in their present plight. But that is where ideological and political unity stops and differences begin. Militant Islam is currently represented by a diversity of views, such as those of the Taliban in Afghanistan, who follow reactionary medieval practices, and the Refah (Welfare) Party in Turkey, which briefly came to power through parliamentary elections and carried out many progressive reforms. To label both groups as fundamentalist would only cover up our own ignorance. Similarly, to consider the Saudi regime in the same category as the Iranian regime, namely, fundamentalist, simply suggests that we have lost our sense of history. These two regimes belong to two different historical eras, one to a premobilized society and the other to a postmobilized state. In Saudi Arabia women have no right to vote or drive a car. In Iran women vote, serve in the Majlis (parliament) and the cabinet, sit on the bench as judges, are employed as film producers and directors, and generally make life difficult for a regime that still wishes to keep them in chador, the veil.

To speak of Muslim fundamentalist terrorists displays even more ignorance. The 1997 Organization of Islamic Conference (OIC) held in Tehran condemned terrorism as contrary to Islamic principles and practice. Fifty-five Muslim states representing a population of over 1 billion people, encompassing about 20 percent of the world, were unanimous in this condemnation. Nevertheless, contrary to their own religious precepts, individual Muslims, like individual Jews, Christians, Buddhists, and Hindus, continue to act as terrorists. What is worse, states that claim loyalty to one or a combination of these creeds also engage in state terrorism. No one can forget the U.S. government's use of napalm bombs and Agent Orange in the Vietnam War, which indiscriminately killed almost 1 million innocent civilians and poisoned their sources of livelihood. Nor can we forget Saddam Hussein's use of chemical weapons against the Iraqi Kurds in the 1980s. The massacre of hundreds of women and children in the Palestinian refugee camps of Sabra and Shattila in Lebanon by the Maronite militia forces, under the supervision of Israeli troops, is a reminder that even Jewish high standards of moral conduct fall apart in times of war. All states have thus had bloody hands and none can claim moral superiority, but that does not stop any of them from making such claims. As demonstrated in Egypt and Algeria, state and oppositional terrorism continues to be the weapon of the morally and politically weak and bankrupt parties.

The issue of terrorism, as well as others, divides the Muslim world, which stretches from Gibraltar in the westernmost tip of North Africa to the Philippine Islands in the Pacific. It comprises over 1 billion people of all races, languages, nationalities, and cultures. It includes all manner of socioeconomic and political systems, from monarchical absolutism to republican and socialist regimes with varying degrees of claims to religious or secular adherence. It shows an extraordinary level of diversity and complexity of social situations and movements on at least five continents, Asia, Africa,

Europe, North and South America, and Oceania. Given this diversity and versatility, there is no single answer to the question of the direction of the Muslim world.

However, there are elements of unity that make it possible to discern some possible uniformity. These include a common faith in the oneness of God and his message (*tawhid* and *nabbuwat*) as well as some common hopes and fears. Under the impact of Western domination, the common hopes and fears of the last two centuries have sometimes favored a revolutionary and militant interpretation of the faith. But to assume that this is peculiar to Islamic countries is to confuse the symptoms for the cause. Other Third World societies with a variety of historical and religious traditions have also shown some of the same symptoms. Love and hate relations with the oppressor, periods of infatuation and emulation followed by periods of spite and defiance, have characterized the struggle of the colonized to liberate themselves both politically and psychologically from the colonizers in all ages of human history. The Mau-Mau movement in sub-Saharan Africa, the anti-U.S. sentiments in the Latin Catholic theology of liberation, the Mahdist revolt in Sudan, and the current Islamic resurgence against Western domination all stem from fundamentally the same set of social, economic, political, and cultural imbalances and inequities.

What is uniquely Islamic, of course, is that the anti-imperialist sentiments are being expressed in a powerful ontological symbolism understandable to millions of the faithful. The deeper the level of the social and political struggle, the greater the Islamic ideological casting it has had to assume. This is demonstrated in part by the fact that after a long period of elitist disdain for religion in general and Islam in particular, secularists such as Saddam Hussein, Hosni Mubarak, and Hafez Assad have begun to appear more Muslim than the ayatollahs. Witness the Mujahedin Khalq, which represents itself as Islamic Marxist and is currently acting against the Islamic regime in Iran from its Iraqi military bases. Nevertheless, the truth of Islam (like the truth of all other great religions) rests not so much on its current social and political doctrines as on its ability to give solace to humanity and its enduring ontological insecurities. Religion is the sigh of the oppressed and the hope of the disenfranchised. On that score, Islam seems to have proved itself sufficiently deep and adaptable to suit different historical and social circumstances, from the most primitive to the most advanced.

A militant interpretation of the faith is therefore just another phase in the evolution of Islam. This evolution must be understood not so much in terms of abstract notions of what a utopian Islamic society is (as the proponents and opponents of Islamic ideology would have us believe) but in terms of the historically specific circumstances out of which these interpretations have emerged.

ISLAMIC RESPONSES TO WESTERN DOMINATION

Clearly, not all of the Islamic responses to the challenges of Western domination and modernization have been revolutionary in nature. On the contrary, despite its revolutionary origins (and which world religion cannot claim some revolutionary origin?), Islam, until the nineteenth century, could on the whole be considered a conservative social and cultural force in the life of most Muslim societies. Subsequent to Islam's rapid and spectacular expansion in the first century of the Islamic Era (622–722 A.D.), the energies of Islamic rulers were spent more on consolidation than on colonial or revolutionary expansion. In India, the Far East, Central Asia, Eastern Europe, and Africa, as well as North and South America, Islamic expansion took place rather peacefully. The expansion was achieved largely through conversions prompted by trade and cultural contact (as in Southeast Asia), Muslim rule over largely non-Muslim populations (as in Mogul India and Ottoman Europe), and the appeal of Islam as a multicultural faith against the predominantly white Christianity (as in Africa and North America).

Given a history of spectacular early success in world conquest followed by a long period of territorial stability and relatively peaceful expansion of the faith, the shock of defeat and colonization at the hands of the new industrial West was excruciatingly painful. Insult was added to injury when Muslims realized that their civilization was, materially if not spiritually, inferior to that of the West.

Muslim responses to these series of defeats, which stretch for nearly two centuries, have been complex and manifold. Initially, of course, the Western threat was conceived primarily in military terms. The Ottoman and Persian Empires, the two states that still enjoyed some measure of autonomy in the early nineteenth century, turned to a series of military reforms for resistance. It was soon discovered, however, that a modern military force is contingent on the acquisition of modern science, technology, training, and methods of organization. Muslim reformers such as Abbas Mirza and Amir Kabir in Persia and Midhat Pasha in the Ottoman Empire advocated the education of students at European schools and educational and administrative reforms. In the meantime, Western economic and political penetration of the Muslim world continued unabated. The struggle against Western domination was commensurably deepening in those sectors of the population that were more directly threatened, that is, the merchant class, the ulema, and the liberal revolutionary intelligentsia.

In the second half of the nineteenth century, the anticolonialist and reformist movements in the Islamic world gathered momentum, led by a charismatic leader, Seyyed Jamal ed-Din Asadabadi (known as al-Afghani). Afghani traveled widely throughout the Islamic world and some parts of Europe; he thus gained firsthand knowledge of the conditions of European progress and Muslim subjugation. He even joined the Freemasons and engaged in a debate with Ernest Renan, in which he acknowledged the obscurantist role of religion in history. As a bona fide member of the ulema, however, he could speak with authority on religious matters. His response to Muslim subjugation consisted essentially of two parts: dealing with the conditions of Western domination and calling for Pan-Islamic unity and reform. He addressed himself not only to the elite, the ulema and the Muslim rulers, but also to the revolutionary enthusiasts of the late-nineteenth-century Muslim societies.

Wherever he went, Afghani left his mark. Friend and foe credited him with having fomented revolts in India, Iran, and Egypt against the British and local potentates; he was clearly a man whose influence was far-reaching. The themes of his oratory and active politics have become the dominant themes of modern Islam. They include Islamic unity (Pan-Islam), modernist reform through the opening of the "gates of *ijtihad*," an impulse to return to the purity of pristine Islam, and an unparalleled revolutionary militancy against foreign domination and the un-Islamic rulers of Muslim lands. This agenda for modern Muslims has not been without its problems and contradictions. In an age of nationalism, when Muslims, among other peoples of the world, have increasingly become conscious of their own separate languages, cultures, and ethnic and national identities, the message of Pan-Islam has fallen largely on deaf ears. But perhaps the Pan-Islamic diagnosis of the historical problem was faulty to begin with. Having awakened to the Western threat, the Pan-Islamists perceived the West in traditional, dualistic terms of Dar-al-Islam (Domain of Islam) versus Dar-al-Harb (Domain of War). It therefore called for Muslim unity against the Christian West. Medieval Christendom, however, had already broken up into separate and often competing nation-states in Europe and North America. Pan-Islam as a political program could not answer the challenges and opportunities of a new nationalist world.

Pan-Islamism was for some time the rallying cry of the beleaguered Muslims, but it was soon exploited by cynical rulers (such as Sultan Abdul Hamid of the Ottomans) to justify their own claims for universal loyalty. Pan-Islamic ideology soon merged into separate nationalist and constitutional movements that most clerics joined. With the clerics, the nationalist movements could not have received mass support, but as soon as the secular nationalists won the day, the clerics were pushed aside and, in some cases, such as in Iran, Turkey, and Central Asia, were branded as reactionary and unworthy of leadership.

By contrast, Islamic modernism found fertile soil in some of the more advanced Muslim countries, such as Egypt, and thus developed some roots and branches. Two eminent Muslim scholars, Mohammed Abduh and Rashid Reda of the Al-Azhar University (the most famous center of Sunni

Islamic scholarship, located in Cairo), continued the work of Afghani. They took up the painstaking challenge of reform of the Shari'a through a judicious exercise of *ijtihad*. Their work is a continuing challenge to other Muslim modernists.

CAN THE ISLAMIC REVOLUTION BE EXPORTED?

The five major world religions (Confucianism, Hinduism, Buddhism, Christianity, and Islam) and the two modern secular ideologies of progress (liberalism and Marxism) may be considered not only as modes of explication of the world and codes of conduct but also as competing strategies for world integration. These seven belief systems all have claims to universal validity and application. All seven (but particularly the last two) have also attempted at one time or another to spread their faith and message universally. They have also initially underestimated and have subsequently had to come to terms with the racial, ethnic, and cultural diversity of the world, which divides humanity into tribes, nations, castes, and classes. Under the impact of modernization, the processes of global mobilization and fragmentation have been at least as strong as the processes of assimilation and integration; consequently, these messages of world unity (whatever their origins and claims to validity) have often fallen on deaf ears.

We may respond in the negative, therefore, to the question of whether or not the Islamic revolution can be exported. The evidence of history seems to be against such a possibility. The eighteenth-century European and American liberal revolutions and the twentieth-century Marxist revolutions attempted to export their messages and organizations. Similar material conditions, of course, gave rise to similar ideological trends, but in no instance could a revolution in one country be automatically reproduced in another. Revolutions, like wars, are more frequently lost than won. It is frequently the moral, political, economic, and physical exhaustion of the ancien regime that brings about the triumph of a group of often disorganized, incoherent, inexperienced but energetic oppositions to fill the new power vacuum.

What has been brought about as a result of a unique set of historical circumstances in one country cannot be wished into reality in a different set of unique historical circumstances. Old enmities and rivalries among neighbors also often militate against the universal revolutionary calls. Lenin's attempt to export the Russian revolution to the rest of Europe or at least to neighboring colonial Asia was a partial success in Eastern Europe and Central Asia primarily because of Russian might. Che Guevara's heroic endeavors to export the Cuban revolution to the rest of Latin America and the Ayatollah Khomeini's call for an Islamic uprising in the Muslim world against "corrupt and tyrannical" rulers are only the more recent historical examples of failures to export revolutionary ideologies and movements effectively.

Western worries about the export of the Islamic revolution are therefore unwarranted, but concerns about indigenous conditions that give rise to political instability, terrorism, and revolt are well justified. There is much in the revolutionary situation of a given country that corresponds to conditions in other countries with a similar set of historical circumstances. These corresponding conditions keep revolutions spreading gradually and often autonomously. The Islamic revolution in Iran owed its genesis to two overriding factors that are present throughout most of the Muslim world.

First, there are the material and social conditions of foreign economic and political domination reinforced by indigenous Western-oriented elites who owe their power and prominence to the military and technological support systems that come mainly from the liberal West. Sometimes these secular elites and their sponsors also exhibit an extraordinary degree of social ostentation, political insensitivity, and intellectual arrogance, inflaming the moral and political sensibilities of their Muslim underlings. The regimes in Algeria, Egypt, and Turkey are currently the prime examples.

Second, Islam as a religious belief system presents possibilities for revolutionary interpretations unparalleled in the other world religions (Smith 1957). Islam is the closest rival to Marxism in its revolutionary ideological potential. Like Marxism, Islam believes in the unity of theory and practice. Unlike Marxism, it provides a belief in the afterlife that gives ontological security to the human conditions of death, suffering, and evil. Islam, like Marxism and unlike Buddhism, takes history seriously and believes in the possibility of salvation here and now. Unlike Christianity, Islam recognizes no demarcation between the spiritual and temporal realms. The unity of temporal and spiritual authorities in early Islam is the ideal state to which modern Islam would like to return. This can be achieved either by the imposition of the rule of the ulema as practiced in the clerical domination in Iran or as suggested by Maulana Abdul al-Maududi in Pakistan or, alternatively, by the leadership of such lay Islamic organizations as the Mujahedin Khalq or Ikhwan al-Muslimun (Muslim Brotherhood).

Furthermore, two of Islam's first articles of faith are the unity of God (universalism) and the brotherhood of humanity (egalitarianism). In some branches of Islam (particularly but not exclusively in Shiism), there is also the expectation of a Second Coming. Mahdism or the messianic expectation of a religious redeemer to save the world from corruption and injustice has provided the Muslim world, both Shia and Sunni, with a powerful ideology that is used to galvanize mass movements on behalf of a variety of social and political causes. This ideology has served revolutionary causes in recent times (as in Sudan, Iran, or Algeria) largely because pro-pitious revolutionary circumstances existed in those countries.

A revolutionary Islamic ideology, like all other modern totalistic ide-ologies, contains some seeds of its own self-destruction. By uniting the legislative, executive, and judicial functions into a monolithic ideology and organization, totalistic ideologies (if successful politically) run the risk of closing all possibilities for social and political feedback and self-correction. Quite apart from its aesthetic value, political and ideological tolerance opens the doors for co-optation and delivers the incalculable and practical rewards of political longevity for a regime. However, when a rev-olutionary ideology, such as that of political Islam, is also based on claims of moral purity and eschatological hopes for salvation, the inevitable cor-ruption of power and gain on the part of the rulers in the name of religion can have disastrously disillusioning effects on the believers. In this way, the ruling clerics in Iran have demythologized Islam as effectively as the shah demythologized monarchy. In the presidential election of 1997 in Iran, 70 percent of the electorate voted for Mohammed Khatami, a candi-date who has called for full equality of women, more liberal media and cultural policies, and a dialogue of civilizations between Islam and the West. These are policies that run against the views of the dominant con-servative clerics, led by the supreme *Faqih* (jurist) Ayatollah Sayyed Ali Khamenei. More radical leaders such as Abdol-Karim Soroush, Ayatollah Hosseinal Montazeri, and the Islamic Student Organization of Tehran Uni-versity have been calling for the separation of religion and politics, a sym-bolic rather than a political role for the chief of state (the Ayatollah Khamenei), and election to that position by universal suffrage. These new revolutionary rumblings promise a bitter struggle in the years to come be-tween the conservative and liberal clerics, with each side seeking allies in the military and civil societies.

None of the foregoing problems need be as detrimental as they seem to the progress of Islam. The experience of Iran seems to have been taken to heart in other parts of the Muslim world. The intellectual and moral ca-pacity of the ulema will grow as their educational and practical attain-ments in the modern world increase. A more sophisticated if less militant approach to the problems of the modern world may also result. Islam has shown itself adaptable enough for the past fourteen centuries and will continue to adapt itself to the historical challenges of another fourteen centuries. After all, Islam is a young religion in comparison with other world religions. In terms of longevity, Islam is now where Christianity was at the time of the Reformation. Some of the militancy, pain, and fac-tionalism of modern Islam may similarly be considered as the rebirth pangs of a medieval religion coming into a cold, hostile, and challenging modern world.

WESTERN PERCEPTIONS AND REACTIONS

Islam and the West suffer from the perceptual problems of an adversary relationship going far back into history. Prejudices and myths difficult if not impossible to overcome have thus distorted Western perceptions of Islam and, indeed, Islamic perceptions of the West. Since the pendulum of power has swung back and forth at least twice in the past fourteen centuries, the dominant themes in this relationship have been mutual fear, imitation, rejection, and, ultimately, grudging acceptance and sometimes respect. The swings of power and civilization from the Roman and Persian empires to the Islamic empires of the seventh to thirteenth centuries, and back again to modern industrial Europe after the Renaissance and Reformation, are reminders to both sides that history does not stand still.

Nor can historical situations, sui generis, be repeated. Nevertheless, the myths continue. The myths of the Crusades are powerful indeed in the minds of some modern Muslims and Christians. As late as the 1920s, when the French general Gouraud entered Damascus following the battle of Maissaloun, one of the first things he did was to visit the famous tomb just outside the Omayyad mosque. He knocked on its door and said to its inmate: "Saladin, listen, we have returned." A recent volume by an "expert political writer and commentator" is entitled *The Dagger of Islam,* invoking the memory of the Crusades to make its point.

The Crusaders returning to Europe from Syria in the twelfth and thirteenth centuries brought with them the word "assassin," the name they gave to an Ismaili sect led by Hassan Sabbah ("The Old Man of the Mountain") that practiced religious terrorism under the influence of hashish, a hullucinogen derived from marijuana. The terrorists were called *hashashin* (hence assassin). Gradually, the word became synonymous with murderer, though "assassin" is the stronger term. Seven centuries after the Crusaders startled Europe with the first stories of the assassins, the world is now viewing through global television networks such as CNN Muslim assassins at work again. In the period since the end of World War II, these assassins are supposed to have killed in every part of the Islamic world and as far away from it as London, Paris, Hamburg, and New York. Frequently, the assassins are alleged to be Arabs, Iranians, or Pakistanis, who are encouraged by their ayatollahs to be dedicated killers. Such a media image of Islam represents what is in fact a universalist and humane world religion as parochial, monolithic, reactionary, and pathological and as having a crusading spirit. Offering irrefutable evidence in defense of this sometimes explicit and sometimes implicit message, the media uncritically assume that the Islamic religion is based on the pursuit of domination and power. In retaliation, the West is often portrayed in the militant Islamic media as greedy, corrupt, and imperialist.

In such unidimensional views, Islam and the West are essentialized, dichotomized, dramatized, and demonized. A careful reading of Islamic and Western histories and ideologies would teach us that we cannot make grand generalizations about their inherent and unchanging qualities. Ideologies are inextricably tied to the historical conditions out of which they emerge; they evolve with the changes in the historical conditions to which they have to adapt. Islam began as a universal rather than parochial message of hope in the Judaic and Christian prophetic traditions. It soon developed into a political and religious community at Medina, with the prophet Muhammad as its founding temporal and spiritual authority. Although Muhammad was and still is considered by Muslims as the last of the prophets and the single most important source of authority after the Koran, he never regarded himself as a divinity, nor have his followers. To call Islam "Muhammadanism," as some Orientalist scholars have done, is misleading and, from a Muslim point of view, a sacrilege. The young Islamic community split into factionalism and civil war soon after the death of Muhammad and to this day has not recovered from the deep ideological divisions that pluralize Islam. Views of Islam as a monolithic ideological and political force, therefore, fly in the face of historical and contemporary realities.

Similarly, the West is an imaginary construct of modern vintage that was invented and popularized by European opinion leaders and poets such as Kipling who wished to construct a collective historical self against "the other" (the East), whom they regarded as their inferior. As late as the eighteenth century, much of the so-called East (China, India, Egypt, Persia, and Mesopotamia) was still considered a fountain of civilization to be emulated rather than subjugated. But Asian military defeats in successive battles changed the balance of power and perception. It fortified the collective consciousness of the industrial world of Western superiority to the rest of the world in the areas of science, technology, culture, and civilization. However, the vanquished in history often cooperates in its own subjugation. A psychological study of victims of hostage taking has shown how they come to admire their captors, a phenomenon known as the Stockholm syndrome. Similarly, the so-called East gradually adopted a conception of the so-called West as politically, economically, culturally, and morally superior to itself and worthy of emulation. But the conception gave rise to a love-hate relationship between the two that to this day provides a serious obstacle to authentic communication among the diverse peoples and traditions of these two giant and diverse cartographies of imagination.

Islam and the West have thus been caught up in a fourfold vicious circle of misunderstanding: Western misunderstandings of Islam, Islamic misunderstandings of the West, Western misunderstandings of the West, and Islamic misunderstandings of Islam. The roots of these misunderstandings are historical as well as contemporary. Although I have touched on the first set of misunderstandings, the limits of this volume preclude the possibility of examing the three other sets. Yet they are equally important to an understanding of the depth and intensity of the problems at hand.

Islamic militancy has been a blessing in disguise. It has shocked us and brought into historical relief the interconnections of these four sets of misunderstandings. By failing to understand the depth and intensity of the Islamic peoples' struggles for independence, democracy, and development, the West has sided with those social and political forces that have been subservient to its short-term interests. By their preoccupation with vengeance at a time when historical circumstances call for international reconciliation and national reconstruction, the Islamic militants have often alienated domestic and international opinion.

However, the Western powers' singular inability to acknowledge their own part in bringing about such tragedies as those in Palestine and Israel, Iran, Iraq, and Algeria presents another obstacle to reconciliation. Shortsighted economic and political policies in the Persian Gulf, for instance, have often created leaders such as Saddam Hussein, whose greed and ambition violate their own people as well as their neighbors.

Narrow and anachronistic interpretations of Islam continue to strip this great religion of its ability to deal imaginatively and creatively with the problems of religious faith and practice in the modern world. By succumbing to the totalitarian temptation, some factions of militants also run the risk of alienating the most intelligent and patriotic sectors of the population away from Islam and toward rival ideologies or, worse yet, cynicism and opportunism. As a religious faith and as a social and political worldview, Islam has a vital part to play in the modern world alongside those competing and complementary worldviews embedded in modern sciences and ideologies. If, however, Islam tries to usurp the functions of science and political ideologies, it will fail to fulfill the role for which, as a great universal religion, it is uniquely suited.

CONCLUSION

In March 1997 I had the privilege of acting as a rapporteur at a UNESCO-sponsored conference in Paris focusing on a dialogue between European and Islamic civilizations. The participants included eminent political, economic, cultural, academic, media, and religious leaders from both sides. My own participation at the conference was in my capacity as the director of a peace institute, the Toda Institute for Global Peace and Policy Research. The institute has chosen for its motto "Dialogue of Civilizations for World Citizenship." I was therefore most grateful to Emma Nicholson, the British parliamentarian who led the conference, for inviting the Toda Institute to cosponsor it. As a Muslim heading an organization that is sponsored by a lay and pacifist Buddhist organization, Soka Gakkai International, I have been actively engaged in this kind of dialogue and have learned an immense amount from it. My report to the conference may therefore provide a fitting conclusion to this chapter.

In a parliamentary style, the conference was given several different resolutions to debate. The resolution on cultural diversity stated: "This conference believes that the post-globalization era can only protect mankind's diverse cultures and vulnerable communities if specific mechanisms to achieve that essential goal are created and put in place now." There were four main speakers on this topic, two European and two Islamic scholars. Although all of the main speakers were men, four of the ten participants who joined the subsequent discussion were woman. The opinions expressed in this extraordinary debate ranged from devout theism and secular skepticism to strong atheism. But the common ground reached was equally extraordinary. It proved that women and men of goodwill, coming from different ideological perspectives but engaging in sincere dialogue, could in fact agree on some essential principles for human decency and cultural diversity. I shall try to summarize the debate in the form of fifteen main propositions expressed in one form or another during the debate. These propositions were sometimes contradictory, but more often they were complementary. In the interest of developing common ground, I took the liberty of combining several different expressions of the same points into unified propositions. In conclusion, I have proposed a revised motion that seems to capture the essense of our dialogue.

- In Islam, God knows and commands, but humans possess only partial knowledge and err. Divine truth can therefore be absolute, but human truths are only relative. The metaphor of the elephant and the blind men quarreling among themselves as to the shape of the elephant applies to all human affairs.
- It is empirically misleading to speak as if there is a single Islamic (or European) civilization. It is more useful to speak of Arab, Persian, Turkish, African, Malay, or other national cultural traditions in the Islamic world.
- Despite differences in perspectives, dialogue between European and Islamic peoples is possible provided that it is not accompanied by cultural and political domination. A good example of such an exchange is the recent dialogue between the Ayatollah Taskhiri and the Archbishop of Canterbury.
- Whereas a true global culture requires genuine dialogue and exchange, globalization has become a synonym for Westernization.

- Without their own cultural identity, no people can enter into any kind of cultural exchange.
- Cultural tolerance of diversity is another precondition for cultural exchange. The example of the Abbasid era in Islamic history, during which Muslims, Christians, and Jews as well as Arabs, Persians, Greeks, and Turks worked together, is a good model for cultural tolerance. These cultures produced an Islamic synthesis and renaissance that served as a bridge between classical Greek, Roman, and Persian cultures and the modern European Renaissance. This was principally accomplished by the establishment of a Dar al-Hikmah by the Khalifa Ma'mun, which operated during the third and fourth centuries of the Islamic era (eighth and ninth centuries of the Christian era).
- It is a mistake to think of cultures as static. Cultures change as humans change, biologically, socially, and intellectually. It is therefore both simplistic and unfortunate to view others and ourselves in terms of fixed stereotypes.
- The moral task is to see ourselves as others see us, and that takes a great deal of education and intercultural dialogue. But the dialogue must be rational, avoid domination, and refrain from the kind of stereotyping that attributes, for example, the strange behavior of the Taliban to the entire Islamic world.
- Reflection and dialogue are necessary but not sufficient; they must be followed up by actions that take into account the following three central facts of the contemporary world: The world has become far too complex, it is changing too rapidly, and its problems are too large to lend itself to any solutions devised by any single cultural or national group.
- War is easy; peace is difficult. To build peace among cultures, we need massive public education. Such education requires financial resources enabling us to produce a vast range of educational materials accessible to all.
- Fundamentalism, defined as cultural intolerance and violence, comes in all forms and shapes, including secular and religious kinds. The bombing of the Russian Parliament in 1993 was, for instance, a form of liberal fundamentalism. The denial of freedoms of belief and speech in any country is another example of so-called fundamentalism.
- Fundamentalism as a label has become an insult. It covers a vast and complex range of ideas, from sincere beliefs in the fundamentals of a religious tradition to all kinds of intolerant attitudes toward others. It has also become a psychological scapegoat for those who

refuse to acknowledge and take responsibility for the real international and intercultural problems. The term should therefore be avoided in serious discourse.

• In some European countries, there is a general hostility toward Islam fed by media stereotypes and anti-immigrant sentiments caused by conditions of unemployment. To correct this, we need to address the prevailing economic and cultural conditions of disparity between rich and poor.

• The word "protect" in the motion sounds patronizing and should be discarded. We must enhance and cross-pollinate cultures. In fact, some of this is already happening in Europe, as exemplified by the impact of Arab melodies on French popular music.

• The media can be a source of cultural stereotyping as well as cultural cross-pollination and enrichment. We must provide financial incentives for the latter kind of multimedia creativity.

In light of the above, the motion on cultural diversity should be amended to read as follows: "We believe that the postglobalization era can enhance humankind's diverse cultures and develop common ground for global human rights and responsibilities. To achieve these goals, rules of civility in dialogue, tolerance in practice, and protection of vulnerable communities must be observed and specific mechanisms must be created and put in place now."

6

DEAFENING DISSONANCE

There is a tide in the affairs of men,
Which, taken at the flood, leads on to fortune;
Omitted, all the voyage of their life
Is bound in shallows and in miseries.

—William Shakespeare, *Julius Caesar*

In his polemic *The Image: A Guide to Pseudo-Events in America,* Daniel Boorstin (1975) has identified and diagnosed a new malady of modern civilization: mediacracy. Boorstin argues that the new, complex apparatus of image making in the United States (and by now throughout the world) is systematically creating not only serious distortions of life but also a distinct cultural preference for lively illusions over dull facts, colorful celebrities over honest citizens, media politicians over statesmen, commercialized tourism over inquisitive traveling, shortcuts to salvation over long spiritual journeys, and glittering images over challenging ideals. The arguments against "hidden persuaders," "mind managers," "captains of consciousness," "electronic colonialists," "consent manufacturers," and "media imperialists" have become so familiar by now that even the media pundits themselves have begun adopting them. In contrast to this pessimistic view of the media, Daniel Dayan and Elihu Katz (1992) have focused on the positive and integrative role that certain events dramatized by the media can play in the lives of viewers and nations. Media events have brought home the dramatic moments of history to millions of viewers

---

This chapter is a revised version of my article "International Communication: A Dialogue of the Deaf?" *Political Communication and Persuasion* 2, no. 1 (1982).

around the world. They may have also produced a catharsis of the tensions and conflicts that divide humanity. Examples of such events include President John F. Kennedy's assassination, man's landing on the moon, Anwar Sadat's journey to Jerusalem, Pope John Paul II's trip to Poland, and Princess Diana's funeral. Whether or not these momentary sentiments and revelations on our common destiny can result in lasting consensus remains a question.

The purpose of this chapter is fourfold. It examines the controversy on the role of the media, presents an argument on the media's critical role in international conflicts, offers some historical evidence in support of that argument, and draws conclusions on the limits and possibilities of international communication in conflict management. Among a number of contemporary examples, the Iranian hostage crisis perhaps best illustrates how competing interests are practically and symbolically served in domestic and international politics. Through a case study of the hostage crisis, this chapter provides an analysis that goes to the roots of increasing dissonance in international communication. It concludes with some warnings on the potentials and menaces of image politics.

A DIALOGUE OF THE DEAF?

There is a baffling paradox in contemporary international relations that can hardly escape the attention of discerning observers. Although there is an exploding technological abundance in the availability and use of telecommunication facilities, international discourse is often drowned in a flood of abusive words, images, and noise that limits the possibilities for a meaningful negotiation of conflicts. Some argue that the mass media and its practitioners are at least partially responsible for this state of affairs. Others point to the constructive role that the media can play and have played in furnishing direct and unadulterated reportage of international events and providing channels of international communication hitherto unknown and unexplored.

One of the unintended consequences of the advancements in telecommunications is the rise of terrorism as an instrument of state and opposition policy. Historical evidence shows that terrorism has always been an instrument of state policy (witness Hitler, Stalin, and Mao), but thanks to the publicizing power of the new international communication media, we tend to know more about it. The opposition has learned to resort to terrorism and the media as instruments of political struggle. Although the states attempt to hide their terrorism from the public, opposition parties have employed the media to publicize their causes. Oppositional terrorism includes such events as the attack at the Munich Olympics, the hijacking of civilian planes in the 1980s and 1990s, the Unabomber's attacks on scientists and engineers, the attack on the Al-Aqsa mosque, and the bombings of the

World Trade Center in New York and the federal building in Oklahoma City. State terrorism is illustrated by such events as the U.S. chemical spraying of Vietnamese villages, the Israeli-Maronite militia massacre in Sabra and Shattila, the ethnic cleansing in Bosnia, the Argentinean and Chilean mass arrests and executions, the Indonesian massacres during the coup of 1965 and in East Timor, the Tiananmen Square massacre in China, the Pol Pot massacres in Cambodia, and the Mexican government attacks on the Chiapas. There are few states in the world that can claim innocence in this respect. Opposition parties also have increasingly resorted to terrorism because television broadcasting of the drama of terror presents the least costly way of bringing attention to their cause. Terrorism seems at times to be the weapon of the feeble, at other times the weapon of the strong. But terrorism is at all times the weapon of moral bankruptcy.

EIGHT IMAGES IN SEARCH OF REALITY

In the controversy on the role of the media and journalists in international relations, there are many hidden assumptions and prototheories of news that are rarely made explicit. The conflicting conceptions of news can be best understood in the context of the competing structural and ideological orientations of the media in the contemporary world. An early and influential book on the subject, *Four Theories of the Press* (Siebert, Peterson, and Schramm 1956), provided a Cold War version of the ideological conflicts in news formations. Presented as theories, the four ideologies were labeled as follows:

- Authoritarian theory, which began in the late Renaissance and was based on the idea that truth is the possession of a few wise men.
- Libertarian theory, arising from the works of liberal pundits such as John Milton, John Locke, John Stuart Mill, and Thomas Jefferson, who considered the search for truth as a natural right and argued against interference by the state.
- Social responsibility theory of the modern day, which allows some government regulation to ensure certain media standards, such as avoidance of media monopoly, equal radio and television time for political candidates, the obligations of the newspaper in a one-paper town, and rules on children's programming.
- Soviet Communist theory, an expanded version of the old authoritarian theory that ensures totalitarian control of all media.

Since the publication of *Four Theories of the Press*, the international communication system and its corresponding ideological apparatus have seen dramatic changes, including the end of the Cold War and the four-way division of the world. The MacBride Report (UNESCO 1980) and its surrounding controversies pointed to the presence of at least eight competing normative theories or ideologies of the news that have permeated all debate on the subject. I may dramatize these conceptions by focusing on the images they present on the role of international journalists. The following typology examines both journalistic practice and its ideological rationalizations. The first five models correspond to societal types, and the last three reflect critical views of the dominant commercial and government-media systems.

Selfless Revolutionaries

This image of an ideal journalist is presented primarily in the revolutionary literature. Marxism and other revolutionary doctrines (Islamic militancy, Christian theology of liberation, anarchism) view the ideal journalist as a revolutionary dedicated to helping the poor, the oppressed, and the colonized and exposing the powers that be. In Leninist parlance, the function of journalism is "organization, agitation, and propaganda" directed at unmasking the enemy and sharpening the consciousness of the masses. It is small wonder that most classical revolutionary leaders have practiced journalism at some point in their career. Such figures as John Jay, James Madison, and Alexander Hamilton (authors of *The Federalist Papers*), Benjamin Franklin, Marx, and Lenin started with journalism and moved on to organizing revolutions. As midwives of history, their central function was not only to understand historical opportunities but also to seize upon them by enlightening and mobilizing their audiences.

Fearless Truth Seekers

This is the self-image held most often among professional journalists in liberal democratic societies. The presumption of this model is the existence of a pluralistic society in which conflicting power centers, interests, and views clash while a dynamic equilibrium is achieved through the processes of public discussion and political compromise. Investigative journalism is central to this model, which views the task of reporters as researching and reporting the facts without fear or favor. Mill's classical defense of liberty on pragmatic grounds and Franklin's well-known dictum "Such is the power of truth that all it wants and all it seeks is the liberty of appearing" lie at the theoretical foundations of this model. There is, however, a close affinity between liberal economics and liberal politics; their respective doctrines of "free flow of goods and services" and "free flow of ideas" clearly converge. The metaphor of information as a commodity in "the marketplace of ideas" (a term coined by U.S. Supreme Court Justice Oliver Wendell Holmes) both upholds and justifies private ownership of the media. In the interest of naked truth, muckraking is a central concept in this tradition in which the journalist exposes the dominant powers and myths. Such figures as John Reed (*Ten Days That Shook the World*), Upton Sinclair (*The Jungle*), Edgar Snow (*Red Start Over China*), I. F. Stone (*I. F. Stone Weekly*), and Bob Woodward and Carl Bernstein (*All the President's Men*) are the archetypes of such journalists.

Responsible Agenda Setters

This view of journalism is an extension of the former image that has evolved out of the liberal democratic tradition. However, the journalist in this model views the role as an autonomous membership of the power elite with special responsibilities to provide critical comments on current policies. The emergence of the public as a factor in domestic and international politics introduced such concepts as social responsibility, public opinion leadership, and agenda setting into the literature of journalism. The emergence of mass society and mass culture in industrial societies also gave rise to elite theories of public opinion formation in which opinion leaders were believed to perform the function of shaping mass consciousness in a multiple flow of messages (Lippmann 1930; Lazarsfeld, Berelson, and Gaudert 1948; Katz and Lazarsfeld 1955). The new publics have also created a new class of journalists known as "publicists" (in the American Revolutionary tradition) and "columnists" (in the more contemporary practice) whose task is to interpret rather than report the news. This image puts some journalists on par with politicians, clergy, and academicians as leaders of public opinion. In the U.S. tradition of journalism, such figures as Walter Lippmann, James Reston, and David Border typify this role.

Benign Gatekeepers

In a less visible but no less powerful role, some journalists, particularly those in positions of editorial responsibility, act as gatekeepers of what filters through the eyes of the editors to finally appear in press and broadcasting (Van Ginneken 1988: 78). Every reporter is, of course, acting in the same capacity when selecting the facts to report as news. But in this school of thought, the motto "All the news that's fit to print," adopted by a prestigious newspaper such as the *New York Times,* suggests that benign objectivity is the highest principle of journalism. That idea is also what is taught in most journalism schools. News is thus filtered through the mind of the reporters and editors with a view to selecting those items that best reflect the proverbial two sides of the story—even if there are many sides.

Veracity, accuracy, confidentiality, and credibility of sources have become the criteria in this school of journalism.

Development Promoters

This school of thought has emerged primarily out of the Third World but has a close affinity to the first model in its postrevolutionary phase. As the tasks of national integration and socioeconomic development have assumed importance in postcolonial periods, a school of thought known as "developmental journalism" has dominated the Third World media. In this model, journalists are viewed as servants of the state and its efforts to further national independence and unity, economic progress, and social welfare (Gunaratne 1978). In the UN system and the USAID programs, this school of thought has found its corollary in concepts such as development communication or development support communication, suggesting the use of communication technologies and methods to support national developmental objectives (Schramm 1964; Rogers 1976; Hornik 1980).

Hidden Persuaders

Propounding this model are critics of commercial journalism who believe that it is primarily at the service of commercial interests. A journalism that is controlled by business interests directly or indirectly through advertising is thus presumed to cater to the subliminal while employing sex and violence to add to its audience ratings and revenues (Packard 1957; Ewen and Ewen 1982).

Consent Manufacturers

An even stronger indictment of the commercial media comes from theorists who view it as subservient to the hegemonic designs of global capital (Herman and Chomsky 1988; Schiller 1973; Said 1981). From this perspective, the central function of news is the manufacturing of consent by systematic distortion and manipulation of facts to produce legitimation in commercial and state media systems. The sinister motives of journalism are thus attributed to either monopoly interests or totalitarian power.

Citizen Muckrakers

With the Internet and the World Wide Web, a radically new form of journalism has been born. The historical antecedents to this new type of citizen journalism are the Committee of Correspondents in the American Revolution, the Russian *zemizdat*, and Persian *shabnameh,* all of which served the function of providing underground channels of communication for the opposition under conditions of severe censorship. The new electronic channels of interactive communication have provided an embarrassment of riches in such channels of democratic and authoritarian societies. Although there is currently a large and increasing number of listservs, chat lines, bulletin boards, and Web pages for the new citizen journalists to exploit, the limitations are also apparent. First, authenticity of facts and reliability of interpretations greatly vary from one Internet site to another. Second, countries such as China have already created firewalls through which what the government considers obscene or subversive cannot pass. Third, all electronic communication is vulnerable to eavesdropping, and security agencies are not reluctant to collect data on criminals and dissidents. Fourth, the reach of the Internet is limited in its access and availability only to the computer literate. Nevertheless, the new citizen muckrakers, the student democrats in China and the Mexican Zapatistas, have already shown their effectiveness by employing fax machines and using laptop computers and the Internet.

EMERGENCE OF IMAGE POLITICS

In domestic politics as in international politics, the media are thus playing a multiple role at the service of the state, the market, and civil society. By contrast, the traditional realist, state-centric theories of international relations consider the media as part of the propaganda apparatus in the nation-state's struggle for power (Morgenthau 1985). In this view, the international system is perceived as a primitive political community still largely devoid of the essential properties of sovereignty and therefore prone to violence. Fragility of moral consensus and low levels of rule making, rule adjudication, and rule enforcement characterize the system. The realist theorists have maintained that the pursuit of naked national interest through military strength can best achieve a balance of power that can guarantee peace far more effectively than the idealist pursuits of human rights, social justice, national self-determination, world disarmament, etc. In such a view, the media and the ideological apparatus (i.e., public opinion, diplomacy, ideology, propaganda, morality) of a realistic foreign policy must be subordinated to the considerations of power politics.

In light of the media's omnipresence in international conflicts, however, the realists have had to rethink the issue and acknowledge the importance of image politics. As one realist scholar has noted, "It is perhaps no exaggeration to say that today half of power politics consists of 'image making.' With the rising importance of publics in foreign affairs, image making has steadily increased. Today hardly anything remains in the open

conduct of foreign policy that does not have a propaganda or public relations aspect, aiming at presenting a favorable image to allies, opponents,
neutrals, and, last but not least one's own domestic audiences" (Hertz
1981: 187). In the last twenty-five years, at least three major technological, socioeconomic, and political forces have altered the structure of the
international system to such a degree that even a realistic view would have
to consider the vital role that the apparatus of image making is playing in
international relations.

First, the accelerating technological explosion in communications has
both universalized *and* personalized world communication (Dordick,
Bradley, and Nanaus 1981). The convergence of several somewhat separately developed technologies (printing, broadcasting, point-to-point telecommunications, computers, satellites, coaxial cable, fiber optics, cellular
phones, and laser) into a single flow of digital zeros and ones has been
characterized as the second industrial revolution, a postindustrial society,
and the information age (Bell 1973; Porat 1977; Kumar 1978). The accelerating processes of digitalization and miniaturization have put mass-
produced information and communication devices at the disposal of increasing numbers of people. They have also allowed the less developed
countries to leapfrog into the information age without going through historical stages of development from print to the Internet.

As a result, traditional notions of national sovereignty have been seriously undermined by the ability of the superpowers and transnational corporations to conduct constant surveillance of national resources (both sub-
terranean and suboceanic), military personnel movements, changing
patterns in weather and crops, and transborder information data flows. The
domination of world news and cultural industries by a few countries and
companies has created real anxieties about the preservation of cultural autonomy and national identity in smaller countries (Nordenstreng and
Schiller 1979). However, the extraordinary achievements in telecommunications have made it possible for world leaders to directly and simultaneously reach untold millions across the world; millions of individual citizens
can also interactively communicate with one another. The new communications technologies have thus exhibited both centralizing (the global village) and fragmenting (the global chaos) potentialities. Since the world
system is primarily organized around the state and the market, the centralizing effects of the new communications have dominated the scene, but access to the new technologies by individuals and civil society is equally important in the process. The new communications technologies have
brought the world closer together in friction as well as cooperation.

Second, however, the small media and expanding educational opportunities are empowering millions of people in a democratizing process that
questions the dominant world system. The exposure to the mass media

through print and broadcasting has created rising levels of expectation, envy, and frustration. The macromedia (national newspapers, broadcasting, satellites, central data processing) have provided channels for elite communication, decisionmaking, dissemination, and legitimation of their views and interests. The micromedia (small and underground press, copying machines, transistor radios and tape recorders, and personal computers) have facilitated the channels of communication among a diversity of disenfranchised groups. The mesomedia (desktop publishing, Internet chat lines, and listservs) have expanded the communication capacity of the civil society. The pluralization of epistemic communities has thus created competing claims for identity and political community that utilize the expanding channels of communication. Such groups as the Islamic revolutionaries in Iran, the Irish Republican Army, the Kurds, and the Palestinians can attract the attention of the world to their own cause for sustained periods. Concentrations of power in world politics through cooperative arrangements among the Group of Eight is thus countered by its fragmentation into a series of local, national, or regional groupings that divide world public opinion.

In the meantime, a third set of forces has been at work to provide for integration in the world community. The media have served as channels of world ideological conflicts and consensus building. Major global crises have contributed to the emergence of a new tribe of world citizens and world organizations that transcend national loyalties and boundaries. The possibility of an accidental or designed nuclear war of total annihilation, the changing balance between world population and world resources, and the increasing cleavage between (information) rich and poor—all threaten to unleash violence and untold suffering in the coming decades. International communication encompasses both mediated and unmediated channels that have contributed to the conduct of international relations in basically three ways: (1) by providing expanding channels of communication, (2) by setting norms and values of global significance beyond narrow national or regional interests, and (3) by mobilizing support for or opposition to certain policies and projects such as nuclear war or genocide.

Traditional diplomacy was heavily dependent on realist calculations of power and secrecy of negotiations. The new international communication environment, however, has made secrecy increasingly difficult if not impossible. Power politics has thus been progressively supplemented or supplanted by image politics, questioning traditional boundaries between domestic and international politics and creating image fixations that have proved occasionally inimical to the accommodation of real interests. The symbolic uses of images have in turn served at least four kinds of cognitive rationalities and interests: practical, instrumental, critical, and communicative, corresponding to the purposes of domestic solidarity, foreign policy, ideological projects, and global community building.

INTERESTS AND COGNITION

The confluence of image and power politics in international relations is perhaps nowhere better illustrated than in the Iranian hostage crisis of November 4, 1979–January 20, 1981. This crisis is not, however, alone in the annals of contemporary affairs. In every international conflict, television's powerful image has mobilized public opinion in favor of certain policies and against others. States, even the most powerful and least democratic, cannot be totally impervious to such mobilization of opinion. It is generally acknowledged, though it has not been proved empirically, that televised coverage of the Vietnam War had an enormous impact on mobilizing the peace movement in the United States and the government's ultimate decision to withdraw from that country. The landing on the moon dramatically justified the enormous spending on U.S. space programs before and after the event. The intense media exposé of the Watergate cover-up led to President Nixon's resignation from office. Similarly, Sadat's dramatic trip to Jerusalem paved the way for the Camp David peace accords between Israel and Egypt. The handshake between Yasir Arafat and Yitzhak Rabin put a seal of approval on a peace accord between Israel and the Palestine Liberation Organization that was a bitter pill for both.

If "bread, circus, and roots" are the essence of politics, the media largely supply the last two components in image politics. The high ratings of media events are a testimony to their theatrical value for commercial television, and the projection of national or group identity into the arena of international politics is what manufactures legitimation for the actors. However, as projected images of "strong and unwavering allies," "terminated and relentless revolutionaries," and "reasonable and peace-loving states" are aggrandized by the media into larger-than-life mental pictures, media manipulation becomes problematical. Every image freezes its own constructed reality into an inflexible position. Certain postures that were perhaps valuable at certain stages of a conflict become impediments at other stages. Thus, reified images can prove as serious an obstacle to negotiations as real conflicts of interest. Conversely, when the media manage to break through the barriers of control and censorship to show that the state of affairs is in flux, that there is confusion of facts and ambivalence of minds, international conflict assumes a fluidity that lends itself to transformation into reconciliation. In the Vietnam War, as in the Iran-U.S. conflicts, international conflict assumed such fluidity of form and complexity of substance beyond the relatively conventional calculations of power and interest. In such circumstances, domestic and international audiences, each with its own claims and interests, come into play and blur the traditional boundaries between domestic and international politics.

The basic problem with realism in international relations theory is that its concept of national interest is monolithic and does not recognize the inner contradictions and complexity in the formation of what is perceived to be national interest. It is therefore useful to dismantle the concept. The media serve four different and often contradictory cognitive interests in international conflict situations: practical, instrumental, critical, and communicative. Although these categories are adopted from Jurgen Habermas (1971), John Hertz (1981), and Richard Ashley (1981), I have given them sharper and somewhat different distinctions in order to demonstrate their relevance to the media's role in conflict.

Practical Interests

This category corresponds to Habermas's "practical cognitive interest," an interest in knowledge as a basis for understanding the other. The mass media have provided powerful means for expanding the channels of information on issues of international conflict. In this role, the media give access to self-perceptions of the parties at conflict, including myths, symbols, and rituals that have emerged out of a particular historical and cultural tradition or political situation. They therefore provide interpretations that facilitate orientations of action and formation of foreign policy. The media thus furnish information and interpretation on the objectives, policies, and methods of the actors. Much of this information, however, is framed in terms of the ethnocentric biases of the national media, giving rise to stereotypes and misrepresentations.

Instrumental Interests

This group corresponds to Habermas's category of "technical cognitive interest, an interest in knowledge as a basis for extending control over objects in the subject's environment (possibly including strategic dominance over other human beings)" (Ashley 1981: 208). The media in this role concentrate on the legitimation of material interests (e.g., national security, the price and security of oil supplies) and employ images of power rivalries among nations and corporate groupings that are inherently in conflict over the ownership, control, and manipulation of world resources. From this perspective, the other views the game of international politics as zero sum. Much of Cold War politics was conducted in this mode.

Critical Interests

This set of interests is grounded in normative structures of meaning that legitimize the moral posture of the actors in domestic and international politics. Existing conditions are thus criticized from the perspective of generally accepted moral norms, such as freedom, equality, community, or human rights. Because the actors often generalize their particular interests in terms of publicly accepted norms, instrumental and critical interests are often intertwined in international politics. Thus, for example, Saddam Hussein was "liberating" the people of Kuwait from their tyrannical rulers, and the United States was "liberating" Kuwait from Iraqi occupation. The ideological rhetoric of each side said little about Kuwaiti oil, the main motivation in their moves. Critical interests are closely related to communicative interests when they take account of the rights of the other.

Communicative Interests

This category corresponds to Habermas's "emancipatory cognitive interest, an interest in securing freedom from 'hypothesized forces' and conditions of distorted communication (e.g., ideology)" (Ashley 1981: 208). It also corresponds to Habermas's hypothesized "ideal speech community" in which the actors enjoy equal competence in and access to communication. The function of the media in this role is rooted in the communicative exercise of reflective reason in light of needs, knowledge, and rules. In the international arena, the media have to break through the overpowering ethnocentric pressures of national self-justification and instrumental manipulation in order to focus on the long-term strategic interests of a global community increasingly threatened by what Waltz aptly calls the "four p's" of global self-destruction—pollution, poverty, population, and (nuclear) proliferation (Waltz 1979: 139). To serve communicative interests, the media must focus on adequately reflecting the views of the adversaries, honestly acknowledging the conflicting interests, and earnestly searching for common grounds.

HOSTAGES TO IMAGES

The Iranian hostage crisis, so rich and multifaceted in its global implications, lends itself particularly well to an analysis along the foregoing theoretical framework. At every major point in the decisionmaking process, the media managed to reveal the underlying interests of the parties involved in the conflict and thereby played an important role in the evolution and resolution of the drama. However, the crisis became a media event on both sides with its autonomous political and commercial ratings playing a crucial role in the domestic politics of both nations and in intermedia rivalries. In Iran the event led to the resignation of the liberal prime minister Mehdi Bazargan and the victory of the radical clerics. In the United States, it resulted in the loss by Jimmy Carter and the victory of Ronald Reagan in the presidential election. In the meantime, for 444 days the U.S. television networks competed against one another for access to the sources of news to boost their ratings and revenues.

The crisis served the fourfold interests of both states in (1) practically mobilizing national unity at a divisive moment in their histories, (2) instrumentally controlling each side's political forces domestically and internationally, (3) critically elevating each side's moral position while putting the other side in the worst possible light, and (4) in the end recognizing their common and global strategic interests in the sanctity of diplomatic immunity, the preservation of innocent human lives, and the de-escalation of a local conflict that threatened to turn into a larger conflict detrimental to the interests of all concerned. Let us examine the drama in greater detail and at the major points of its unfolding (see Table 6.1).

Backdrop

The overthrow of the shah's regime in Iran should be considered in the light of the struggles of a small nation for national independence. For some 180 years Iranians had struggled against considerable geopolitical odds to achieve a measure of dignified autonomy in a strategically and economically important region of the world. Dominated by British-Russian (later Soviet) rivalries, modern Iran looked to a third great power (France, Germany, or the United States) to balance the power of the first two. With its anticolonial reputation, the United States presented an ideal candidate in the postwar period for such a role. For its part, U.S. involvement in Iran was motivated by oil interests and Cold War strategic rivalries against the Soviet Union buttressed by a postwar ideology of liberal internationalism and interventionism. However, the role of the United States in Iran underwent a major shift as it replaced Britain and the Soviet Union as the nation's dominant power. The CIA-sponsored coup d'état of 1953 against Mohammad Mosaddeq's liberal democratic government in order to bring the shah back to power punctured the liberal nationalist illusions about the U.S. championship of democracy. The United States became increasingly identified with the shah's dictatorial regime and its excesses, and the shah came to look to the United States as his main ally and benefactor. The Iranian revolution of 1979 combined into a single revolt several repressed revolutionary processes, including anticolonial nationalism, democratic liberalism, communism, and grassroots Islamism. Whereas the anticolonial revolt united the revolutionary force, the ideologies of liberalism, communism, and Islamism divided them. Postures toward the United States significantly differed among the different elements; the liberal Islamists (Bazargan and his allies) were most favorably disposed.

The hostage crisis took place in the context of these historical circumstances. It revived the memories of August 1953, when the shah had fled the country only to be returned to power four days later by U.S. intervention. Under President Carter's administration, the United States was

Table 6.1 The Hostage Crisis: A Schematic View of Symbolic Uses in International Politics

Points of Decision	Cognitive Interests		
	National Solidarity Interests	National or Subnational Instrumental Interests	Global Community Interests
Admission of the shah into the United States, October 22, 1979	United States: To alleviate the feelings of guilt about letting down an ally	United States: To placate "old boy network" of interests posing the question, "Who lost Iran?"	United States: To fulfill human rights claims in providing medical treatment to a dying man
Seizure of the U.S. embassy in Tehran, November 4, 1979	Iran: To mobilize sagging public enthusiasm for the revolutionary cause	Iran: To embarrass and unseat Prime Minister Bazargan's government and his liberal-secular moderate faction from power	Iran: To dramatize Iranian grievances against the shah and U.S. imperialism and to gain support of world public opinion
Abortive negotiations, November 4, 1979– April 11, 1980	Iran: To resolve an embarrassing issue (for the secular faction); to continue to use the issue for national solidarity (for the clerical faction)	Iran: To reverse its own decline (the secular faction); to undermine the credibility of the secular faction (the clerical faction)	Iran: To appear to be the standard bearer of a just cause (bringing justice to a tyrant) without damaging innocent lives
The rescue attempt, April 24, 1980	United States: To assert its military power without endangering innocent lives or causing major conflict	United States: To improve the image of a weak president in an election year	United States: To project an image of a strong yet restrained superpower
	United States: To release the hostages without resorting to military means	United States: To regain influence in a vital region without losing face	United States: To defend the basic rules of international diplomacy

(continues)

Table 6.1 continued

	Cognitive Interests		
Points of Decision	National Solidarity Interests	National or Subnational Instrumental Interests	Global Community Interests
Resumption of negotiations, September 9, 1980–January 20, 1981	Iran: To dispose of an issue that had substantially lost its unifying value after the Iraqi invasion of Iran	Iran: To relieve the clerical faction of accusations of irresponsibility leveled by the secular faction and to prove who the real power is in Iran	Iran: To prove Iranian goodwill and expose U.S. financial interests
	United States: To resume efforts for a peaceful settlement of a national humiliation	United States: To achieve a settlement acceptable to national and parochial financial interests before the end of President Carter's term	United States: To achieve world approval in a just cause
Final settlement and catharsis, January 20, 1981	United States: Joy of homecoming of captive sons and daughters and release from a national ordeal symbolic of the United States' declining powers	United States: The continuity of U.S. foreign policy despite the change in administrations that had two different outlooks and approaches—Reagan's tough words actually helping Carter's conciliatory approach	United States: The honoring of U.S. commitments by the new administration and the refusal to engage in reprisals
	Iran: Shift from an increasingly costly and divisive issue to another unifying issue: the war against Iraq	Iran: Projection of the new clerically controlled government as the real center of power in Iran	Iran: Projection of the revolutionary government as responsible and responsive to global Third World community interests and sentiments

still emerging from a post–Vietnam War syndrome of withdrawal and retrenchment. In the face of the Iranian revolution, the White House was thus divided between the hawks, led by National Security Adviser Zbigniew Brzezinski, and the doves, led by Secretary of State Cyrus Vance. The hawks generally argued for some kind of intervention in the fashion of the 1953 coup d'état, and the doves, for some kind of accommodation with the Iranian revolutionaries. Given his ambivalent position, President Carter was torn between the two camps as events rapidly unfolded. The Iranian revolutionaries were thus deeply suspicious of U.S. intentions. The situation therefore lent itself to profound misperceptions and symbolic politics on both sides. It also provided the media with a captivating human drama endowed with a beginning, middle, and an end—tragic or triumphal.

Enter the Shah

Following the overthrow of the shah in February 1979, the debate on U.S. policy in Iran centered on whether or not to give refuge to the fallen and wandering monarch. Loyalty to an old and faithful ally clearly called for not only his admission but also assistance to regain his throne; this assistance was considered a U.S. tradition upon which the national interest practically converged. However, U.S. instrumental interests dictated otherwise. The revolution in Iran was by all accounts a popular uprising. It manifested strong religious and anti-Communist tendencies and therefore could be manipulated to the advantage of U.S. strategic interests against the Soviet Union in a strategic part of the world. Providing a refuge for the shah would have thoroughly undermined the U.S. position with the new regime. Therefore, U.S. diplomatic dispatches from Tehran as well as policy analysts in Washington recommended against his admission. But the medical diagnosis of his terminal cancer changed the picture. Human rights had been declared a cornerstone of President Carter's foreign policy. U.S. critical interests therefore combined with instrumental interests to argue for the shah's admission into the United States. The "old boy" network of Henry Kissinger, David Rockefeller, and John J. McCloy was pressing for the White House not to let down an old ally lest others take heed. The shah was finally admitted into a New York hospital for medical treatment. This decision was made against the explicit warnings of the U.S. embassy in Tehran, which had been occupied for a few hours on February 14, 1979, by revolutionary militants. President Carter's fateful decision served three symbolic functions at the time: (1) to soothe the guilty feelings of having let down an ally; (2) to placate those who were posing the question, "Who lost Iran?"; and (3) to project an image of a president who was sensitive to human rights but tough on issues of national interest.

The Seizure of the Embassy

On November 4, 1979, the U.S. embassy in Tehran was seized by a group of Islamic student revolutionaries who identified themselves as the Imam's (Khomeini's) Disciples. The seizure was followed by a sit-in to protest the shah's admission into the United States. In Iran's revolutionary politics, the seizure of the embassy served three symbolic functions. First and foremost, it was, for all practical purposes, a coup against Prime Minister Bazargan. The seizure came at a time when the conflict between the liberal moderates led by Bazargan and the revolutionary radicals led by the Ayatollah Khomeini, in alliance with a myriad of leftist parties, including the Tudeh (Communist) Party, had reached a breaking point. A week earlier, Bazargan and Foreign Minister Ebrahim Yazdi had met U.S. national security adviser Zbigniew Brzezinski in Algiers to discuss an improvement in U.S.-Iranian relations. The seizure of the embassy forced Bazargan to resign. By then it was clear that grassroots power was in the hands of the clerics who controlled the revolutionary committees. Thus, opposition to the clerical leadership by the liberals and moderates was successfully silenced by a national frenzy of sentiments against the crimes of the shah and U.S. imperialism. The revolutionaries claimed to have found in the embassy's shredded files evidence of a den of spies, implicating some liberals and moderates.

Second, the threat to put U.S. diplomats on trial on charges of spying provided Iran with a negotiating position demanding the shah's extradition to stand trial and the return of his ill-gotten foreign assets. These demands served the instrumental interests of the Iranian government, and the fact that the seizure of the embassy had been undertaken by an autonomous group of student revolutionaries exonerated the government from having violated the international norms of diplomatic immunity.

Finally, the seizure of the embassy contained elements of enormous international symbolic significance for the revolutionaries. It instrumentally served to dramatize the cause of Iran in international forums and to emancipate the oppressed everywhere from the fear of U.S. omnipotence. These symbolic elements included the release of thirteen women and blacks from among the hostages and the organization of an international conference in Tehran to unmask the crimes of the shah and U.S. imperialism. They also included Khomeini's letter to the pope, which was advertised in some major Western newspapers, and the friendly reception Iran gave to Third World journalists and mediators. The seizure of the U.S. embassy was generally viewed as a success among those nations that had suffered colonial domination; these Third World countries were gleeful, vicariously satisfied by the humiliation of the United States. The international state system as a whole, however, could not accept the violation of its most essential rules of conduct, that is, the protection and immunity of diplomats.

On the domestic front, before the hostage crisis, revolutionary enthusiasm had begun to ebb in the face of mounting economic and political difficulties. There is evidence that both the student militants and their mentors were surprised by the degree of spontaneous national support they received for the seizure of the embassy. The sit-in thus turned into a siege to galvanize further support and serve revolutionary solidarity interests. The hostage crisis had also become an important symbolic factor in the U.S. presidential elections, receiving unprecedented media attention, further encouraging the hostage takers. Some benign neglect by President Carter toward the crisis might have actually helped hasten the hostages' release (Anonymous 1981), but he made the issue a centerpiece of his re-election campaign on which he would stand or fall.

Abortive Negotiations

In the first round of negotiations for the release of the hostages, three factors worked against real progress: U.S. misperceptions of the locus of power in Iran, Iranian misperceptions of U.S. public opinion regarding the fate of the hostages, and the intense symbolic uses made of the issue in the domestic politics of the two countries. Throughout this first round, the United States continued to deal primarily with the wrong faction, that is, the liberal secular moderates (Bazargan, Yazdi, Abolhassan Bani-Sadr, Sadeq Ghotbzadeh), who neither approved of the hostage taking nor had the power to release them. In fact, the U.S. decision to admit the shah into the country had been partly encouraged from assurances by Prime Minister Bazargan and Foreign Minister Yazdi that the U.S. embassy and its personnel would be protected. Although Bani-Sadr and Ghotbzadeh also condemned the hostage taking as detrimental to the good name of Islam and the revolution, they could not afford to be perceived as siding with U.S. imperialists. However, once the leftist and clerical factions had realized the enormous symbolic value of the hostages in unmasking and destroying the liberal "appeasers and lackeys of imperialism," the negotiations for their release were continually and effectively undermined.

The series of bizarre encounters and plans undertaken by a variety of world personalities (Kurt Waldheim, Amadou-Mahtar M'Bow, Sean MacBride, Arafat) as well as by actual negotiators (Jody Powell, Ghotbzadeh, and their go-betweens, Christian Bourguet and Hector Villalon) all came to naught with one significant exception. In a personal intervention with the ayatollah, PLO leader Yasir Arafat is credited with having obtained the release of thirteen black and women hostages only sixteen days after their capture. Neither the source nor the symbolic significance of this act of clemency should have been lost on the negotiators.

The Rescue Attempt

Having almost reached what appeared to be an impasse in negotiations, President Carter on April 11, 1980, decided to embark on a plan to rescue the hostages. The mission was actually undertaken on April 24; it was, however, canceled on April 25 in a grim scene of death and destruction at an airstrip, code-named Desert One, in a remote section of Iran. The rescue mission served three symbolic functions. First, it came at a time when the crisis had become a U.S. obsession; the media and the president had managed to make the crisis a centerpiece of national attention, and the series of fruitless attempts at a negotiated settlement left the public fully frustrated at U.S. impotence. The ill-conceived rescue attempt was an effort by President Carter to avoid the image of the United States as a paper tiger. Second, the mission came at a time when President Carter's popularity and campaign efforts were facing some serious setbacks. Although earlier in the crisis Carter's posture in defense of the hostages' lives had served him well against Senator Edward Kennedy and others in depoliticizing the issue, his inability to solve it was becoming a symbol of his weaknesses in foreign policy. The mission also cost him the services of a respected secretary of state, Cyrus Vance. Finally, the strict limitations he had imposed on the use of force served to symbolize his intentions to contain the conflict, and possibly ensured the failure of the mission from the start.

Resumption of Negotiations

Negotiations were resumed for a second time only at the initiation of the newly constituted Iranian Majlis (parliament) and government, which were both controlled by the radical clerics. For the clerics, the hostages had by now served their threefold symbolic function of whipping up sagging national enthusiasm, undermining the position of the secular liberals, and mobilizing world public opinion in support of the Iranian cause. But in the meantime, they had also paid a heavy price. The United States had frozen Iranian assets. The reputation of the Islamic republic as a responsible state had been tarnished. But most important, the invasion of Iran by Iraq on September 22, 1980, entangled the country in a devastating war that lasted for eight years.

Covertly encouraged by the United States and financially supported by Saudi Arabia and Kuwait, the invasion led to over 1 million deaths and another 1 million injured at a price tag of over $120 billion. Prior to the invasions, Iraq had given assurances to Israel through the U.S. ambassador that Iraqi air force planes had been moved to the Amman airport for protection from possible Iranian retaliation, not for potential use against Israel. All the Western powers and their allies in the region therefore shared an interest in the Iraqi invasion of Iran. The Iran-Iraq War thus dwarfed the hostage issue as a rallying cry, and it brought home to the clerical faction the claims made by the moderates that the issue was increasingly isolating Iran and making it vulnerable. In the negotiations that followed, the positions of the two sides shifted from symbolic to substantive issues, that is, the release of the hostages as a quid pro quo for the return of Iranian assets frozen in U.S. and European banks. The complex settlement reached through the mediation efforts of Algeria had to reconcile Western banking interests with Iran's desire to receive the full return of its assets. Iran's decision to pay off the entire $3.67 billion in outstanding low-interest loans from Western banks and to set aside another $5.1 billion against U.S. and European claims hastened the financial settlement. The financial loss to Iran in this transaction was substantial. Iran thus gained little and paid heavily in political and economic terms, and the United States suffered in national prestige and anguish.

The Catharsis

The tumultuous welcome the hostages received upon their return home symbolized in no uncertain terms the extraordinary significance of the affair in recent U.S. history. However, it also underlined the symbiotic power of the media and the presidency to focus on a single issue for 444 days to the detriment of most other domestic and international issues. In the wake of the humiliations of Vietnam and Watergate, the hostage crisis symbolized yet another facet of a weakening United States. A nation yearning to believe in itself seized upon the hostage crisis and its victims/heroes as symbols of the traditional U.S. virtue of quiet strength under stress. However, the crisis also presented a test case for the Carter presidency. As Steven Weisman has put it, "A president who had risen to office because of his mastery of symbolism, achieving its height in his walk down Pennsylvania Avenue on Inauguration Day, met his fate in large measure because Iran had become a symbol of what Americans had come to dislike about their country—its seeming inability to get control of events and serve as the master of its fate" (Anonymous 1981: 120).

President Carter has to share some of the responsibility for this symbolism with the U.S. media, which often follow the government lead in foreign affairs. In 1968, for instance, when North Korea seized thirty-eight U.S. crew members aboard the intelligence ship the *Pueblo,* the hostages were not made into a media event. "It is true," as George Ball points out, "they were naval personnel, but they were in much worse shape, because they were tortured, and they were kept for nearly a year" (Anonymous 1981: 117). After their release, the media once again responded to the presidency when it relegated the hostages to its back pages. As in the case of Vietnam, the nation wished to forget and opted for collective amnesia. The symbiotic relation between the presidency and the media, particularly on issues of foreign policy, is well observed by Jeff Gralnick, executive producer of ABC's "World News Tonight": "If the government had nothing public to say, except that it would run things as if no crisis existed and we will negotiate quietly until they are released, the media would not have been able to do anything with the Iran story" (Anonymous 1981: 117).

CONCLUSION

This chapter does not argue for a mediacentric view of contemporary international relations. It does suggest, however, that a combination of three circumstances has created an extraordinary role for the media and the image politics that they generate:

- the rapid worldwide expansion of telecommunication facilities, leading to the universalization and personalization of international communication
- the mobilization of untold millions into the position of actors on the historical stage
- the rapid expansion of transnational channels of communication (international news agencies, professional and scientific associations, international forums, DBS, the Internet)

Together these forces have created multiple crossnational actors and audiences, blurring the traditional boundaries between domestic and international politics.

W. Phillips Davison has proposed that "for international or world public opinion to develop as a political force, three requirements must be fulfilled: People in several countries must give their attention to a given issue; they must have sufficient means of interacting so that common and mutually reinforcing attitudes can form; and there must be some mechanism through which shared attitudes can be translated into action" (Davison 1973: 874). The hostage crisis illustrates how under the emerging international communication regime, global public opinion is a factor that states must take into realistic consideration. In addition to the traditional tools of secret diplomacy, the state must now consider public and citizen diplomacy as two new tools that extensively employ the new media channels. For every public act a statesman undertakes today, he must calculate its substantive and symbolic significance for a greater number of interests and audiences that can be reached by the global media. The hostage crises of recent vintage demonstrate the often relentless international attention such events receive and the conflicting views they generate. Other significant international issues also generate attention, controversy, and conflicting political pressures for action. Witness the recurrent controversies in the United States regarding China's most-favored-nation status. An issue that would have been considered a technical question for the experts to resolve is now a matter of practical, instrumental, critical, and communicative interest and scrutiny.

The addition of public diplomacy to the arsenals of international relations is a matter of quantitative growth of the media's reach. With the introduction of interactive media, however, citizen diplomacy is making a qualitative leap forward in the democratization of foreign policy. The ever-expanding worldwide networks of travel, print and electronic media, and the Internet, combined with the growth of an international civil society, are taking foreign policy out of the hands of the so-called experts. During the Iranian hostage crisis, various Iranian and U.S. citizens' groups tried their hand at reconciliation efforts. Some Iranian students and exiles in the United States, U.S. clergymen, journalists, academics, and politicians got deeply engaged in the process of negotiations. These nonstate actors may appear to have been ineffective in the resolution of the conflict, but in fact they opened channels of communication hitherto closed to the two states. The communicative interests of the two nations were thus served by fostering greater mutual understanding of their respective grievances for the development of a common ground. However, a settlement of the conflict did not come until the two sides had exhausted the issue's symbolic uses in their own domestic politics.

For the United States, as a superpower, the hostage crisis marked a turning point in its climate of opinion—from aversion to war and foreign entanglements born out of the Korean and Vietnam experiences to support for assertiveness and military preparedness. As Yankelovich and Kaagan argue on the basis of their 1980 public opinion polls:

> Americans have become surprisingly explicit about how the United States should seek to regain control of its destiny, and in the context of the disquieting realities of the 1980s, these ideas create a new, different and complex foreign policy mandate for the Reagan presidency. The national pride has been deeply wounded: Americans are fiercely determined to restore our honor and respect abroad. This outlook makes it easy for the Reagan Administration to win support for bold, assertive initiative, but much more difficult to shape consensus behind policies that involve compromise, subtlety, patience, restrained gestures, prior consultation

with allies, and the deft geopolitical maneuvering that is required when one is no longer the world's preeminent locus of military and economic power. (Yankelovich and Kaajan 1981: 696–697).

One consequence of this new U.S. determination was the dramatic rise in the U.S. defense budget; another was renewed efforts by the Reagan administration toward public diplomacy—the dissemination of the United States' message abroad that became "Washington's major growth industry" during the media-conscious Reagan years (Adelman 1981: 913).

For Iran, as a small power in the grip of a revolutionary upheaval, the hostage crisis suggested once again the limits of its power. Despite its doggedness, the clerical leadership in Iran finally failed to achieve any of its original objectives: the return of the shah and his wealth, a public apology from the United States for its past interference in Iran, and sympathy for its cause. Despite its seeming resilience to outside opinion, the Iranian leadership had to bow in the end to the pressures for the release of the hostages that were exerted from foes as well as friends. World public opinion in favor of diplomatic immunity also undermined the initial domestic support in Iran for hostage taking.

This chapter also suggests the promises and perils of the new telecommunication facilities for the conduct of international relations. The threat is very real: the menace of unreality. What Daniel J. Boorstin (1975) argued about U.S. society is now perhaps true for an increasingly Americanized world. The hostage crisis, a dramatic illustration of the triumphs and tragedies of the new electronic age, was as much a pseudoevent as a media event, and the number of such events are on the rise. The crisis demonstrated (1) how image politics centering on the uses of new telecommunication facilities can supersede traditional power politics in some situations of international conflict, (2) how old cultural stereotypes and new political fears blown up by the international mass media can sometimes impede progress in negotiations, and (3) how increased awareness by the public of the complexities of an international issue can serve to limit excessive reactions to redress legitimate grievances. On balance, the ultimate outcome of the hostage crisis leaves some room for optimism on the positive contributions of telecommunications to international relations. Neither Iran (which felt aggrieved by U.S. domination) nor the United States (which felt harassed by terrorism) used its ultimate weapons. The hostages came home safely, no serious military actions were taken, and Iranian assets were returned. However, simplistic explanations of a complex political and human drama have left lasting images and stereotypes in the minds of the two nations that continue to be impediments to constructive relations.

During the hostage crisis, the people of Iran were no less victimized by this particular pathology than were the people of the United States. The crisis created both a deafening dissonance and new channels of communication between Iran and the United States. Iranian illusions about mobilizing the oppressed in the United States against their own rulers were punctured; the frenzy of the moment empowered one element of the revolutionaries (the militants) against another (the moderates). U.S. illusions about its government's benign role in international relations by supporting a "progressive" shah were also destroyed. The media have a critical role to play in international conflict by deconstructing the illusions of power and self-righteousness. For this task, professional communicators (politicians, artists, scientists, journalists, publicists, teachers, and clergy) have both a special training and a special obligation.

7

PURSUING PEACE

Politicians, commentators and students of history and politics should, perhaps, all attend divorce courts—before and after briefings, books, lectures and other "learning."

Their essential lesson that diametrically opposed yet equally logical versions of events can be constructed from the same facts, when proceeding from different premises and values, needs constant reminder. This does not mean that we must not judge. It means that we best not judge so absolutely for our knowledge is never absolute, our judgment never incontestable. To pretend otherwise is to embrace the banners of prejudice, partisanship, conflict and war.

—C. G. Jacobsen,
"Myths, Politics and the Not-So-New World Order"

The twentieth century has been the bloodiest century in all known human history (Tilly 1992). Can we turn the twenty-first century into a century of peace? As we continue to make "progress" in the hit/kill ratio of weapons, the next century might be even bloodier. That perplexing problem is at the heart of all efforts to develop a global culture of peace through a dialogue of civilizations. This chapter analyzes the global transformations at the threshold of the new century; it then goes on to propose an outline of communication and cultural policies that could avert tragedies far greater than those we have known in the twentieth century.

This chapter is a revised version of my article "World With/out Wars: Moral Spaces and the Ethics of Transnational Communication," *Javnost/The Public* 1, nos. 1–2 (1994), pp. 77–92.

A CENTURY OF DEATH BY DESIGN

How do you make sense of the collective suicide of thirty-nine Americans, young and old, men and women, in San Diego in late March 1997? The people who took their own lives were not poor, desperate, uneducated, or rebellious. By all accounts, they were highly gifted computer Web designers, making a good income, living in a posh San Diego suburb, in a luxurious mansion, peacefully among themselves and with others. They all belonged to a religious group known as Heaven's Gate, which had started in the 1960s with syncretic beliefs and practices. According to one of its former members, they were the gentlest and kindest group of people one could have ever wished to know. Why, then, the extreme measure of taking their own lives? It is a baffling question, and no one can pretend to have a definitive answer.

Throughout history, the end of each century has prompted hysteric episodes such as collective suicides and apocalyptic predictions, collectively known as the fin de siècle phenomenon. What is special about the twentieth century? It has been a period of death by design. In this century more than any other, responsible government authorities have meticulously designed the death and destruction of millions of people by employing the most advanced information and military technologies to subdue their enemies. In a definitive study of massacres in the twentieth century, Rudolph Rummel (1994) has presented statistics showing that about 170 million people have been murdered from 1900 through 1990 because rulers wanted them wiped out.

Since 1900, about 250 new international and civil wars have been waged in which over 100 million soldiers and another 100 million civilians have died. Counting only military casualties, the eighteenth century had a casualty rate of 50 per 1 million population per year, as compared with 60 per 1 million during the nineteenth century and 460 per million so far for the twentieth century. The end of the Cold War brought forth a ray of hope, but subsequent outbreaks of violence in many parts of the world have chastened that hope. If we add structural violence, which goes on unnoticeably in the slow death of millions suffering from famine, malnutrition, epidemics, or homelessness, the twentieth century could legitimately be called a century of death by design.

In the face of mass murders, the twentieth century also has been a century of spectacular achievements in science and technology outpacing human progress in intellectual and spiritual understanding. As the two recent wars in the Gulf (1980–1988 and 1990–1991) demonstrated, we have improved our technologies and engineering of death well beyond our moral imagination. Human learning is moving at radically different levels and paces. We may identify at least three kinds of cultural learning: *additive, regenerative,* and *transformative.* Additive learning is typical of scientific and technological learning in which knowledge tends to be accumulative and accelerating. Regenerative learning is the moral knowledge that is passed from one generation to another; it often has to be relearned through the pain and suffering of each new generation. That is why wars recur and each generation makes some of the same mistakes as the previous ones. By contrast, transformative learning is a type of moral and spiritual knowledge that comes about sluggishly through the inspirations of a great spiritual leader who takes a giant leap forward by integrating the collective learning of all past generations. Such great moral breakthroughs are the equivalent of big technological breakthroughs. They reverberate in the sinews of society for centuries to come until they are fully institutionalized. Such are the teachings of our great masters, from Zoroaster to Buddha, Confucius, Lao-tze, Abraham, Moses, Jesus, Muhammad, and Gandhi.

In recent years, a number of pundits have apocalyptically warned us of the end of history, geography, modernity, university, journalism, and work. Others have spoken of a coming clash of civilizations that will be characterized by ethnic cleansing on a systematic basis. The UN *Human Development Reports* have demonstrated the gaps in world income by employing the metaphor of a champagne glass, fat at the top and thin at the bottom. According to its statistics, the top 20 percent of the world's population receives over 82 percent of the world's income and the bottom 20 percent receives only 1.4 percent. The 1996 edition of the report tells us that the gaps between rich and poor within and among nations are growing further. Two sets of statistics tell the story:

- "The poorest 20% of the world's people saw their share of global income decline from 2.3% to 1.4% in the past 30 years. Meanwhile, the share of the richest 20% rose from 70% to 85%. That doubled the ratio of the shares of the richest and the poorest—from 30:1 to 61:1.
- "The assets of the world's 356 billionaires exceed the combined annual income of countries with 45% of the world's people" (UNDP 1996: 2).

We are witnessing the rise of a global two-tiered society in which automation and robotics are eliminating repetitive and routine jobs in favor of high-tech, high-skilled jobs. Downsizing and outsourcing have become the dual response of the corporate world to the challenges of global competition. Two new social classes, the underclass and the corporate elite, have emerged at the bottom and the top of the global social structure; the middle classes are routinely downsized to the level of sporadic unemployment. Meanwhile, the social safety nets, absent from the Third World, are being cut away in Europe and the United States.

Under such conditions, moral bewilderment is encountering technological certitude and poverty is confronting plenty. Is it any wonder that
sensitive souls might take refuge in a cult that promises the end of time, a
"recycling of the Planet Earth," the meeting of a UFO hidden behind a
comet, and the transmigration of life into a new paradise? Religion is the
sigh of the oppressed and the stuff of human hope. For centuries, it has re-
nounced the pain and suffering of this world for the coming of a world of
peace and plenty. It is only in the last few centuries that we have come to
expect a ceaseless improvement of our lives here and now. For millions of
people everywhere, the idea of progress has thus come to the end of its
tether. For about half of the human race suffering from worsening conditions of physical and political security, this is fairly obvious. But for the
other half living in societies that are affluent or aspiring to affluence, spiritual poverty is sometimes harder to bear than material poverty. The ceaseless anxieties of atomized societies that reduce the individual to conditions
of abstraction and anonymity can lead to cultist ventures or interethnic
bloodbaths, as witnessed in Bosnia and Rwanda-Burundi.

The technologies of mass murder have progressed much faster than
the technologies of peacemaking. The wars of the twentieth century have
been waged in the name of the colliding moral spaces of tribalism, nationalism, colonialism, and imperialism. The identities and cartographies of violence have been transformed across global times and spaces, from premodern to modern and postmodern formations. From Korea to Vietnam,
Israel and Palestine, the Persian Gulf, Somalia, and Bosnia, the collisions
of spatial claims have been increasingly clothed in greater moral self-
righteousness. The adversaries are playing to an ever-growing gallery of
global audiences watching them on television screens. As the mass media
dichotomize, dramatize, and demonize "them" against "us," reified images
of the "Islamic terrorists," "satanic Americans," "cunning Japanese," "evil
Chinese," and "uncivilized Africans" become frozen in the minds of mass
audiences as justifications for the next cycle of violence.

The new phase in global modernization under pancapitalism is creating new forms of manifest and latent violence. Since 1945, the character of
warfare has changed from direct military confrontations primarily with
military casualties to protracted warfare with more civilian than military
victims. In World War II, 95 percent of the casualties were military; in
more recent wars, 60 percent of the casualties have been civilian (Barnaby 1988: 57). In these invisible wars, global media are performing a role
by providing channels of expression to competing truth claims. Although
the roots of conflicts are structural, paradoxically, the battles are often
politicized in the name of cultural and ethnic identity. A change in the
epistemic framing of conflict and cultural attitudes would thus more effectively deal with the underlying problems.

Rapidly expanding global communication provides hope for achieving greater long-term understanding among nations and cultures, but the cluttering of the channels by episodic news of violence without any serious analysis of its root causes and possible remedies is leading to systematic distortions in communication and knowledge. Most news is framed in narrow partisan and nationalist terms. But a global marketplace and society demand global norms, citizenship, and journalism. In order to go beyond partisan interests and their moral geographies, a new spiritual breakthrough leading to a new ethics of transnational communication is needed. The new ethics would have important implications for the practice of international journalism and peacemaking. It calls for global journalism as an exercise in global citizenship.

Three basic scenarios may be envisioned for the future: continuity, collapse, and transformation. Table 7.1 provides a schematic review of the three scenarios and their variations as reflected in the literature of futures studies. Without going into detail on each variation (M. Tehranian and Ogden 1998), continuity scenarios envision more of the same. In typical capitalist busts and booms, the world system will continue to grow unevenly across the globe, with certain regions and countries growing faster than others. East Asia was the fastest-growing region from 1980 to 1997, but as its economies matured and its comparative advantage in low wages, rents, taxes, and regulation erodes, East Asia is losing its place to Latin America or Africa (Anonymous 1997c: 47; Editorial 1997: 13–14). The basic structures of capitalism, however, will not change. As the most successful form of governance, liberal democracy will dominate, but those countries that are still suffering under dictatorships will have to democratize as the working class demands higher wages and the new middle classes insist on civil liberties (Fukuyama 1992).

The collapse scenario, by contrast, envisions growing gaps within and among countries and regions of the world. These gaps produce their own tensions and conflicts. Capitalism thus breeds inequity and violence. That violence may appear in the form of a "clash of civilizations" (Huntington 1998) on a massive scale or continue to simmer below the surface, breaking out in the form of terrorism or protracted conflicts (Kaplan 1995). The world may end, as T. S. Eliot suggested, "not with a bang but a whimper."

The transformation scenario views neither of these two scenarios as inevitable. It calls for education and intervention to avoid disaster. As H. G. Wells put it aptly, it considers "civilization as a race between education and catastrophe." Such interventions may take radically different forms, including a struggle to establish world government (the World Federalists) in order to establish global law and order or, at the opposite extreme, a fight against all governments as embodiments of domination and exploitation (classical Marxism and anarchism). Alternatively, the efforts for transformation

Table 7.1   A Schematic View of the Post–Cold War Future Scenarios

Scenarios	Corresponding Sources
Continuity Scenarios	
State System Scenario Continuity and restoration of the state system, requiring a balance of power through military strength	Kissinger 1994; Morganthau 1949; Waltz 1979
End of History Scenario Global triumph of liberal capitalism, requiring progressive worldwide democratic and market institutions	Fukuyama 1992
Corporate Hegemony Scenario Transnational corporate domination of the world, requiring democratic resistance	Barnet and Cavanagh 1992
Regionalist Scenario Intraregional cooperation and interregional competition for trade and development, requiring such organizations as NATFA, EU, Southern Cone Common Market (MERCOSUR), ASEAN, APEC, SARC, CIS, and ECO	Fawcett and Hurrell 1996
Collapse Scenarios	
Growing Gap Scenario A widening bifurcation of the world system between rich and poor, leading to increasing intrastate and interstate clashes	Attali 1991; UNDP 1990–1998
Clash of Civilizations Scenario Future conflicts will be among civilizations, notably between the West and the rest	Huntington 1998
Chaos Scenario Disintegration of the world system into anarchy requiring strict antiterrorist strategies	Kaplan 1995
Transformation Scenarios	
End of State Scenario Abolition of social classes and withering away of the state requiring revolutionary struggle	Marx and Engels 1948
Anarchist Scenario Dissolution of the state into a libertarian laissez-faire system, requiring progressive devolution of power	Boaz 1998
World Government Scenario Evolution toward a federal system of world government through a democratic federal constitution	Tinbergen, Dolman, and Van Ettinger 1976
Just World Order Scenario Rule of law and conflict resolution through peaceful means, requiring institutionalization of conflict resolution and legal methods of dispensing justice	Falk 1995
Communitarian Scenario Cooperation for peace, development, and justice on the basis of shared values and interests, requiring world integration and building of dialogical security communities at national, regional, and global levels	Deutsch 1966b; Etzioni 1993; Tehranian 1990b

toward a more just world order may take incremental and reformist forms. It may focus on the building blocs of world governance through the establishment of the rule of law (Falk 1995) or concentrate on the construction of interlocking communities of interest, knowledge, and meaning from local to global (Deutsch 1966a; M. Tehranian 1990b). Clearly, these different approaches are not mutually exclusive. Nor are the three scenarios all right or all wrong. We can change neither the past nor the future. Human agency can be exercised only in the present. But by changing the present, we are changing the future.

ENTER GLOBAL MEDIA

What is the role of global media in this uncertain future? Despite their largely military origins and applications (Levidow and Robins 1989), modern communication technologies have generally had multiple effects. Lags and leads abound, and it takes a while for any technological innovation such as broadcasting, satellites, or computers to be transferred from their military uses to civilian applications. Once they enter the consumer marketplace, however, the users employ them imaginatively, in many intended as well as unintended designs. These applications often lead to dispersion as well as centralization of power, democratic as well as counterdemocratic formations, globalization as well as localization of culture, contestation among conflicting notions of political sovereignty, national identity, and civil rights as well as consensus formation. Although centers by far outrank the peripheries in media ownership and access, control of territorial and cultural spaces is still more or less in the hands of the peripheries. Global media have been deterritorializing communication and territorializing culture. The macromedia are crossing boundaries, and the micromedia are empowering ever-smaller epistemic communities of common language, religion, and ethnicity. The media have thus pitted competing truth claims against each other (clash of civilizations) while opening the way for global negotiations on an ethics of transnational communication (dialogue of civilizations). Such negotiations can potentially reconcile the nativist loyalties with global ecumenicity.

At times of war, cultural and political confrontations become most visible. It is in the acts of violence that the moral arsenals of the belligerents are brought most visibly into the open. In the twentieth century, the first two world wars were fought primarily among Western powers, including a modernized Japan, contesting within a largely common cultural and moral framework. It may be argued that World War III has already begun under a variety of influences in the remotest peripheries, pitting the premodern and modernized localist against the modern and postmodern globalist forces. A protracted World War III began with the Korean War and has continued with the wars in Vietnam, the Suez, Israel and Palestine, Afghanistan, Iraq and Iran, thet Persian Gulf, South Africa, Somalia, Bosnia, and many other forgotten parts of the Third World (e.g., Tibet, Tajikistan, Kashmir, Mexico). The colliding moral spaces of these acts of violence have encompassed belligerents with vastly different worldviews, epistemologies, and codes of honor, shame, or guilt. To treat them as if they all belonged to the same moral space is tantamount to distorting our vision and obstructing the path to a just peace.

The debate on the effects of the mass media on democratic and counterdemocratic formations seems never-ending, but historical evidence largely supports a multiple effects hypothesis (M. Tehranian 1990a). The print, telephony, broadcasting, computer, satellite, and multimedia technologies have each supported both concentrations and dispersions of power. Historical evidence thus negates technological determinism. On the contrary, it suggests that the structure is the message. Through social constructions of technology, social forces lock into particular communication technologies to determine their uses and impact. However, as Harold Innis (1950) and Marshall McLuhan have argued, media technologies also bring with them certain biases toward certain outcomes. The print technology tended to democratize knowledge, propagate the vernacular languages, strengthen nationalism, and undermine the authority of the church and the monarchies. It also encouraged a certain type of linear rationality that gave impetus to the rise of industrial civilization, capitalism, the modern nation-state system, and its ideology of nationalism. Broadcasting's one-way channels of communication seem to have largely supported national integration and control from the centers. Satellites and computers tend to undermine national borders and sovereignties. Interactive multimedia tend to fragment and reconfigure audiences. The small media of communication (copying machines, audio and video recorders, personal computers) tend to empower their users. However, none of these possible effects are automatic or inevitable. In fact, the contrary may happen and has happened in revolutionary situations (M. Tehranian, 1979a). When combined with democratic or counterdemocratic forces, the same technologies can have contradictory consequences.

LANDMINES AND CYBERDEMOCRACY

The new interactive media, in particular, promise more democracy. The most dramatic example of this promise is how a global civil society of concerned citizens and organizations managed to bring some 170 reluctant states to sign a Landmines Ban Treaty in December 1997.

"When two elephants fight," an African proverb says, "it's the grass that suffers." The proverb finds its most fitting example in landmines. Landmines are deadly stuff. The statistics are staggering: The UN estimates that there are 110 million landmines planted around the world in over sixty-four countries. Although 100,000 are removed each year, an additional 2 to 5 million are deployed. An antipersonnel mine costs $3–$30. It costs a hundred times that amount for the international community to destroy those landmines, and there is a considerable risk to the experts who defuse them. In addition, vast tracts of arable land and pastures are designated as forbidden territory. The harvest is grim: 26,000 people are killed or maimed each year by landmines. That is one occurrence every seventeen minutes. Landmines are everywhere, but mostly in poor and war-inflicted countries such as Angola, Cambodia, Mozambique, Somalia, Afghanistan, and Sudan. The victims are mostly children and adult civilians.

Elsa's story is typical. In January 1995, eleven-year-old Elsa Armindo Chela went to pick mangoes with her cousin Osvaldo in the town of Kuito, Angola. Elsa lost her eye and her leg. Both children suffer bouts of depression. Elsa may smile warmly and hold her cousin's hand, but she withdraws in the company of other children. Elsa's parents lost three other children to disease and starvation during the 1993 siege of Angola. Her father worries whether Elsa will finish school. "Angola should buy tractors and seeds, not landmines," he said. "I appeal to the international community to not sell us any more of those weapons."

The 1988 Nobel Peace Prize justly went to a small grassroots disarmament organization that had been fighting for the abolition of landmines for six years. Jody Williams, a forty-seven-year-old U.S. peace activist who heads the International Campaign to Ban Landmines (ICBL), was the recipient of the prize. She began working for the Vietnam Veterans of America Foundation at the end of 1991 to bring together a coalition to ban antipersonnel landmines. The coalition has grown from two organizations to more than 1,000 NGOs in over sixty countries. Williams has spoken and written extensively on the subject, producing a seminal book on the socioeconomic impact of the weapon, *After the Guns Fall Silent: The Enduring Legacy of Landmines*. She and her colleagues have brought to the task a combination of human compassion, political savvy, and communicative competence unparalleled in the history of the peace movement. Princess Diana's championing of their cause was an element in this campaign. But their use of the Internet as a means of communication and mobilization of hundreds of NGOs and millions of world citizens to engage in an informed and effective campaign is a phenomenon worth emulating. This is a historical landmark, a new beginning in world history in which ordinary citizens can be empowered and mobilized to stop the madness of their democratic and undemocratic governments.

Upon receiving the Nobel Peace Prize, the outspoken and feisty Williams said to the reporters, "The main obstacle is President Clinton. I think it's tragic that Clinton does not want to be on the side of humanity and does not want to join the tide of history in bringing about a ban of this indiscriminate killer of civilians." At a September 1997 conference in Oslo to ban landmines, over 100 countries signed a treaty for an immediate ban. The United States, China, and Russia were not among them. However, following the granting of the Nobel Peace Prize, Russia joined the treaty. The United States refused to sign on three grounds. First, the Pentagon considers landmines a "combat multiplier" that frees its forces for other operations. Second, the United States believes that its own so-called smart mines are capable of targeting only tanks. Third, the United States wishes to except the Korean Peninsula from the treaty. All three grounds create loopholes that would render the treaty meaningless.

Fortunately, there are some voices of sanity in the U.S. government speaking for the abolition of landmines. U.S. Senator Patrick Leahy and Representatives Lane Evans and Jack Quinn have introduced legislation in the Senate and the House to bar new U.S. antipersonnel landmine deployments beginning January 1, 2000. Congratulating the ICBL, Senator Leahy predicted that "this award will help encourage the nations of the world to seize this fragile moment to begin banning these weapons forever. I hope it will help convince my country to join this process."

It took sixteen years to achieve a ban on chemical weapons, and twenty-three years to achieve the nuclear test ban treaty. How many hundreds of thousands of deaths and traumatic injuries from landmines must occur before the great powers are willing to forgo this inhumane and indiscriminate weapon? That is a question that recalcitrant governments are not willing to answer. But the answer lies not in individual governments but in a global civil society that is fast building to pressure the governments to recognize the most elementary rules of human decency. The movement to ban landmines demonstrates a new way of conducting international diplomacy, in which middle and smaller powers take the lead in responding to and working with civil society and their NGOs to address urgent humanitarian needs. The global communication system is providing the channels through which an informed global citizenship can take effective action instead of leaving it to the experts. War is too important a matter to be left to warriors.

"In many ways our work has just begun," Williams noted. The international campaign has drafted an action plan for promoting the rapid enforcement of the treaty, as well as universalization and monitoring of the treaty. The same global communication system that has made such a worldwide movement possible also makes monitoring technically more possible. Remote-sensing satellites and ground inspections can detect the violators. In December 1997 these efforts culminated in a conference in Ottawa to sign the international treaty. In twenty-two articles, the treaty banned landmines in all forms without any of the loopholes that the United States had proposed. In all, 123 countries signed the treaty (the United States and China refused to sign it).

As Williams has pointed out, "this campaign will not go away." Indeed, it must not go away. As long as two of the most powerful countries in the world (the United States and China) have not signed the treaty, pressure must be brought to bear on their governments to recognize their moral and political responsibility. The peace movement should insist on the eradication of landmines and assistance to those who must live with this lethal contamination; it must also focus on the elimination of all weapons of mass destruction, including nuclear, biological, and chemical. Abolition 2000, another coalition of NGOs, is working for precisely that objective in the nuclear arms field. Only when these immoral weapons of mass destruction are eradicated can we begin to call ourselves civilized.

The erosion of democracy through a campaign financing system that puts the politicians at the service of donors, including arms manufacturers, rather than citizens can now be partially corrected by a mobilized civil society. But such correction takes active and informed citizens. The Internet provides a new democratic sphere of public discourse in which citizens can be globally informed, empowered, and mobilized on specific issues. The case of landmines illustrates how the new cyberdemocracy can work effectively. All it takes is a compassionate citizen with a computer, including a modem connected to a telephone line and an Internet server, to reach the variety of Websites that would connect with contemporary social movements.

IDENTITIES AND CARTOGRAPHIES OF VIOLENCE

One arena in which such wars of words are conducted is the moral spaces of violent conflicts. Except for deranged acts of random violence, resort to force often has to be legitimated in terms of grander and more generally acceptable moral schemes than the specific situations at conflict. But when the use of violence is a collective act, as in wars, to mobilize the material and moral support of the population, such legitimation also has to be grounded in specific times, spaces, and identities. The wars of the twentieth century have largely been wars of identity, and for that reason all the more ferocious. World Wars I and II were primarily fought on behalf of nationalist causes buttressed by such broader slogans as "to make the world safe for democracy," "Aryan supremacy," "the four freedoms," or "Asia for the Asians." By contrast, wars of the second half of the twentieth century

have often been fought among nations at different stages of historical development with fundamentally different senses of time, space, identity,
shame, and honor. In some ways, these wars hark back to the struggle between the European imperialists and the indigenous populations in Asia,
Africa, and the Americas in the fifteenth to nineteenth centuries, when entire peoples and civilizations were wiped out in the name of the white
man's burden (Stannard 1992).

The rapid spread of global communication in the second half of the
twentieth century has significantly changed the rules of engagement and
cartographies of violence. Its dual effects have both globalized and plural-
ized the voices to be heard. Although the dominant voices are still those
primarily in control of the world media, the new polyphony is creating
both cognitive dissonance and possibilities for cognitive enlightenment on
a global scale. The cartographies of violence, the mental maps of conflict,
are no longer confined to the nation-state borders. They constantly twist
and turn, sometimes referring to the sanctity of borders (as in the case of
the Iraqi invasion of Kuwait) but at other times defending the rights of
"humanitarian intervention" (as in the case of the no-fly zones in Iraq and
Bosnia). By contrast, the so-called terrorist wars know no boundaries at
all. The entire globe is the stage for the exercise of violence at times and
places of the belligerents' choosing—at the Olympics, in the airways, at
the World Trade Center, in a Hebron mosque. The shifting physical spaces
of violence thus call for the juxtaposition of a variety of moral spaces.

Global communication has also reconfigured the identities of violence. The self often defines itself in opposition to "the other." In situations of conflict, the self is frequently imagined as morally righteous or superior, whereas "the other" is frequently cast as morally depraved or
inferior. However, when "the other" is confronted face-to-face in all of
his or her humanity, it is far more difficult to maintain a level of self-
righteousness sufficient to sustain systematic efforts at total annihilation.
An accommodation is often sought in which the enemy is subdued and manipulated to serve the purposes of the victor. Global communication has
thus raised the moral cost of genocides, but it has not ruled them out altogether. The enemy now has to be abstracted rather than identified. Instead
of talking about how many Germans or Vietcong have been killed, the new
language of the military speaks of "body counts" or "collateral damage,"
referring, respectively, to the military and civilian casualties. The new high
technologies of warfare have distanced, abstracted, and further alienated
the aliens. The enemy can now be totally anonymous while the laser
weapons and guided missiles are showered on "military targets" with some
"collateral damage." During the Gulf War, the only significant time that an
individual was hinted at on television screens was when General Norman
Schwarzkopf pointed to a car driving across a bridge before Patriot

missiles hit their target. The driver was called "the luckiest man alive in Iraq." For the most part, the war was reconstructed in powerful images as a high-tech video game with few human casualties and consequently little moral cost. The abstracting power of technologies has combined with the cognitive dissonance of colliding moral spaces to render postmodern warfare nearly incomprehensible and thus morally ambiguous.

Shifting moral spaces, cartographies of violence, and imaginary boundaries have thus made the understanding of postmodern warfare extremely difficult. In place of the moral clarity of the premodern face-to-face combat and the modern war of nation-state against nation-state, we are now facing new forms of violence. They include nuclear fallouts (as in Hiroshima, Nagasaki, and the Pacific Islands), biological and chemical weapons (such as Agent Orange in the Vietnam War and chemical weapons in the Iran-Iraq and Gulf wars), high-tech weapons (such as the U.S. Patriot missiles showered on Iraq and the Iraqi Scud missiles showered on Israel), and guided missiles that hit innocent civilian targets (such as the U.S. automated missile attack on a civilian Iranian airplane during the Gulf War that killed 286 passengers).

A TRANSFORMATION OF WAR?

Table 7.2 presents a schematic view of the main perceptible differences between premodern, modern, and postmodern forms of warfare, identity, organization, and legitimation. A few caveats are in order. First, the table should be viewed as more suggestive than definitive. It is constructed primarily for analytic and heuristic purposes, to open rather than close considerations of significant differences. Second, although the table may suggest otherwise, this is *not* a stage theory of warfare. Clearly, most contemporary wars are a complex mix of all three "pure types." History is conjunctural rather than linear. Like all historical events, each war is unique but also a conjunction of elements from the old and new technologies, strategies, and tactics. Last, in certain respects, there seems to be a curious resemblance between the premodern and postmodern forms. That raises a question: Are we facing a historical regression, conjunction, or transformation?

Table 7.2 suggests significant transitions in warfare. In the premodern world, times of warfare tended to follow seasonal changes or great migratory movements. For instance, in the native Hawaiian civilization before European contact, periods of peace coincided with times of harvest ruled by the god Lono (four months of the year), and periods of tribal warfare followed times of rest and hunting ruled by the god Ku (eight months of the year). From prehistoric times, great population movements have also

Table 7.2 Models of Warfare: Identity, Organization, and Legitimation

	Premodern	Modern	Postmodern
Time	Sporadic	Discrete	Permanent
	Periodized	Declared (overt)	Undeclared (covert)
Space	Tribal	National	Global
	Prestate	State	Poststate
	Agrarian empires	Nation-states	Global systems
Identity	Tribalist	Nationalist	Globalist-localist
	Tribal member	Civilian soldier	Professional soldier
	Identity security	Identity anxiety	Identity panic
	Embodiment	Coembodiment	Disembodiment
Organization	Spiritual-temporal	Secular-civilian	Military-industrial
	Existential	Bureaucratic	Technocratic
	Ritualized	Regularized	Totalized
	Immanent	Visible	Invisible institutions
	Tribal institutions	Military institutions	Total institutions
Institutions	Warriors	Mobilized population	Expert population
	Individual combat	Mass assault	Technical targeting
	Medium-intensity conflict	High-intensity conflict	Low-intensity conflict
	Physical-political violence	Political-economic	Cultural-environmental
Legitimation	Prelegitimation	Legitimation	Postlegitimation
	Dictates of nature	Reasons of state	Economic motivations
	Ontological	Ideological	Praxiological
	Naturalist	Instrumentalist	Naturalized
	Manliness	Patriotism	Acquiescence

Sources: Clausewitz (1976), Creveld (1989 and 1991), Levidow and Robins (1989), Galtung (1990), Hassig (1988), Nietschmann (1987), Shapiro (1993a, 1993b, and 1997), K. and M. Tehranian (1992), K. Tehranian (1995), and Tilly (1992).

involved great warfare. This was true of the periodic tribal encroachments upon sedentary populations (e.g., the Aryan, Arab, Mongolian, Teutonic, and Turkish tribes descending upon the fertile, settled, agricultural lands of West and South Asia as well as Eastern and Western Europe) and the European encroachments on native populations of the Americas, Australia, and New Zealand. The emergence of the multinational, agrarian, and bureaucratic empires (Persian, Greek, Roman, Arab, Chinese, Mongolian, and Ottoman) witnessed an anticipatory modernization of warfare. Wars were no longer strictly seasonal or sporadic; they began to involve territorial and sphere-of-influence disputes. They thus followed the reasons of the state rather than the dictates of nature. Following the Peace of Westphalia in 1648 and the creation of the modern nation-state system with distinct and internationally agreed boundaries, modern warfare followed *raison d'état* even more vociferously. In contrast to the premodern wars, which tended to be periodized, modern warfare was discrete, with a declaration of war and overt hostilities across international borders. However, the start of the Cold War in 1947 between the Communist and capitalist worlds introduced an element of permanency in warfare, characterized by intense rivalries, proxy violence, undeclared wars, covert operations, and low-intensity conflicts.

The spaces of warfare also commensurably changed from tribal in premodern to national in modern, and global in postmodern formations. The prestate nature of tribal and feudal societies left the boundaries rather ill-defined, whereas state formations in the modern world imposed borders sanctified by international agreements. The transnationalization of the world economy and the worldwide reach of advanced military technologies, along with global communication, have considerably weakened the state system. Thus, warfare is more often than not conducted as if state borders did not exist. Shipments of arms, supplies, and technical advisers to the client states or armed guerrillas have been a normal practice of the superpowers and their allies in the postwar period.

The identity of warfare has similarly shifted from tribalist to nationalist and increasingly to a struggle between globalist powers and a diversity of localist forces based on religious, tribal, or ethnic solidarity. Although the identity of the combatants was often collectivist in premodern warfare, it became individualized through citizen armies and universal military service in the modern world. In the postmodern world, military forces are decisively professionalized. This transitional process is, of course, gradual and still interlocking with the citizen armies in most countries. Whereas the combatants in the premodern world tended to enjoy a high measure of identity security as bona fide members of their tribes, the citizen soldier is under pressure to prove his or her identification with the state through patriotic acts of self-sacrifice. Thus, the Japanese Americans in the U.S. armed forces during World War II had to fight especially hard to earn the trust of their superiors, nation, and state as true patriots. The most decorated U.S. division in World War I was Japanese American. Whereas the tribal warrior proved his worth through acts of manliness by taking bodily risks, the citizen soldier is coembodied with a mass of his cocombatants, who are collectively commemorated by the grave of the Unknown Soldier. In postmodern wars, by contrast, the combatants on both sides are disembodied, as if the wars were being fought between two impersonal fighting machines. In the Gulf War, for instance, the Pentagon talked of the enemy as if it were one huge piece of meat to be tenderized by saturation bombing before being encircled and devoured. The Pentagon's metaphor of tenderizing was reminiscent of the premodern Aztec wars, in which the flesh and blood of the enemy were devoured by the victors to gain their manna, or spiritual power (Shapiro 1997). The postmodern war will increasingly be fought not by citizen armies but by professional warriors and mercenaries. The logic of pancapitalism pushes wars toward increasing commercialization. The formation of mercenary armies for hire by South African and U.S. veterans fighting in Africa and Bosnia is a testimony to this trend. In the case of Bosnia, the engagement of mercenaries has been approved by the U.S. government, which is reluctant to undertake the costs of warfare but wishes to pursue its foreign policy objectives forcefully.

The organization of the premodern wars was based on a unity of spiritual and temporal authorities. In the modern world, democratic formations have led to a separation of church and state and of the civilian and military branches of the government, with civilians constitutionally in a position of authority. As the great theoretician of modern warfare Clausewitz suggested, war is "the pursuit of politics by other means." However, postmodern warfare has significantly shifted the locus of authority from civilian to a routinized "military-industrial complex" (Eisenhower 1960) that defines the enemy and devises global strategies and tactics in cold and hot wars toward the enemy's constant harassment and ultimate defeat. Whereas warfare in the premodern world was considered existential, under modernity it becomes bureaucratized in the military branches of the government. In postmodern times, warfare seems to have become thoroughly technocratic through the use of exclusively professional armies assisted by a complex of defense industries and corporations such as Dow Chemical, Hughes Aircraft, and Grunman. The organization of warfare was thus ritualized in the premodern world, it was regularized with modernity, and it has been totalized by involving every social institution in society. Paradoxically, warfare was immanent in tribal societies but became visible and specialized by modernization. In postmodern warfare, it seems to have become invisible in situations of low-intensity conflict except for occasional flare-ups. Commensurate with its technocratic character, postmodern wars also feign to be engaged in "military targeting" with only "collateral (i.e., civilian) damage." The objects of violence in premodern wars were the physical bodies of the enemy and the literal decapitation of the chief or the king. In modern warfare, the locus of violence shifted not only to mass populations but also to the enemy's economic resources, that is, its industrial infrastructure and factories. In postmodern warfare, there is yet another shift to the cultural and environmental resources. Following World War II, the Japanese were to be re-educated into democratic ways. Similarly, during the Vietnam War, the Vietnamese were to be taught democracy even if by force. In the Gulf War, Saddam Hussein inflamed the oil wells in Kuwait, and in the Vietnam War, the United State sprayed poisonous chemicals on the farmlands and forests presumed to be inhabited by the enemy.

Finally, legitimation of wars has significantly changed from premodern to modern and postmodern forms of warfare. Insofar as war was a way of life, a dictate of nature, and an ontological condition, premodern warfare required little legitimation. War in modern times was ideologized; to mobilize the masses for the struggle, it needed to be legitimated in terms of some higher nationalist, imperialist, or universalist goals, such as carrying out the white man's burden, saving the world for democracy, or advancing the cause of the international proletariat. With postmodern warfare, the permanent, low-intensity, professionalized nature of conflict makes legitimation not as necessary except in times of high-intensity warfare. Postmodern warfare is thus routinized, naturalized, and practiced in pursuit of unabashedly economic or political objectives. It requires the acquiescence of one's own population rather than its acts of manliness (as in premodern wars) or patriotism (as in modern warfare). As routinized affairs, postmodern wars depend on systematic information gathering. The Anglo-Saxon countries (the UK, United States, Australia, and New Zealand, for example) collaborate in a project called Echelon to spy on countries throughout the world through the Internet and share their findings (Anonymous 1988).

THE MORAL AMBIGUITY
OF POSTMODERN WARFARE

Modern and postmodern warfare have thus exhibited several mutually reinforcing features, including globality (Tilly 1992), totality (Aron 1954), representationality (Virilio 1989), invisibility (Nietschmann 1987), unwinnability, and moral ambiguity. The globality and totality of modern wars are matters of consensus. World Wars I and II fully demonstrated the global and total nature of modern warfare. Since 1945, however, wars have been simultaneously fought at several fronts: global (the Cold War), national (civil wars), regional (Central America, Middle East), and local (Kurdish revolt). But as threats to the prevailing world order, most wars have been infiltrated and manipulated by the great powers during the Cold War and since its end in 1989. The smaller belligerents have been ready and willing to acquire weapons and financial support from the larger.

Global communication has made wars more global, total, and representational than ever before. The unprecedented peace among the European and North American states since 1945 has led some observers to call this an era of long peace. However, that designation completely ignores the protracted violence that has continued to plague the Third World nations in the same period. Wars have appeared in a variety of guises, ranging from wars of national liberation against the colonialists, to multilateral wars (in Korea, Vietnam, the Middle East, Somalia, Bosnia) and bilateral wars (Israel and Palestine, Iran and Iraq), to many insurgencies and civil wars. These "little wars" have already resulted in over 20 million casualties, mostly civilian, and have inflicted some of the most brutal forms of violence, such as ethnic cleansing, forced migration, rape, and chemical, biological, and environmental warfare. As Sinathamby Rajaratnam prophetically noted during a meeting of the Non-Aligned Movement:

> The ending of colonialism does not automatically inaugurate an era of peace and prosperity for the liberated peoples. It could equally be the prelude to fraternal wars and new inhumanities. . . . It is my considered opinion that the third world war has already begun—in the Third World. The new era is likely to be a compilation of the little wars rather than one big war. Though the form is new, it is basically a war between the great powers and one fought for the realization of their ambitions and the promotion of their national interests. However, this is not obvious because in this new world war, the great powers are invisible. (Barnaby 1988: 56)

Television screens have brought the images of this kind of protracted violence to teeming audiences around the world. They have sometimes distorted its reality, as in the Gulf War, and, at other times, mobilized governments and nations into belated action, as in Somalia and Bosnia. However, television screens have at all times provided only a manufactured representation of what goes on. TV news is typically episodic, dichotomizing conflict stories into goodies and baddies, friends and enemies, demonizing the enemies, and desensitizing moral sensibilities. In an age of professional, technocratic wars, the enemies in remote moral spaces tend to be viewed as subhuman and barbaric people to be civilized by force if necessary. Such mystifications of the enemy would not be a readily available moral option except in a postmodern age dominated by glossy images covering many complex realities. Although all reality is socially constructed, when the commercial media manufacture it to achieve high entertainment value and ratings, the sensational and abnormal take precedence over the routinized forms of human suffering, such as malnutrition, child mortality, forced migration, and short life expectancy. Because audiences have little access to alternative constructions of reality, the overpowering mediated images of television are readily accepted as truth, particularly when that truth also uplifts the national pride. Eighty percent of U.S. audiences, for example, receive their news primarily through television. It should occasion no surprise, therefore, that the Gulf War as manufactured on television screens (high tech, low casualty, high returns, low cost) was supported by about 80 percent of the U.S. people.

Despite its high profile during major flare-ups, postmodern violence tends to be structural and invisible. Over 500,000 children die each year of malnutrition and chronic diseases, as compared with about 400,000 adults who die violent deaths, yet the stories of the children rarely reach audiences (Kent 1993). Many of the conflicts of the postwar era have persisted for years with heavy casualties, yet media coverage is scant until something dramatic happens. Table 7.3 provides a somewhat incomplete picture of protracted conflicts, some stretching back some seventy years. The vast majority of wars worldwide have been between established states and nascent nations struggling for recognition and sometimes statehood.

As organized systems of violence, states are the root of the problem, yet the general impression conveyed by the mass media is that sporadic

Table 7.3 Duration and Casualties of Protracted Conflicts, 1925–1997

Conflict	Duration of Conflict	State	Number Killed
National Liberation Wars			
Algeria FLN	17 years (1945–1962)	France	500,000
Afghan mujahidin	10 (1979–1989)	USSR	1,000,000
Kurdistan	72 (1925)	Turkey, Iran, Iraq	500,000
Kashmir	52 (1949)	India	
Euskidi	60 (1937)	Spain	
Kawhoolei	49 (1948)	Myanmar	
Shan	49 (1948)	Myanmar	
Nagaland	42 (1955)	India	
Chakma	33 (1964)	Bangladesh	
North Ireland	36 (1961)	Britain	160,000
Western Sahara	22 (1975)	Morocco	
Tigray	22 (1975)	Cuba/Ethiopia	
Kalinga	22 (1975)	Philippines	
Pathan	10 (1979–1989?)	USSR/Afghanistan	
Kirghiz	10 (1979–1989?)	USSR/Afghanistan	
Miskitos	15 (1981)	Nicaragua	
Hutu-Tutsi	?	Burundi	200,000
Mayas	?	Guatemala	80,000
Moros	?	Philippines	100,000
Baluchs, Pathans	?	Pakistan	9,000
Tamils	?	Sri Lanka	4,500
Tibet	47 (1950)	China	
Uighurs	?		
Multinational Wars			
Palestine	60 (1937)	Britain/Israel	
Eritrea	36 (1961)	Cuba/Ethiopia	100,000
West Papua	35 (1962)	Indonesia	200,000 (50% of population)
East Timor	22 (1975)	Indonesia	
Lebanon	30 (1967)	Israel, Syria	200,000 (33% of population)
Tajikistan	6 (1991)	Russia, Uzbekistan	
Afghanistan	18 (1979)	Russia, U.S. Pakistan, Iran	125,000
Insurgency Wars			
M19, etc.	49 (1948)	Colombia	
URNG	33 (1964)	Guatemala	
MNLF	18 (1979)	Philippines	
Various parties	18 (1979)	Vietnam/Kampuchea	
FMLN	18 (1979)	El Salvador	
FSLN	15 (1982)	Nicaragua	
Islamic parties	7 (1990)	Algeria	
Islamic parties	45 (1952)	Egypt	
State Wars			
Arab states			
Ethiopia	49 (1948)	Israel	
Libya	33 (1964)	Somalia	
Iran	21 (1973–1994)	Chad	
Israel	8 (1980–1988)	Iraq	1,000,000+
	15 (1982)	Lebanon, Syria	

Notes: FLN refers to the National Liberation Front; URNG refers to Unidad Revolucionario Nacional Guatemalteco; MNLF refers to Moro National Liberation Front; FMLN refers to the Farabindo Martí National Liberation Front; FSLN refers to Sandanista National Liberation Front.

violence by terrorist groups or insurgencies are primarily to blame. The state system has privileged the dominant nations often at the expense of minority ethnic groups within their boundaries. Repressed nations such as the Palestinians, Kurds, or Tibetans have long struggled for statehood or autonomy to no avail. For this reason, the history of nationalism is a history of glorified mass murder. In the prenationalist era, the city-states, the feudal fiefdoms, and the multinational empires cared more about collecting taxes than about homogenized ethnicity. The nation-state system was the first to focus its attention on the total control of a population (Shapiro 1997). A total of 82 percent of protracted conflicts have involved nascent nations. In February 1997, UN membership stood at 185 states. If we consider that there are anywhere from 3,000 to 7,000 linguistic groups in the world in search of nationhood and possibly statehood, we can foresee what types of conflict will predominate in the decades to come.

The unwinnability and moral ambiguity of postmodern warfare may be a matter of dispute. However, if we consider the colossal damage a nuclear war would inflict on both victors and vanquished, unwinnability can be acknowledged as an unmistakable feature of at least a nuclear confrontation. The direction of the wind would largely determine the extent of casualties on either side. The nuclear balance of terror between the two superpowers kept them from unleashing a global war for some forty-four years (1945–1989). Since the end of the Cold War, it has spurred their efforts toward nuclear disarmament and against nuclear proliferation. No conceivable moral cause could justify a nuclear holocaust. Nuclear wars are thus ultimately unwinnable and indefensible (Lifton and Falk 1982). Protracted struggles between the dominant state system and the nascent nations have also demonstrated that such wars are unwinnable. The Kurdish, Palestinian, Tibetan, and Kashmiri struggles for civil rights and national independence have been waged for long periods of time. The cycles of violence generated by these protracted conflicts have undermined whatever moral justification either side of the conflict may have had for its actions. When two equally righteous causes are at stake for the conquest of a single territory, as is the case in many interethnic wars, moral ambiguity and unwinnability become twin features of conflict. Political expediency and moral imperative thus call for pacific settlements, yet the warring parties are caught in escalating cycles of violence from which it has proved extremely difficult to extract themselves.

WARS AND CONTESTING MORAL SPACES, 1945–1994

To fully appreciate the moral and political complexities of postmodern warfare as it has evolved in the last few decades, it might be useful to briefly review the moral spaces of the conflicting parties in the major international conflicts of the post–World War II era.

The Korean War was perhaps the last of the conventional wars fought in this century. It pitted two clusters of globalist adversaries against each other. Under the aegis of the UN, the war was legitimated as the moral defense of democracy against world communism. The fact that neither North Korea nor South Korea could be defined as a democracy did not diminsh the ferocity of the war, which was essentially a geopolitical struggle between the United States, Soviet Union, and China. North Korea's crossing of the 38th parallel into South Korea was the ostensible reason for the Western engagement. From North Korea's view, this move was a legitimate continuation of a war of liberation against the Japanese and U.S. colonialists and their "henchmen" in Seoul, the Syngman Rhee regime. The two sides in the Cold War fought in the name of two competing truth claims organized around two globalist ideologies, capitalism and communism. Following a few skirmishes in Greece, Turkey, and Iran, Korea became the first real arena for their tests of strength. The confrontation became more deadly when UN forces crossed the 38th parallel into North Korea. With the aid of the Soviet Union and the entry of the People's Republic of China on the side of North Korea, the war became a stalemate, ending finally in a truce in 1953. The moral and political claims of the two sides had to find another arena for another engagement.

The war in Vietnam provided that arena. Although Vietnam superficially resembled Korea in its division between north and south, Communist and capitalist, the country had persisted in a protracted war of national liberation against Japan, France, and the United States. In this prolonged war, a national hero, Ho Chi Minh, had led the people in their defeat of the Japanese and the French. As leader of the Communist Party, Ho Chi Minh had captured the nationalist movement as well. The United States decided to support the French in their vain efforts to recolonize Vietnam. The defeat of the French in 1954 led to a division of the country into north and south, with the latter under U.S. protection. The anti-imperialist movement, however, continued. The escalation of the war in the 1960s pitted U.S. globalist strategies against Vietnamese nationalist aspirations. From the U.S. perspective, the war represented another theater of confrontation between Communist tyranny and the free world. The United States assumed that if Vietnam fell, it would have a domino effect on the rest of Southeast Asia, where Communist parties were still strong. From the North Vietnamese perspective, the United States represented yet another imperialist power attempting to subjugate its people. U.S. withdrawal and the fall of Saigon in 1975 entailed no domino effect, but the war had devastated Vietnam and left its relations with the United States embittered for years to come. Yet the colliding moral spaces of globalism and nationalism sought other theaters in which to continue their struggles.

That theater turned out to be in the Persian Gulf and Central Asia. The next three big wars were fought between Iran and Iraq, Iraq and the United States, and the Afghan Mujahidin and the USSR. Although the three wars were fought separately, they constituted three acts in a single drama. The Islamic revolution of 1979 in Iran created a new dynamic in the Persian Gulf and Central Asian regions. Its messianic message called on oppressed Muslims everywhere to rise up against U.S. and Soviet imperialism. As in past major social revolutions, such as the French and Russian revolutions, the neighboring conservative states were deeply alarmed by the revolutionaries' rhetoric calling for the export of their idea. In the Persian Gulf states of Iraq, Kuwait, Saudi Arabia, the United Arab Emirates, and Bahrain, the Shiite Muslims have also been long repressed by the Sunni ruling elites. The message of the Iranian revolution thus met with receptive ears. As the most ambitious Arab leader in the region, Saddam Hussein saw an opportunity in Iran's postrevolutionary chaos to strike a blow.

In apparent collusion with Jordan, Israel, the United States, and the Arab Persian Gulf states, Iraq invaded Iran in 1980. Within a short period of time, Iraq made serious inroads into Iranian territory by conquering the oil-rich province of Khuzistan, which Saddam quickly renamed Arabistan. However, Iran's battered regular forces as well as the newly recruited and ill-trained revolutionary guards soon beat back the Iraqi forces into their own country. A tug-of-war ensued in which the messianic Shia Islamic moral appeals were pitted against the secular, Arab nationalist ideology to win over people and territory. The war was ostensibly being fought between Iran and Iraq. But, in fact, the entire Arab world (with the exception of the radical states of Syria and Libya) as well as Western and Soviet powers were on the side of Iraq. Despite deep ideological rifts among them, their common interest was to avert the threat of a possible spillover of the Islamic revolution into Central Asia and Afghanistan (the Soviet spheres) and the other Persian Gulf states (the Western sphere). As a result of Kuwaiti and Saudi Arabian support of the Iraqi war effort (to the tune of some $60 billion) and shipments of arms from France, Germany, and the Soviet Union, Iraq managed to reverse Iran's initial superiority in military arsenal. By the mid-1980s, however, Iraq appeared to be on the verge of defeat in its southern marshes, where the Shiite population predominates. Iranian warships and planes had also started a campaign of intimidation against the Kuwaiti and UAR shipments of oil in the Persian Gulf. To protect their allies, the United States virtually entered the war on the side of Iraq by sending a naval fleet to defend "the free flow of oil" out of the gulf. The direct encounter between the United States and Iran on several occasions, the rapid arms buildup in Iraq, the continuing stalemate, and the exhaustion of the populations on both sides finally led to a truce in 1988. Having initially approved of Saddam's invasion, the two superpowers now saw great risks in its continuation and jointly called for its cessation. Nevertheless, the colliding moral spaces of Islamism, nationalism, and globalism continued to prevail in the Persian Gulf, Afghanistan, and Tajikistan.

Thanks to his Arab and Western allies, Saddam Hussein had now acquired a new powerful war machine and tested armed forces. He therefore turned his attention to Iraq's old territorial ambitions against Kuwait, which was now demanding repayments for its wartime loans. Iraq invaded and occupied Kuwait in August 1990 by a blitzkrieg. The ambiguity of the United States' position on the Iraq-Kuwait conflicts was followed by a rapid deployment of forces to oppose the Iraqi invasion, a move that was probably unanticipated by Saddam. With the end of the Cold War and the disappearance of the Soviet Union as a superpower, Saddam was gambling on an easy victory. During the Iran-Iraq War, he had assumed a new stature as a Pan-Arab nationalist and was hoping to cash in on his prestige by championing the cause of a united Arab world against all enemies. But he had miscalculated for a second time.

From the globalist perspective of the United States and its allies, the emergence of a hostile regional superpower in the Persian Gulf would have proved disastrous for Western oil and strategic interests. From a domestic perspective, the Republican Party in power in Washington wished to exorcise the "Vietnam syndrome" in the United States that had deterred it from playing a more activist global, military role. The invasion of Kuwait had also assumed a symbolic significance in the post–Cold War era. Should a regional potentate be allowed to assume power by virtue of Western default? President Bush quickly responded to that question by deploying the largest postwar military forces into Saudi Arabia. Following fruitless peace negotiations in which the United States was unwilling to allow Saddam even a face-saving withdrawal, UN forces led by the United States reconquered Kuwait with the tacit approval of all five great powers and restored its monarchy back to power. Iraq itself came under UN occupation, economic sanctions, and no-fly zones in the north and the south in order to protect the dissident Kurds and Shiites. Following Egyptian president Gamal Abdel Nasser's challenges of the 1950s and 1960s, the colliding moral spaces of Western globalism and Pan-Arabism thus led in 1991 to a decisive defeat for the latter.

The third theater of confrontation between globalism and Islamism has been situated in Afghanistan and Tajikistan. Following the revolution in Iran, Soviet anxieties about the threat of a spreading Islamic revolution in Central Asia led the nation to invade Afghanistan in 1979 to assist their client Communist regime against the mujahidin guerrillas. A brutal war subsequently ensued in which two globalist forces, the Soviet Union and the United States, took the two opposing sides in the Afghan civil war. Central Asia and Pakistan served as conduits for the shipment of Soviet and U.S. weapons and matériel to Afghanistan. But the direct Soviet military involvement turned Afghanistan into the USSR's Vietnam. Following a ten-year bloody war, the Soviet troops finally had to withdraw their troops in 1989, admitting to some 15,000 casualties on their side and over 1 million on the Afghan side, both military and civilian. Some 5 million to 6 million Afghan refugees had also been forced into Iran and Pakistan. A thriving drug traffic through Afghanistan and Pakistan was also another legacy of the war. When the Communist government finally fell to the mujahidin in 1992, the country had been splintered into so many warring tribes and political groupings armed by the Soviet Union and the United States that it has not yet been able to regain its national unity. The struggle between the two globalist forces led to a tribalization of politics in Afghanistan. In 1996, supported by Pakistan, a newly formed ultrafundamentalist group, the Taliban, overran Kabul and most of the country. Mostly Pushtu, the Taliban defeated the Tajik government of President Burhanuddin Rabbani, supported by Iran, and the Uzbek general Abdul Rashid Dostum, supported by Uzbekistan. With the aid of the superpowers and its neighboring countries, Afghanistan has thus sunk into a protracted civil war of unparalleled intensity and cruelty. In 1998, the Taliban managed to control 90 percent of Afghanistan, pushing women out of schools and the workplace while massacring anyone in opposition.

Similarly, in Tajikistan, following its independence in 1991, a civil war between the Communists and the Islamist nationalists has led to Russian intervention in that country. Since the Soviet policy of divide and rule had drawn the national boundaries among its Central Asian Muslim republics across ethnic divisions, the conflict in Tajikistan soon erupted into a quasiregional war involving Russia, Iran, Afghanistan, and Uzbekistan. The moral space of Russian hegemony is thus colliding with Islamist and nationalist claims. Although competing with the Soviet Union during the Cold War years, the United State now shares a common interest with Russia in containing Islamic militancy. Despite a 1996 peace accord between the Tajik government and its opposition led by Abdullah Nuri, Tajikistan continues to face serious problems of national unity and integration.

The same fate befell Somalia in the Cold War years. Following its independence in 1960, Somalia came under Soviet influence but continued to be plagued by tribal conflicts. However, when Somalian troops attacked Ethiopia in 1972, the Soviet Union took the side of the new Ethiopian Marxist regime. The Somalian invasion was thus repelled, but after 1978, Somalia became a U.S. sphere of influence. The spread of Soviet and U.S. arms into the hands of rival tribes and warlords has made national unity a nearly impossible task to achieve. In December 1992, after a severe drought had led to widespread starvation and a population of 2 million refugees, the United States under the authority of the UN began Operation Restore Hope, in which 28,000 ground troops were deployed. But attacks on UN forces by rival factions led to a complete withdrawal of U.S. troops in March 1994, followed by most of the other peacekeeping forces. Devoid of much strategic or economic value, Somalia now appears to be largely left to its own devices. When confronted with unmanageable tribalism, as in Afghanistan and Somalia, globalism is therefore ready to retreat from its moral space.

The war in Bosnia provides another tragic example of the colliding moral spaces of imperialism, nationalism, and globalism. The three warring parties (the Serbs, Croats, and Muslims), in fact, fundamentally belong to the same linguistic and nationality group—Slavonic. However, they have been deeply divided by religion, script, and political loyalties. The Serbs are primarily Orthodox Christians writing in the Cyrillic alphabet and are sympathetic to Russia. The Croats primarily practice Roman Catholicism, write in the Roman alphabet, and historically have been close to Western Europe. The Muslims primarily practice Sunni Islam, speak Bosnian, and write in the Latin script. They are the leftover allies of the Ottoman Empire when it ruled most of the Balkans. During World War I, imperial rivalries between Russia, Germany, and Ottoman Turkey played a very important part in the Balkanization of the Balkans. That in turn inflamed the national rivalries contaminated by religious and linguistic prejudices. President Josip Tito (a Croat), however, managed to bring the six republics of Serbia, Croatia, Bosnia and Herzegovina, Macedonia, Slovenia, and Montenegro together into a socialist federal republic. With Tito's death in 1980, the various pieces of the republic drew apart and, following the dissolution of the Soviet Union in 1991, Yugoslavia broke up into its constituent parts. The war in Bosnia is thus as complex as any other in the world today. The colliding "imaginaries" (B. Anderson 1983) of several nations are providing moral spaces that are ill-defined both territorially and culturally. In the meantime, the international community is torn apart by historic loyalties (Russians with the Serbs, Western Europeans with the Croats, Turkey with the Muslims) while struggling to define its globalist role.

Last but not the least, the protracted struggles waged by the unrepresented nations and peoples organizations (UNPOs) present a variety of localist moral spaces that often collide with the globalist pretensions of the superpowers. Labeled as "low-intensity conflicts" (LICs) by the Pentagon, these wars of national liberation have been increasingly waged globally by acts of violence such as hostage taking, kidnapping, and terrorism. The Jews, Armenians, Kurds, and Palestinians have waged the best known of these struggles throughout this century. The least known are beginning to surface in the post–Cold War era as ethnic and religious conflicts throughout the world, including those of the Tibetans, Tajiks, Tatars, Kashmiris, and Shiites. Because of the technological vulnerability of the advanced industrial societies, the increasing sophistication of the militant groups, and the proliferation of nuclear, chemical, and biological weapons, the acts of state terrorism and people's counterterrorism will continue to plague the world in the twenty-first century.

A STRUCTURAL-CULTURAL THEORY OF VIOLENCE

Our views of the future are thus present constructions that predict resource scarcity or abundance, conflict or harmony, war or peace. Contemporary theories of war and peace have gravitated toward either materialism or idealism, economic or cultural determinism. But such dichotomies exist only in the mind of the analyst; realities are far more entangled and complex. Are wars caused by the struggle for territories and resources or by ideological prejudices and historical hatreds? The answer is not "either/or," but "both/and." Can we speak of a culture of peace and a culture of war independently of economic and political conflicts? Whether it be Aztec, U.S., or Islamic, the danger of essentializing and labeling any culture as a "culture of violence" is to forget that all cultures reflect the universal human propensity toward peace as well as violence. Anthropologists have persuasively argued that certain social conditions are more prone to violence than others and bring out those cultural traits that legitimate competition and conflict rather than cooperation and harmony. Political scientists (Arendt 1958) have argued that in the modern world, a political formation known as "totalitarianism" is particularly prone to domestic and international violence.

Totalitarian temptations may be viewed as an inherent feature of the passage to modernity. In their modern history, liberal, Communist, and communitarian societies have all shown themselves prone to this temptation. The temptation is strongest wherever the state is strong and the market and civil society are weak. Under such conditions (as in Germany, Italy, Spain, Argentina, Portugal, the Soviet Union, China, and Cambodia), millions have been persecuted and have died in the name of purity of some type or another. Typically, in such circumstances, the state becomes the chief instrument of mobilization of resources for modernization in the name of an ideological purism defined in racial, political, or religious terms. This gives the state the authority to centralize all political and economic power while repressing civil society and its voluntary associations of resistance. The totalitarian state is also typically imperialist in its ambitions, inflicting violence or threats of violence on its neighbors often in the name of a crusading ideology.

In this context, a distinction between authoritarian and totalitarian states is useful. While authoritarianism is a premodern phenomenon, totalitarianism is thoroughly modern. Totalitarian regimes depend upon the apparatus of an industrial economy for their surveillance of society while enforcing their total control of ideology, market, means of violence, and political organization. They also depend on charismatic leadership to obtain mass popularity. Some theories focus on this particular aspect of totalitarian regimes to explain the phenomenon, but cult of personality should be more properly considered as a symptom rather than a cause. To the extent that modernizing regimes such as those in Indonesia, Iran, Iraq, Egypt, Algeria, and Libya lack the industrial wherewithal, the attempt on their part to be totalitarian cannot fully succeed. This does not, however, imply that they cannot pursue partial surveillance and inflict crude violence.

Can a modernizing society resist the totalitarian temptation? Yes, if international conditions are not threatening and civil society institutions are strong vis-à-vis the state. For this reason, Western liberal democratic regimes have so far succeeded in bypassing totalitarian formations, but in their imperialist ventures, they largely externalized and inflicted their violence upon the indigenous and colonial peoples. Nevertheless, as witnessed by the Puritan and segregationist states, as well as McCarthyism in the United States, Calvinism in Geneva, and the Jacobin period in the French Revolution, Western liberal democracies have also gone through their own totalitarian phases.

Theories of mass society have focused particularly on cultural and psychological variables to explain totalitarian formations (Arendt 1958; Lacquer 1966). But mass society itself is a modern phenomenon. Under both capitalism and communism, modernization has atomized societies by driving the rural population into cities. It has also led to vertical and horizontal social mobility from traditional to modern professions and social groups and classes. The psychological conditions of abstraction, anonymity, and homelessness fostered by such physical and social mobility give rise to a desperate yearning for totalizing mass movements. Such movements, even though democratic or populist in their initial impulses, often lead to mass organizations and leaders who can respond to people's identity anxiety by providing them with an illusory sense of community, meaning, and dissolution of individual identity in the mass.

CULTURAL REMEDIES TO VIOLENCE

Despite the foregoing structural perspective on violence, remedies to violence can, paradoxically, be more readily assumed by a cultural approach entailing structural reforms. Emanating from a universal human condition, all human cultures contain within themselves contradictory propensities to both peace and violence. However, conditions of rapid growth, inequity, and relative deprivation give rise to greater violence than relative stability and perceptions of equity. Social and cultural learning about conditions of violence can preempt them. Such learning requires dialogical communication among different social classes, ethnic groups, and religious and political persuasions. Framing the problems from a single perspective leads to ideological rationalizations. Entering into dialogue in the public sphere under conditions of relative equality of competence and access to the means of communication can enhance a more dispassionate understanding of the existing social conditions.

At the risk of oversimplifying the complexities of cultural phenomena, Table 7.4 identifies the main features of cultural tendencies toward violence and peace. The table classifies human attitudes under seven major categories: attitudes toward life, self, others, society, nature, the supernatural, and death. As webs of meaning, cultures orient the human action toward one pole or the other. The attributes catalogued here are clearly the opposite extremes of seven continua. No human society, culture, or individual can be found to exclusively possess all the attributes of one or the other extreme. Most human societies, cultures, and individuals possess a complex configuration of these attributes. But each society, culture, and individual has the potential to move in one or the other direction. By

Table 7.4 Cultural Tendencies Toward Violence and Peace: A Schematic View

Attitudes Toward	Propensity to Violence	Propensity to Peace
Life	Carelessness or contempt	Reverence
Self	Self-doubt	Self-respect
	Self-negation	Self-affirmation
	Self-hatred	Self-love
Others	Closed	Open
	Exclusionary	Inclusionary
	Indifferent	Compassionate
	Greed	Generosity
	Revengefulness	Forgiving
	Exploitative	Giving
	Sarcasm (at others' expense)	Humor (at one's own expense)
Society	Totalitarian	Communitarian
	Hierarchical	Egalitarian
	Competitive	Cooperative
	Conflict generator	Consensus generator
	Monoculturalist	Multiculturalist
	Ethnocentric	Universalist
Nature	Domination of nature	Preservation of nature
	Ecologically irresponsible	Ecologically responsible
Supernatural	Positivist: letter of the law	Mystical: spirit of the law
	Sectarian	Ecumenical
	Exclusionary god(s)	Inclusionary god(s)
	Transcendence-immanence	Immanence-transcendence
Death	Necrophilic	Biophilic
	Glorification	Remembrance

strengthening the cultural tendencies toward peace, we may build societies that reward peace and discourage violence.

FROM HUMAN RIGHTS TO HUMAN CARING

Cultural remedies are necessary but not sufficient. It is ultimately in the construction of democratic institutions that violence can be contained. Table 7.5 provides a schematic view of six generations of human rights that have evolved over the centuries to guarantee the sanctity of life. The postwar discourse on human rights may be viewed as a dialogue of civilizations on human security issues. The first generation of rights, natural rights, are ancient in their religious origin but were most aptly formulated by a secular document, the Declaration of Independence, as "life, liberty, and the pursuit of happiness." As embodied in the Universal Declaration of Human Rights, natural rights and a second generation of human rights focused on civil and political liberties, including freedoms of speech, conscience, petition, assembly, and organization. By contrast, the third generation was primarily introduced into the international discourse by the social democratic and Communist revolutions focusing on social and economic rights, including the rights of employment, social security, labor strikes, compensatory hiring, and social welfare. An alliance of the socialist countries with the increasing voting power of the newly independent countries in the UN put these rights on the international agenda. They were thus gradually legislated into the Declaration of Social and Economic Rights. The fourth generation came to be recognized primarily through the struggles of the colonized peoples who viewed the cultural domination of their former colonizers as a threat to their own collective cultural life. Whereas the first, second, and third generations of rights were primarily conferred on individuals, the fourth generation recognized the rights of collectivities. Among them, the right to communicate became an important category of rights, recognizing the right to speak, teach, and be taught in one's own native language—a right that continues to be violated by many dictatorial and so-called democratic regimes. The first four generations of human rights have been codified in the Universal Declaration of Human Rights, which was adopted by the UN in 1948, and the International Bill of Human Rights, including the International Covenant on Civil and Political Rights, an optional protocol attached to this covenant, and the International Covenant on Economic, Social, and Cultural Rights. They collectively came into force in 1976.

Although largely uncodified, a fifth generation of human rights, associated with environmental issues, has entered into the international discourse. In contrast to the previous generations of rights, which focus on

Table 7.5   Cultural Policies with Respect to Diversity and Democracy

Policies Toward Diversity	Extermination	Segregation	Assimilation	Amalgamation	Integration
Democratic Rights	Denied	Denied	Denied	Denied	Fulfilled
Natural Rights Life, liberty, and the pursuit of happiness, including national self-determination	Indigenous peoples under colonial rule; Jews in Hitler's Germany; Bahai's in Iran	Slave societies; the Harijans in India	Colonized peoples	Kashmiris in India	?
Civil Rights Suffrage and freedoms of speech, media, assembly, and association	Indigenous peoples under colonial rule; Jews in Hitler's Germany; Bahai's in Iran	African Americans in the U.S. South until the 1960s; apartheid in South Africa until the 1990s; women in some societies	Colonized peoples	Immigrants in Great Britain and the United States	?
Social and Economic Rights Equal opportunity employment, unemployment compensation, social security, health insurance	Indigenous peoples under colonial rule; Jews in Hitler's Germany; Bahai's in Iran	Koreans in Japan; apartheid in South Africa until the 1990s; women in some societies	Colonized peoples	The underclass and slum dwellers everywhere	?
Cultural Rights Freedoms of identity, language, religion, and customs	Indigenous peoples under colonial rule; Jews in Hitler's Germany; Bahai's in Iran	Koreans in Japan; apartheid in South Africa until the 1990s	Colonized peoples; immigrants in Europe; Kurds in Turkey; Tibetans in China	Immigrants in Great Britain and the United States	?
Ecological Rights Care of natural environmental resources for present and future generations by adopting sustainable development strategies					
Human Caring					

Notes: Columns show the dominant cultural policies. Rows show denial of democratic rights to specific sectors of the population. Switzerland presents a model of a fully integrated multinational, multicultural, multilingual society among the Swiss Germans, French, Italians, and Romansh, allowing each community its autonomy within a federal, canton system of government. The brevity of the cells should be read with some indulgence.

humanity, the new generation of rights may be considered interspecies rights. The environmental disasters of the last few decades (Chernobyl, Three Mile Island, Bhopal, the Exxon *Valdez,* the Kuwaiti oil fires) have brought the point home that humanity cannot survive, let alone prosper, without the living earth, skies, oceans, and their multitude of species. An increasing appreciation of the wisdom of traditional civilizations is renewing the fundamental principles needed for greater harmony between the human and natural worlds. The hubris of the Enlightenment, which put humans above nature, has been challenged by an environmentalist view that places humanity in nature. The interdependencies of the natural and human worlds are therefore the focus of this fifth generation of rights.

We may even speak of a sixth generation of human rights, yet to be developed and articulated, that no longer refers to rights but rather to human caring, compassion, and love. Emerging out of the most profound spiritual traditions of civility in the world, this generation of rights will recognize that human security cannot be ultimately achieved in its totality unless and until we see the individual as an integral part of the larger human community. The tradition of libertarian rights, with its emphasis on individual rights, social contracts, and legal obligations, has positioned the individual against society rather than in society. It has thus led us to forget all too often that humans do not feel fully safe and secure until and unless they are loved and cared for. A communitarian perspective on rights therefore would begin rather than end with satisfying the conditions of ontological security (Laing 1969). As children demonstrate unabashedly when they are left alone, ontological insecurity is the root cause of our most desperate cries. Humans can realize their full human potential only in communities of caring, beginning with the family and going on to school, workplace, and retirement. As Hillary Rodham Clinton has aptly pointed out, it takes a village to raise a child. But in our own increasingly interdependent world, it must also be recognized that it takes an entire world to sustain the planet Earth for future generations.

DIVERSITY, DEMOCRACY, AND DISCOURSE

Although diversity is a condition of all planetary life, much of the violence in history against humans and nature has attempted to eliminate it. Table 7.5 correlates the evolution of human rights with the cultural policies that have changed from extermination to segregation, assimilation, amalgamation, and integration. Policies of extermination have been pursued in the cases of Native Americans in early U.S. history, Jews in Hitler's Germany, and Muslims in Bosnia. Policies of de jure segregation were pursued in the South of the United States until the 1960s and in South Africa until the dismantling of apartheid in the 1990s. But such policies continue in many parts of the world through de facto social segregation in neighborhoods, schooling, and professions. They have been the dominant policies of many societies in which a single group enjoys a position of privilege but is not readily willing to accept talented individuals from other aspiring groups. Exceptional individuals who are assimilated must forgo their own cultural heritage and adopt the cultural norms and practices of the dominant group(s). This has been the implicit policy in most European and North American societies in the postwar period. Assimilation policies begin with the premise that, in the words of Theodore Roosevelt, "we do not want hyphenated Americans." Amalgamation policies represent the next level of tolerance. Since the 1960s, when cultural roots and identity were generally revived in the United States, hyphenated Americans have become an accepted norm. Instead of simply tolerating cultural diversity, however, integration policies celebrate it. They therefore require a high degree of social and economic leveling. Such policies rest on the institutions of equal opportunity laws and compensatory hiring and social welfare. Although such policies were pursued in the United Sates and some European countries during the 1960s and 1970s, rising unemployment and resentment against immigrants and welfare recipients are currently placing those policies on the defensive.

DIALOGUE OF CIVILIZATIONS FOR PEACE

"It is possible to live in peace," Gandhi once said. Peace is not therefore an end to be reached; it is a process to be generated; it is a path to be taken; it is a culture to be adopted. Pursuing peace with violent means has historically proved self-defeating. But pursuing peace with peaceful means requires a value system that puts the preservation of life forms above all else. It also requires a form of communication that is dialogical in character and transnational and intercivilizational in its epistemological reach. In such an endeavor, the following seven propositions on the practicality of peace may prove useful:

1. In human relations, conflicts of interests and perceptions are ubiquitous. Peace is not the absence of conflict. Peace, in fact, welcomes the inevitability of human conflict as a reality that makes reconciliation possible through communication and conflict resolution.

2. Conflict can be less destructive and even creative if channeled into understanding and accommodating the interests and perceptions of others. Conflict can serve functional or dysfunctional purposes. If accompanied by violence—physical, political, economic, cultural, or environmental—

human conflict can become dysfunctional by developing into a cycle of violence. But if conflict is expressed through open, equal, and interactive communication, it can lead to greater understanding and accommodation of interests and perceptions of the conflicting parties.

3. *Dialogical communication and conflict mitigation, regulation, and resolution can fulfill this purpose through a variety of methods.* Dialogical communication, defined as open, equal, and interactive, can facilitate conflict mitigation, regulation, and resolution. The methods of conflict resolution are of necessity culture bound and can themselves become subjects of conflict. But in a world of colliding cultural and moral spaces, we have no choice except to negotiate and develop synthetic, third cultures in order to bridge the gaps in meaning and understanding between the conflicting parties. A number of conflict resolution methods have, however, become universal in their application, including negotiation, adjudication, arbitration, mediation, and satyagraha (nonviolent resistance). Education and training in such methods and any others emerging in the future would be of immense value to the mitigation, regulation, and resolution of conflicts at all levels.

4. *Individuals and collectivities are ontologically prone to project the dark side of their contradictory selves onto other(s), providing "legitimate" grounds for dichotomizing, demonizing, and devouring the enemy within and without.* Conflicts often result in framing, labeling, and name-calling of the enemy. If such grounds of legitimation of conflict are routinized for a few generations, they are reified in the consciousness of the conflicting parties and form prejudices that are difficult to overcome. Such are the racial, religious, and ethnic hatreds of several centuries.

5. *The propensity to self-hatred, other-hatred, and violence also rises with increasing atomization of society, identity anxiety, and intensifying low self-esteem.* The modern industrial world, with its dislocating, atomizing, and abstracting effects on individuals, has become a breeding ground for such collective hatreds. Low self-esteem, bred by ontological insecurity and identity anxiety in the modern world, has proved a powerful force in the development of mass movements that have encouraged an "escape from freedom" (Fromm 1941) and a social psychology of scapegoating.

6. *Propensity to peace rises with increasing family and community bonding, identity security, self-respect, and respect for others.* Conversely, ontological and identity security often leads to feelings of respect for self and others. That, in turn, often paves the path to peace. Caring families and societies are thus generally peaceful families and societies. To cultivate a culture of peace, we must cultivate a just and caring society.

7. *A culture of violence constantly dichotomizes self and others, separating ends and means, and a culture of peace identifies the self significantly with the other, viewing ends and means as a never-ending chain.* As

Gandhi taught, we must open the windows of our house to all cultural currents without being swept off our own cultural feet. We can best discover global unity through exposure to and celebration of its diversity. Any worldview that dichotomizes the self and other is vulnerable to obscurantism and fails to recognize that the human mind is now more than ever before a constellation of centuries of the human collective unconscious. Any worldview that also draws a sharp distinction between ends and means, speaking of just and unjust wars, legitimate and illegitimate uses of violence, is laying itself open to a culture of violence feeding on self-serving moral pretensions. Moral self-righteousness is the first step in descending into the fire of anger and violence. Intellectual humility and moral self-criticism are the first lessons into the recognition and acknowledgment of the truth claims of others.

CONCLUSION

Marshall McLuhan's global village has proved to be a place not of harmony but of colliding moral spaces. The lords of the electronically moated opulent castles and the rebellious serfs, shamans, and jesters surrounding them have confronted one another through a variety of violent encounters: physical, political, economic, cultural, and environmental. Some 3,000 nationalities around the world that have not yet received political recognition from the international community are increasingly clamoring to be subjects rather than objects of history. The global state-corporate system of organized violence will continue to be challenged by sporadic but persistent acts of counterviolence unless the world learns to respect and celebrate diversity by devolving power to the smallest levels of human communities. In place of states of violence in which the world has learned to acquiesce, zones of peace must be built. Such zones, however, would have to rethink the problems of sovereignty, governance, economy, human rights, and civic responsibilities in order to accommodate a human diversity that can be homogenized only to the detriment of peace and justice.

8

TURNING TIME

When the forms of an old culture are dying, the new culture is created by a few people who are not afraid to be insecure.

—Rudolf Bahro,
German Green Party leader

As do all measurements of time, centuries punctuate our fragility, finitude, and failure. But they also occasion reflection on that fragility, finitude, and failure. It is no surprise, therefore, to find a cottage industry growing at the end of each century in general and this one in particular that apocalyptically proclaims the end of history (Fukuyama 1989), geography (Mosco 1995), modernity (Vattimo 1991), work (Rifkin 1995), university (Noam 1995), and journalism (Katz 1992). What would life look like without the fun and frolic of history, geography, modernity, work, university, and journalism?

Rest assured that nothing is ending except a century, which is a figment of our own imagination anyhow. In the midst of this clutter of voices, the reflections of a Buddhist leader, Daisaku Ikeda, represent a message of hope rather than despair. Recalling the Russian philosopher Nicolai Berdyayev (1874–1948), Ikeda makes a critical distinction among three kinds of time: cosmic, historical, and ontological. Cosmic time (light-years) marks the evolution of the universe; historical time punctuates human days, weeks, years, and centuries; ontological time celebrates the timelessness of being. Ikeda suggests that enlightenment is awakening to the timelessness of ontological time, seizing the moment for its joy of life. The great thirteenth-century Sufi poet Rumi (1959: 10) has a similar view:

Consciousness mirrors past memories.
Past and future are curtains concealing God.

189

Burn the curtains, for how long indeed
Will you continue as a knotted reed?

Natural spirituality can lead us to liberation from the burdens of time. Nevertheless, we also live in cosmic and historical times that bring us suffering. It is through natural spirituality that we can overcome this suffering by assuming cosmic and historical responsibility for the celebration and continuation of life. When Buddha was asked, "Who are you—a God, an angel, or a prophet?" he replied simply, "I am awake!" The term for God in Persian (*Khodaa*) could mean "self-awakening." Cosmic and historical time cannot therefore be dismissed without serious damage to our natural spirituality that connects with and cares for all beings. As we strive to transcend historical time, we must also be children of our own time by taking responsibility for all forms of life.

This brings us to our own historical moment. Globalization may be characterized as the most powerful trend of our own time. The process has been going on for the past 2,500 years and will perhaps continue for the next 2,500. However, since the end of the Cold War, it has gained considerable momentum by drawing the former Sino-Soviet bloc, Asia, Africa, and Latin America into the vortex of pancapitalist development. The abstract and anonymous forces of global markets, electronic communications, and military domination appear to leave little room for individual human agency. Yet our natural spirituality ceaselessly calls for our involvement to preserve life against the forces that threaten it.

Three historical forces are currently at odds: markets, states, and civil societies. In recent decades, markets have led the way through the global reach of some 30,000 transnational corporations. Superstates, such as the G7, have collaborated with the TNCs to open up new markets, such as those in the former Sino-Soviet bloc. Smaller and medium states, such as those in the less developed countries, have tried—often unsuccessfully—to defend their national interests vis-à-vis superstate and TNC encroachments. Intergovernmental organizations have become the main arena in which the conflicting interests of the large, medium, and small states are negotiated. In the meantime, the global civil society has organized itself into some 40,000 nongovernmental organizations, such as Greenpeace and Amnesty International. The struggle among the three protagonists is an unequal one. Of the leading economic units in the world, over 50 percent are TNCs. A typical TNC has larger assets and more income than a typical small or medium state. In this struggle, the NGOs have little if any clout. That is why economic globalization is far ahead of political and cultural globalization. As we have witnessed in the recent Asian economic debacle, political institutions have not been able to regulate and moderate the excesses of financial markets. Similarly, market forces have debased global cultural institutions. In one arena, for instance, this has resulted in the Coca-Colanization and McDonaldization of the world. Global advertising is whetting the appetite for consumption well beyond the Earth's capacity. As UN reports show, growing gaps in wealth and income among and within nations are also dangerous outcomes of this state of affairs.

As Gandhi once remarked, this world has enough for all of us but not enough for the greed of a single person. How can the imbalance among economic, political, and cultural globalization be redressed? There are those who argue that we must return to an earlier age of strict national sovereignty, economic barriers to trade and investment, and cultural protection of national identity. However, that solution appears to be neither realistic nor necessarily desirable. As a globalist, Ikeda has proposed the formation of an NGO organ within the UN to represent the views and interests of civil society. To follow the same logic, the General Assembly could have two branches consisting of a People's Assembly and a State Assembly. For the UN to become an organization of nations rather than states, such reform is absolutely necessary. Elected directly by the peoples of the European Union, the European Parliament has already set a successful precedent for such a transnational institution. To be a time of peace rather than strife, the next century must bring its global political, social, and cultural institutions into sync with its economic institutions.

References

Abu-Lughod, Janet. 1989. *Before European Hegemony: The World System* A.D. *1250–1350*. New York: Oxford University Press.

Addo, Herb, et al. 1985. *Development as Social Transformation*. Boulder, CO: Westview Press.

Adelman, Kenneth L. 1981. "Speaking of America: Public Diplomacy in Our Time," *Foreign Affairs* 59:4, pp. 913–936.

Algar, Hamid. 1969. *Religion and State in Iran, 1785–1906*. Berkeley: University of California Press.

———. 1973. *Mirza Malkam Khan: A Study in the History of Iranian Modernism*. Berkeley: University of California Press.

Anderson, Benedict. 1983. *Imagined Communities: Reflections on the Origins and Spread of Nationalism*. London: Verso.

Anderson, Christopher. 1995. "A Survey of the Internet," *The Economist*, July 1.

Anonymous 1981. "America in Captivity: Points of Decision in the Hostage Crisis," *The New York Times Magazine*, Special Issue, Spring.

Anonymous 1994. "America's Information Highway," *The Economist*, December 25–January 7, pp. 35–38.

Anonymous 1995. "A Survey of Telecommunications," *The Economist*, September 30.

Anonymous 1996. "Arachnophobia," *The Economist*, August 10, p. 28.

Anonymous. 1997a. "Disappearing Taxes," *The Economist*, May 31, pp. 15, 21–23.

Anonymous. 1997b. "Don't Ban the Bomb," *The Economist*, January 4, pp. 15–16.

Anonymous. 1997c. "An African Success Story," *The Economist*, June 14, p. 47.

Anonymous. 1998. "U.S. kept Secret Files on Diana," *The Honolulu Advertiser*, December 13, 1998, p. A1.

Appadurai, Arjun. 1990. "Disjuncture and Difference in the Global Cultural Economy," *Public Culture* 2:2, Spring, pp. 1–22.

———. 1993. "Patriotism and Its Future," *Public Culture* 5, pp. 411–429.

Arendt, Hannah. 1958. *The Origins of Totalitarianism*. New York: Meridan Books.

Arjomand, Said. 1988. *Authority and Political Culture in Shi'ism*. Albany: State University of New York Press.

———, ed. 1984. *From Nationalism to Revolutionary Islam*. Albany: State University of New York Press.

Arno, Andrew, and Wimal Dissanayake, eds. 1984. *The News Media in National and International Conflict*. Boulder, CO: Westview Press.

Aron, Raymond. 1954. *The Century of Total War*. Garden City, NY: Doubleday.

Ashley, Richard K. 1981. "Political Realism and Human Interests," *International Studies Quarterly* 25:2, June, pp. 204–236.

Attali, Jacques. 1991. *Millennium: Winners and Losers in the Coming World Order*. New York: Times Books.

Barber, Benjamin. 1995. *McWorld vs. Jihad*. New York: Random House.

Barfield, Thomas J. 1989. *The Perilous Frontier: Nomadic Empires and China*. Cambridge, MA: Basil Blackwell.

Barnaby, Frank, ed. 1988. *The Gaia Peace Atlas*. New York: Doubleday.

Barnet, Richard J., and Roland E. Muller. 1974. *Global Reach*. New York: Simon and Schuster.

Barnet, Richard J., and John Cavanagh. 1992. *Global Dreams: Imperial Corporations and the New World Order*. New York: Simon and Schuster.

Bartlett, Donald L., and James B. Steele. 1992. *America: What Went Wrong?* Kansas City, MO: Andrews.

Baudillard, Jean. 1994. *The Illusion of the End*. Stanford, CA: Stanford University Press.

Bell, Daniel. 1960. *The End of Ideology: On the Exhaustion of Political Ideas in the Fifties*. Glencoe, IL: Free Press.

———. 1973. *The Coming of the Post-Industrial Society: A Venture in Social Forecasting*. New York: Basic Books.

Beniger, James R. 1986. *The Control Revolution: Technological and Economic Origins of the Information Society*. Cambridge: Harvard University Press.

Bentley, Jerry H. 1996. "Cross-Cultural Interactions and Periodization in World History," *American Historical Review* 101:3, June, pp. 749–770.

Berger, Peter. 1977. *Facing Up to Modernity: Excursions in Society, Politics, and Religion*. New York: Basic Books.

Berlin, Isaiah. As quoted by Colin Rowe and Fred Koetter. n.d. *Collage City*. Cambridge: MIT Press, p. 86.

Biggs, Morris I. 1971. *Learning Theories for Teachers*, 2nd ed. New York: Harper and Row.

Blomstrom, Magnus, and Bjorn Hettne. 1984. *Development Theory in Transition: The Dependency Debate and Beyond: Third World Responses*. London: Zed Books.

Boaz, David, ed. 1998. *The Libertarian Reader: Classic and Contemporary Writings from Lao-Tzu to Milton Friedman*. New York: Free Press.

Boorstin, Daniel J. 1975. *The Image: A Guide to Pseudo-Events in America*. New York: Atheneum.

Boulding, Elise. 1988. *Building a Global Civic Culture: Education for an Interdependent World*. New York: Teachers College Press.

———. 1991. "The Zone of Peace Concept in Current Practice: Review and Evaluation," paper presented at the Inaugural Conference of the Centre for Peace Studies, Curtin University and University of Western Australia, January 14–16.

Brandt, Willy, et al. 1985. *Common Crisis: North-South Cooperation for World Recovery*. Cambridge: MIT Press.

Branscomb, Anne Wells. 1994. *Who Owns Information?: From Privacy to Public Access*. New York: Basic Books.

Campbell-Smith, Duncan. 1991. "A Survey of Telecommunications," *The Economist*, October 5.

Caracas Report on Alternative Development Indicators. 1990. *Redefining Wealth and Progress*. Indianapolis: Knowledge Systems.

Carr, Edward. 1990. "A Survey of Telecommunications," *The Economist*, March 10.

Chase-Dunn, Christopher, and Thomas D. Hall. 1977. *Rise and Demise: Comparing World-Systems*. Boulder, CO: Westview Press.

Clausewitz, Carl von. 1976. *On War*. Translated and edited by Michael Howard and Peter Paret. Princeton, NJ: Princeton University Press.

Cohen, Eliot A. 1996. "A Revolution in Warfare," *Foreign Affairs* 75:2, March/April, pp. 37–54.

Commission on Global Governance. 1995. *Our Global Neighborhood*. New York: Oxford University Press.

Creveld, Martin van. 1989. *Technology and War From 2000 B.C. to the Present*. New York: Free Press.

———. 1991. *The Transformation of War*. New York: Free Press.

CRTNET #900. December 22, 1993. E-mail: CRTNET @psuvm.psu.edu.

CRTNET #915. January 12, 1994. E-mail: CRTNET @psuvm.psu.edu.

Davison, W. Phillips. 1973. "International and World Public Opinion," in Ithiel de Sola Pool et al., eds. *Handbook of Communication*. Chicago: Rand McNally.

Dayan, Daniel, and Elihu Katz. 1992. *Media Events: The Live Broadcasting of History*. Cambridge: Harvard University Press.

Derian, James, and Michael J. Shapiro. 1989. *International/Intertextual Relations: Postmodern Readings on World Politics*. Lexington, MA: Lexington Press.

Deutsch, Karl W. 1966a. *Nationalism and Social Communication*, 2nd ed. Cambridge: MIT Press.

———, ed. 1966b. *International Political Community: An Anthology*. New York: Anchor Books.

———. 1988. *The Analysis of International Relations*, 3rd ed. Englewood Cliffs, NJ: Prentice-Hall.

Docherty, Thomas. 1993. *Post-Modernism: A Reader*. New York: Columbia University Press.

Dordick, Herbert S., Helen G. Bradley, and Burt Nanaus. 1981. *The Emerging Network Marketplace*. Norwood, NJ: Ablex.

D'Souza, D. 1995. *The End of Racism*. New York: Free Press.

Duncan, Emma. 1998. "Wheel of Fortune: A Survey of Technology and Entertainment," *The Economist*, November 21, p. 118.

Editorial. 1997. "Emerging Africa," *The Economist*, June 14, pp. 13–14.

Eisenhower, Dwight D. 1960. "Presidential Farewell Address."

Etzioni, Amitai. 1993. *The Spirit of Community: Rights, Responsibilities, and the Communitarian Agenda*. New York: Crown Publishers.

Ewen, S., and E. Ewen. 1982. *Channels of Desire: Mass Images and the Shaping of American Consciousness*. New York: McGraw Hill.

Falk, Richard. 1995. *On Humane Governance: Toward a New Global Politics*. University Park: Pennsylvania State University Press.

Fawcett, Louis L'Estrange, and Andrew Hurrell, eds. 1996. *Regionalism in World Politics: Regional Organization and International Order*. Oxford: Oxford University Press.

Flourney, Don. 1992. *CNN World Report*. London: John Libbey and Co.

Foucault, Michel. 1979. *Discipline and Punish: The Birth of the Prison*. New York: Pantheon Books.

———. 1980. *Power/Knowledge: Selected Interviews and Other Writings 1972–1977*. New York: Pantheon Books.

Frank, Andre Gundar. 1969. *The Development of Underdevelopment*. New York: Monthly Review Press.

———. 1992. *The Centrality of Central Asia*. Comparative Asian Studies No. 8. Amsterdam: VU University Press.

———. 1988. *Re-Orient*. Berkeley: University of California Press.

Frank, Andre Gundar, and Barry K. Gills, eds. 1993. *The World System: Five Hundred Years or Five Thousand?* London: Routledge.

Frederick, Howard H. 1993. *Global Communication and International Relations*. Belmont, CA: Wadsworth Publishing Co.

Freire, Paolo. 1972. *Pedagogy of the Oppressed*. Translated by Myra Bergman Ramos. New York: Herder and Herder.

Frey, Frederick. 1973. "Communication and Development," in Ithiel de Sola et al., eds. *Handbook of Communication*. Chicago: Rand McNally.

Friedman, Jonathan. 1994. *Cultural Identity and Global Processes*. Newbury Park, CA: Sage Press.

Fromm, Erich. 1941. *Escape from Freedom*. New York: Holt, Rinehart and Winston.

Fukuyama, Francis. 1989. "The End of History," *National Interest* 16, Summer.

———. 1992. *The End of History and the Last Man*. London: Hamish Hamilton.

———. 1995. "Social Capital and the Global Economy," *Foreign Affairs* 74:5, September/October, p. 103.

Galtung, Johan. 1990. "Cultural Violence," *Journal of Peace Research* 27:3, pp. 291–305.

Galtung, Johan, and Richard Vincent. 1992. *Global Glasnost: Toward a New Information and Communication Order*. Cresskill, NJ: Hampton Press.

Gandhi, Mahatma. 1957. *An Autobiography: The Story of My Experiments with Truth*. Boston: Beacon Press.

Ganley, Gladys D. 1992. *The Exploding Political Power of Personal Media*. Norwood, NJ: Ablex.

———. 1996. *Unglued Empire: The Soviet Experience with Communications Technologies*. Norwood, NJ: Ablex.

Ganley, Oswald H., and Gladys D. Ganley. 1987. *Global Political Fallout: The VCR's First Decade*. Norwood, NJ: Ablex.

———. 1992. *To Inform or to Control: The New Communications Networks*, 2nd ed. Norwood, NJ: Ablex.

Geertz, C. 1973. *The Interpretation of Cultures: Selected Essays*. New York: Basic Books.

Gerbner, George, ed. 1981. "The Information Society," *Journal of Communication* 31:1, Winter, pp. 131–194.

Giddens, Anthony. 1984. *The Constitution of Society: Outline of the Theory of Structuration*. Berkeley: University of California Press.

Grimes, Barbara F., ed. 1992. *Ethnologue: Languages of the World*, 12th ed. Dallas: Summer Institute of Linguistics.

Gunaratne, Shelton A. 1978. "Media Subservience and Development Journalism," *Communication and Development Review* 2:2, Summer, pp. 3–6.

Haas, Michael. 1992. "A Paradigm of Community for the Post–Cold War World," in Katharine and Majid Tehranian, eds., *Restructuring for World Peace*. Cresskill, NJ: Hampton Press.

Habermas, Jurgen. 1971. *Knowledge and Human Interests*. Translated by J. Shaprio. London: Heinemann.

———. 1973. *Legitimation Crisis*. Boston: Beacon Press.

———. 1983. *A Theory of Communicative Action*, 3 vols. Boston: Beacon Press.

Hall, John Whitney. 1964. "Japan: The Nature of Traditional Society," in Robert E. Ward and Dankwart A. Rustow, eds., *Political Modernization in Japan and Turkey.* Princeton, NJ: Princeton University Press.

Hall, Thomas D. 1996. "The World-System Perspective: A Small Sample from a Large Universe," *Sociological Inquiry* 66:4, November, pp. 440–454.

———. 1997. "The Effects of Incorporation into World-Systems on Ethnic Processes: Lessons from the Ancient World for the Modern World," paper presented at ISA Conference, Toronto, March 18–22.

Hamelink, Cees J. 1983. *Cultural Autonomy in Global Communications: Planning National Information Policy.* New York: Longman.

Harvey, David. 1990. *The Conditions of Post-Modernity: An Inquiry into the Origins of Cultural Change.* Cambridge, MA: Blackwell.

Harvey, John. 1988. "Information Service in the Islamic Republic of Iran," *International Library Review* 20, pp. 273–306.

Hassig, Ross. 1988. *Aztec Warfare.* Norman: University of Oklahoma Press.

Herman, Edward S., and Noam Chomsky. 1988. *Manufacturing Consent.* New York: Pantheon Books.

Hertz, John H. 1981. "Political Realism Revisited," *International Studies Quarterly* 25:2, June, pp. 182–197.

Hitler, Adolf. 1941. *My New Order.* New York: Reynall and Hitchcock.

Hoffmann, Stanley. 1990. "A New World and Its Troubles," *Foreign Affairs* 69:4, Fall, pp. 115–122.

———. 1996. "In Defense of Mother Teresa: Morality in Foreign Policy," *Foreign Affairs,* March/April.

Hornik, Robert C. 1980. "Communication as Complement in Development," *Journal of Communication* 30:2, Spring, pp. 10–24.

———. 1988. *Development Communication: Information, Agriculture, and Nutrition in the Third World.* White Plains, NY: Longman.

Huntington, Samuel P. 1993a. "The Clash of Civilizations," *Foreign Affairs,* Summer.

———. 1993b. "The Clash of Civilizations: A Response," *Foreign Affairs,* November–December.

———. 1998. *The Clash of Civilizations and the Remaking of the World Order.* New York: Touchstone Books.

Ibn Khaldun. 1958. *The Mugaddamah: An Introduction to History,* 3 vols. Translated by Franz Rosenthal. New York: Pantheon Books.

Innis, Harold. 1950. *The Bias of Communication.* Toronto: University of Toronto Press.

Jacobsen, C. G. 1993. "Myths, Politics and the Not-So-New World Order," *Journal of Peace Research* 30:3, August, pp. 241–250.

Jameson, Frederick. 1991. *Postmodernism: The Cultural Logic of Late Capitalism.* Durham, NC: Duke University Press.

Jayaweera, Neville, and Sarath Amunungama. 1987. *Rethinking Development Communication.* Singapore: The Asian Mass Communication Research and Information Centre.

Juergensmeyer, Mark. 1994. *The New Cold War? Religious Nationalism Confronts the Secular State.* Berkeley: University of California Press.

Kaplan, Robert D. 1995. "The Coming Anarchy," *Atlantic Monthly,* February. On the Web at http:www.theatlantic.com/election/connection/foreign/anarchy.htm.

Katz, Elihu. 1981. "In Defense of Media Events," in Robert W. Haigh, George Gerbnel, and Richard B. Byrne, eds., *Communication in the Twenty-first Century.* New York: John Wiley and Sons.

————. 1992. "The End of Journalism: Notes on Watching the War," *Journal of Communication* 42:3, pp. 5–13.

Katz, Elihu, and Paul F. Lazarsfeld. 1955. *Personal Influence: The Part Played by People in the Flow of Communications.* New York: Free Press.

Katz, Elihu, and George Wedell. 1978. *Broadcasting in the Third World: Promise and Performance.* Cambridge: Harvard University Press.

Kennan, George. 1993. "Somalia, Through a Glass Darkly," *New York Times*, September 30, p. A25.

Kennedy, Paul M. 1987. *The Rise and Fall of the Great Powers: Economic Change and Military Conflict from 1500 to 2000.* New York: Random House.

————. 1993. *Preparing for the Twenty-first Century.* New York: Random House.

Kent, George. 1993. "Analyzing Conflict and Change," *Peace and Change* 18:4, October, pp. 373–398.

Keohane, Robert O., and Joseph S. Nye. 1989. *Power and Interdependence*, 2nd ed. Glenview, IL: Scott Foresman.

Khomeini, Ruh Allah. 1981. *Islam and Revolution.* Translated and annotated by Hamid Algar. Berkeley, CA: Mizan Press.

————. 1989. "Imam Khomeini's Last Will and Testament," *Kayhan International* 10: 2446, June 24, p. 6.

Kissinger, Henry. 1994. *Diplomacy.* New York: Simon and Schuster.

Kuhn, Thomas S. 1962. *The Structure of Scientific Revolutions*, 2nd ed. Chicago: University of Chicago Press.

Kumar, Krishna. 1978. *Prophecy and Progress: The Society of Industrial and Post-Industrial Society.* New York: Penguin.

————. 1993. "Hindu Revivalism and Education in North-Central India," in Martin E. Marty and R. Scott Appleby, eds., *Fundamentalism and Society: Reclaiming the Science, the Family, and Education.* Chicago: University of Chicago Press.

Lacquer, Walter. 1966. *Fascism: Past, Present and Future.* Oxford: Oxford University Press.

Laing, R. D. 1969. *The Divided Self.* New York: Pantheon.

Lapham, Lewis H. 1994. "Notebook: Dungeons and Dragons," *Harper's* 288: 1725, February, pp. 9–11.

Lash, S., and J. Urry. 1987. *The End of Organized Capitalism.* Madison: University of Wisconsin Press.

————. 1994. *Economies of Signs and Space.* Thousand Oaks, CA: Sage Press.

Lazarsfeld, Paul, Bernard Berelson, and Hazel Gaudert. 1948. *The People's Choice.* New York: Columbia University Press.

Lee, Chien-yi. 1993. "DBS Issues in the Asia-Pacific," unpublished paper. Communication Seminar, University of Hawaii–Manoa.

Lee, Philip, ed. 1985. *Communication for All: New World Information and Communication Order.* Maryknoll, NY: Orbis Books.

Lenin, V. I. 1917. *Imperialism: The Highest Stage of Capitalism.* London: Lawrence and Wishart (1969).

Lerner, Daniel, and Lucille W. Pevsner. 1958. *The Passing of Traditional Society: Modernizing the Middle East.* Glencoe, IL: Free Press.

Levidow, Les, and Kevin Robins, eds. 1989. *Cyborg Worlds: The Military Information Society.* London: Free Association Books.

Lifton, Robert Jay, and Richard Falk. 1982. *Indefensible Weapons: The Political and Psychological Case Against Nuclearism.* New York: Basic Books.

Lippmann, Walter. 1930. *Public Opinion.* New York: Macmillan.

Livingston, Steven, and Todd Eachus. 1995. "Humanitarian Crises and U.S. Foreign Policy: Somalia and the CNN Effect Reconsidered," *Political Communication* 12, pp. 413–429.

MacBride, Sean, et al. 1980. *Many Voices, One World: Communication and Society Today and Tomorrow.* Paris: UNESCO Press.

Mahathir, Mohamad. 1994. "Religion and Society," in *The Role and Influence of Religion in Society.* Kuala Lumpur: Institute of Islamic Understanding, Malaysia.

Maitland, Donald. 1994. "Forging New Links: Focus on Developing Economies," Plenary Presentations, Pacific Telecommunications Council Sixteenth Annual Conference, Honolulu, Hawaii, January 16–20.

Manahian, David. 1998. "The World is Watching: A Survey of Human Rights Law," *The Economist,* December 9, pp. 1–16.

Mandel, Ernest. 1978. *Late Capitalism.* London: Verso.

Mandelbum, Michael. 1996. "Foreign Policy as Social Work," *Foreign Affairs* 75:1, January/February, pp. 22–49.

Marty, Martin E. 1988. "The Phenomenon of Fundamentalism," *Bulletin of the American Academy of Arts and Science.*

Marty, Martin, and Scott Appleby, eds. 1991. *Fundamentalism Observed.* Chicago: University of Chicago Press.

———, eds. 1992. *Fundamentalism and State,* vol. 1. Chicago: University of Chicago Press.

———. 1993. *Fundamentalism and Society: Reclaiming the Science, the Family, and Education,* vol. 2. Chicago: University of Chicago Press.

Marx, Karl. 1959. "Toward the Critique of Hegel's Philosophy of Right," in L. S. Feuer, ed., *Marx and Engels: Basic Writings on Politics and Philosophy.* New York: Doubleday.

Marx, Karl, and Frederick Engels. 1948. "The Communist Manifesto," in Lewis S. Freuer, ed., *Marx and Engels: Basic Writings on Politics and Philosophy.* New York: Doubleday.

Masuda, Yoneji. 1981. *The Information Society: A Post-Industrial Society.* Washington, D.C.: World Future Society.

Matsuda, Mari J., Richard Delgado, and Charles R. Lawrence, eds. 1993. *Words That Wound: Critical Race Theory, Assaultive Speech, and the First Amendment.* Boulder, CO: Westview Press.

Mattleart, Armand. 1979. *Multinational Corporations and the Control of Culture.* Atlantic Heights, UK: Harvester Press.

———. 1983. *Transnationals and Third World: The Struggle for Culture.* South Hadley, MA: Bergin and Garvey.

Mazlish, Bruce. 1993. *The Fourth Discontinuity.* New Haven, CT: Yale University Press.

McAnany, Emile G., ed. 1980. *Communication in the Rural Third World: The Role of Information in Development.* New York: Praeger.

McClelland, David C. 1961. *The Achieving Society.* Princeton, NJ: Van Nostrand.

McLuhan, Marshall, and Quentin Fiore. 1968. *War and Peace in the Global Village.* New York: Bantam.

McPahil, Thomas. 1993. "Television as an Extension of the Nation State: CNNI and the Americanization of Broadcasting," paper presented at the annual conference of the French Association of American Studies, Paris, May 21–23.

Morgenthau, Hans J. 1949. *Politics Among Nations.* New York: Alfred Knopf.

————. 1985. *Politics Among Nations: The Struggle for Power and Peace.* New York: Alfred K. Knopf.

Mosco, V. 1995. "Will Computer Communication End Geography?" Cambridge: Program on Information Resources Policy, Harvard University.

Mowlana, Hamid, and L. J. Wilson. 1990. *The Passing of Modernity: Communication and the Transformation of Society.* New York: Longman.

Mowlana, Hamid. 1979. *Evolution of Social Communication in Iran.* Tehran: College of Mass Communication Publications.

————. 1996. *Global Communication in Transition: The End of Diversity?* Newbury Park, CA: Sage Publications.

Mowlana, Hamid, and Mehdi Mohsenian Rad. 1990. *Japanese Programs on Iranian Television: A Study in International Flow of Information.* Washington, D.C.: International Communication Program, School of International Service, The American University.

Nietschmann, Bernard. 1987. "Militarization and Indigenous Peoples," *Christian Science Quarterly* 11:3, pp. 1–11.

Noam, Eli. 1995. "Electronics and the Dim Future of the University," *Science* 270, October 13, pp. 247–249.

Nordenstreng, Kaarle, and Herbert I. Schiller. 1979. *National Sovereignty and International Communication.* Norwood, NJ: Ablex.

————, eds. 1993. *Beyond National Sovereignty: International Communication in the 1990s.* Norwood, NJ: Ablex.

Nye, Joseph. 1990. *Bound to Lead: The Changing Nature of American Power.* New York: Basic Books.

Nye, Joseph S., Jr., and William A. Owens. 1996. "America's Information Edge," *Foreign Affairs*, March/April, pp. 20–36.

Okigbo, Charles C. 1985. "Is Development Communication a Dead Issue?" *Media Development*, no. 4.

Packard, Vance. 1957. *The Hidden Persuaders.* New York: D. McKay Co.

Pai, Sunny. 1993. "The Cable News Network," unpublished paper. Communication Seminar, University of Hawaii–Manoa.

Porat, Mark. 1977. *The Information Economy.* Washington, D.C.: U.S. Department of Commerce, Office of Telecommunication Policy.

Poster, Mark. 1990. *The Mode of Information.* Chicago: University of Chicago Press.

Pye, Lucien W., ed. 1963. *Communications and Political Development.* Princeton, NJ: Princeton University Press.

Rifkin, J. 1995. *The End of Work: The Decline of the Global Labor Force and Dawn of the Post-Market Era.* New York: G. P. Putnam.

Riggs, Fred W. 1994. "Ethnonationalism, Industrialism and the Modern State," *Third World Quarterly* 15:4, pp. 583–611.

————. 1997. "The Malady of Modernity: Some Remedies," paper presented at the Toda Institute Conference, Honolulu, Hawaii, June 6–8.

————. 1998. "The Modernity of Ethnic Conflict and Identity," *International Political Science Review* 19:3, July, pp. 269–288.

Robinson, Deanna, Elizabeth B. Buck, and Marlene Cuthbert. 1991. *Music at the Margins: Popular Music and Global Cultural Diversity.* Newbury Park, CA: Sage Publications.

Rogers, Everett. 1962. *Diffusion of Innovations.* New York: Free Press.

————, ed. 1976. *Communication and Development: Critical Perspectives.* Beverly Hills, CA: Sage Publications.

Rousseau, Jean Jacques. 1968. *The Social Contract.* New York: Penguin Books.

Rowe, C., and F. Koetter. 1992. *Collage City.* Cambridge: MIT Press.

Rumi, Jalad ed Din. 1394/1959. *Mathnawi.* Tehran: Jaridan. Translated by the author.

Rummel, Rudolph J. 1994. *Death by Government.* New Brunswick, NY: Transactions Publishers.

Said, Edward. 1981. *Covering Islam: How the Media and the Experts Determine How We See the Rest of the World.* New York: Pantheon.

Samarajiwa, Rohan. 1987. "The Murky Beginnings of the Communication and Development Field: Voice of America and 'The Passing of Traditional Society,'" in N. Jayaweera and Sarath Amunungama, eds., *Rethinking Development Communication.* Singapore: The Asian Mass Communication Research and Information Centre.

Schelling, Thomas. 1992. "The Global Dimension," in Graham Allison and Gregory F. Treverton, eds. *Rethinking America's Security.* New York: Norton.

Schiller, Herbert I. 1973. *The Mind Managers.* Boston: Beacon Press.

———. 1976. *Communication and Cultural Domination.* New York: International Arts and Sciences Press.

———. 1981. *Who Knows: Information in the Age of Fortune 500.* Norwood, NJ: Ablex.

———. 1985. *Information and the Crisis Economy.* Norwood, NJ: Ablex.

Schlesinger, James. 1993. "Quest for a Post–Cold War Foreign Policy," *Foreign Affairs* 72:1, January/February, pp. 17–28.

Schramm, Wilbur. 1964. *Mass Media and National Development: The Role of Information in Developing Countries.* Stanford, CA: Stanford University Press.

Schramm, Wilbur, and L. Erwin Atwood. 1981. *Circulation of the Third World News: A Study of Asia.* Hong Kong: Press of Chinese University of Hong Kong.

Shah, Sonia. 1992. "The Roots of Ethnic Conflict," *Nuclear Times*, Spring, pp. 9–15.

Shapiro, Michael J. 1993a. "Moral Geographies and the Ethics of Post-Sovereignty," unpublished paper. December.

———. 1993b. "Warring Bodies and Bodies Politic: Tribal Warriors Versus State Soldiers," unpublished paper. May.

———. 1997. *Violent Cartographies: Mapping Cultures of War.* Minneapolis: University of Minnesota Press.

Siebert, Frederick S., Theodore Peterson, and Wilbur Schramm. 1956. *Four Theories of the Press.* Urbana: University of Illinois Press.

Singer, Max, and Aaron Widavsky. 1993. *The Real World Order: Zones of Peace/Zones of Turmoil.* Chatham, NJ: Chatham House Publishers.

Smith, Anthony. 1980. *Geopolitics of Information: How Western Culture Dominates the World.* London: Faber and Faber.

Smith, Barbara. 1997. "A Survey of Iran," *The Economist*, January 18, pp. 1–16.

Smith, Huston. 1958. *The Religions of Man.* New York: Harper and Row.

Smith, W. G. 1957. *Islam in Modern History.* Princeton: Princeton University Press.

So, Alvin. 1990. *Social Change and Development: Modernization, Dependency, and World System Theories.* Newbury Park, CA: Sage Publications.

Soroush, Abdul-Karim. 1995. *Farbehtar as Ideology* (Stronger than Ideology). Tehran.

Stannard, David E. 1989. *Before the Horror: The Population of Hawaii on the Eve of Western Contact.* Honolulu: Social Science Research Institute, University of Hawaii.

————. 1992. *American Holocaust: The Conquest of the New World.* New York: Oxford University Press.

Stecklow, Steve. 1993. "Cyberspace Clash: Computer Users Battle High-Tech Marketers over Soul of Internet," *Wall Street Journal*, September 16, p. A1.

Tarjanne, Pekka. 1994. "The Missing Link: Still Missing," Plenary Presentations, Pacific Telecommunications Council Sixteenth Annual Conference, Honolulu, Hawaii, January 16–20.

Tawney, R. H. 1984. *Religion and the Rise of Capitalism: A Historical Study.* New York: Penguin Books.

Tehranian, John. 1995. "The Political Economy of Famine in Africa: Ethiopia, Kenya, and Zimbabwe, 1982–85," B.A. thesis, Harvard University.

Tehranian, Katharine Kia. 1995. *Modernity, Space, and Power: The American City in Discourse and Practice.* Cresskill, NJ: Hampton Press.

————. 1998. "Global Communication and Pluralization of Identities," *The Futures* 30:2/3, March.

Tehranian, Katharine, and Majid Tehranian, eds. 1992. *Restructuring for World Peace: On the Threshold of the 21st Century.* Cresskill, NJ: Hampton Press.

Tehranian, Majid. 1972. "Iran," in Abid Al-Marayati et al., *The Middle East: Its Governments and Politics.* Belmont, CA: Duxbury Press.

————. 1974. *Toward a Systematic Theory of National Development.* Tehran: Industrial Management Institute.

————. 1976. *Andishe daneshgah* (The Idea of the University). Tehran: Bu-Ali Sina University.

————. 1979a. "Communication and International Development: Some Theoretical Considerations," *Cultures* 6:3, pp. 30–38.

————. 1979b. "Development Theory and Communication Policy: The Changing Paradigms," in G. J. Hanneman and Melvin Voigt, eds., *Progress in Communication Sciences*, Vol. 1. Norwood, NJ: Ablex.

————. 1979c. "Iran: Communication, Alienation, Revolution," *InterMedia* 7:2, March, pp. 6–12.

————. 1980a. "Communication and Revolution in Iran: The Passing of a Paradigm," *Iranian Studies* 13:1–2, Spring, pp. 5–30.

————. 1980b. "The Curse of Modernity: The Dialectics of Modernization and Communication," *International Social Science Journal* 32:2, pp. 247–263.

————. 1981. *Socio-Economic and Communication Indicators in Development Planning: A Case Study of Iran.* Paris: UNESCO.

————. 1982a. "Communications Dependency and Dualism in Iran," *InterMedia* 10:3, May, pp. 40–45.

————. 1982b. "International Communication: A Dialogue of the Deaf?" *Political Communication and Persuasion* 2:2, pp. 21–46.

————. 1989. "History Finished? It's Just Begun," *The Honolulu Advertiser*, October 7, A-11.

————. 1990a. "Communication, Peace, and Development: A Communitarian Perspective," in F. Korzenny and S. Ting-Toomey, eds., *Communicating for Peace.* Newbury Park, CA: Sage Publications.

————. 1990b. *Technologies of Power: Information Machines and Democratic Prospects.* Norwood, NJ: Ablex.

————. 1992a. "Communication and Theories of Social Change: A Communitarian Perspective," *Asian Journal of Communication* 2:1, pp. 1–30.

————. 1992b. "Khomeini's Doctrine of Legitimacy," in Anthony J. Parel and Ronald C. Keith, eds., *Comparative Political Philosophy.* New Delhi: Sage Publications.

———. 1993a. "Ethnic Discourse and the New World Dis/order," in Colleen Roach, ed., *Communication and Culture in War and Peace.* Newbury Park, CA: Sage Publications.

———. 1993b. "Fundamentalist Impact on Education and the Media: An Overview," in Martin E. Marty and R. Scott Appleby, eds., *Fundamentalism and Society: Reclaiming the Science, the Family, and Education.* Chicago: University of Chicago Press.

———. 1993c. "Islamic Fundamentalism in Iran and the Discourse of Development," in Martin Marty and Scott Appleby, eds., *Fundamentalism and Society*, vol. 2. Chicago: University of Chicago Press.

———. 1995. "Creating Spaces for Peace: A Comparative Overview of Zones of Peace," in Michael Jalla, Walter Tonetto, and Enrique Martinez, eds., *Essays on Peace.* Rockhampton: Central Queensland University Press, pp. 247–254.

———. 1996a. "Webs of Modernity: The Transformation of Central Asia," ms.

———. 1996b. "The End of University?" *The Information Society* 12:4, October–December, pp. 441–447.

———. 1997. "Global Communication and International Relations: Changing Paradigms and Policies," *International Journal of Peace Studies* 2:1, January, pp. 39–64.

———. 1999. "Human Security and Global Governance: Power Shifts and Emerging Security Regimes," in Majid Tehranian, eds., *Worlds Apart: Human Security and Global Governance.* London: E.B. Tauris.

Tehranian, Majid, Farhad Hakimzadeh, and Marcello Vidale, eds. 1977. *Communications Policy for National Development: A Comparative Perspective.* London: Routledge & Kegan Paul.

Tehranian, Majid, and Michael Ogden. 1998. "Uncertain Futures: Changing Paradigms and Global Communications," *Futures* 30:1, pp. 199–210.

Tehranian, Majid, and Laura Reed. 1996. *Human Security and Global Governance: The State of the Art.* Honolulu: Toda Institute for Global Peace and Policy Research.

Tilly, Charles. 1992. "War and the International System, 1900–1992," paper presented for the Hannah Arendt Memorial Symposium on Peace and War, New School for Social Research, New York, N.Y., March 26.

Tinbergen, Jan, Antony J. Dolman, and Jan Van Ettinger, eds. 1976. *Reshaping the International Order: A Report to the Club of Rome.* New York: Dutton.

Toffler, Alvin. 1970. *Future Shock.* New York: Bantam.

———. 1980. *Third Wave.* New York: Bantam.

Traber, Michael, ed. 1986. *The Myth of the Information Revolution: Social and Ethical Implications of Communication Technology.* London: Sage Publications.

Traber, Michael, and Kaarle Nordenstreng. 1992. *Few Voices, Many Worlds: Towards a Media Reform Movement.* London: World Association for Christian Communication.

United Nations Development Programme (UNDP). 1990. *Human Development Report 1990.* New York: Oxford University Press.

———. 1991. *Human Development Report 1991.* New York: Oxford University Press.

———. 1992. *Human Development Report 1992.* New York: Oxford University Press.

———. 1993. *Human Development Report 1993.* New York: Oxford University Press.

———. 1994. *Human Development Report 1994.* New York: Oxford University Press.

———. 1995. *Human Development Report 1995.* New York: Oxford University Press.

———. 1996. *Human Development Report 1996.* New York: Oxford University Press.

United Nations Educational, Scientific, and Cultural Organization (UNESCO). 1980. *Many Voices, One World: Communication Society Today and Tomorrow.* Paris: UNESCO.

United Nations High Commissioner for Refugees (UNHCR). 1995. *The State of the World's Refugees*. Oxford: Oxford University Press.

Van Ginneken, Jaap. 1998. *Understanding Global News*. London: Sage.

Vattimo, Gianni. 1991. *The End of Modernity: Nihilism and Hermeneutics in Post-modern Culture*. Baltimore: Johns Hopkins University Press.

Virilio, Paul. 1989. *War and Cinema: The Logistics of Perception*. Translated by Patrick Camiller. London: Verso.

Von Sivers, P. 1984. "National Integration and Traditional Rural Organization in Algeria, 1970–80: Background to Islamic Traditionalism," in S. A. Arjomand. ed., *From Nationalism to Revolutionary Islam*. Albany: State University of New York Press.

Wallerstein, Immanuel. 1974. *The Modern World-System*. Vol. 1, *Capitalist Agriculture and the Origins of the European World-Economy in the Sixteenth Century*. New York: Academic Press.

———. *The Capitalist World-Economy*. Cambridge: Cambridge University Press.

Waltz, Kenneth N. 1979. *Theory of International Politics*. New York: Addison-Wesley.

Wang, Georgette, and Wimal Dissanayake, eds. 1985. *Continuity and Change in Communication Systems*. Norwood, NJ: Ablex.

Ward, R. E., and D. A. Rustow. 1964. *Political Modernization in Japan and Turkey*. Princeton, NJ: Princeton University Press.

Waught, Patricia, ed. 1992. *Post-Modernism: A Reader*. New York: Edward Arnold.

Weber, Max. 1958. *The Protestant Ethic and the Spirit of Capitalism*. Translated by Talcott Parsons. New York: Scribner's.

Wriston, Walter B. 1992. *The Twilight of Sovereignty: How the Information Revolution Is Transforming Our World*. New York: Scribner's.

Yankelovich, Daniel, and Larry Kaagan. 1981. "Assertive America," *Foreign Affairs* 59:3, pp. 696–713.

Index

205

About the Book

Reflecting the profound changes that are taking place in the world system, this book charts a conceptual framework for understanding emerging patterns of global politics and communication.

Tehranian begins by tracing the evolution of the world system from its agrarian origins into today's postindustrial, information-based "pancapitalism." He then draws out the implications of that evolution for global systems of domination, development, and discourse in the context of fragmentation. A study of the complexities of relations between the Islamic and Western worlds demonstrates how systemic distortions in cross-cultural communication have led to tragedies in world politics.

The concluding chapter, addressing the pathology of physical and cultural violence, reflects on the possibility of transforming existing conflicts into creative tensions based on the acknowledgment of differences.

Majid Tehranian is professor of international communication at the University of Hawaii at Manoa and director of the Toda Institute for Global Peace and Policy Research. He has also served as director of the Iran Communications and Development Institute (Tehran), trustee of the Institute of International Communications (London), and director of comunication research and planning for UNESCO (Paris). His numerous publications include *Technologies of Power: Information Machines and Democratic Prospects* and *Restructuring for World Peace*. In 1998, he received the Distinguished Service Award of the International Communication Division, Association for Education in Journalism and Mass Communication.